Hellenic Studies 54

THE THEORY AND PRACTICE OF LIFE

THE THEORY AND PRACTICE OF LIFE

Isocrates and the Philosophers

Tarik Wareh

CENTER FOR HELLENIC STUDIES
Trustees for Harvard University
Washington, DC
Distributed by Harvard University Press
Cambridge, Massachusetts, and London, England
2012

The Theory and Practice of Life: Isocrates and the Philosophers
    By Tarik Wareh
Copyright © 2012 Center for Hellenic Studies, Trustees for Harvard University
All Rights Reserved.
Published by Center for Hellenic Studies, Trustees for Harvard University,
    Washington, D.C.
Distributed by Harvard University Press, Cambridge, Massachusetts and
    London, England

Library of Congress Cataloging-in-Publication Data

Wareh, Tarik.
    The theory and practice of life : Isocrates and the philosophers / by Tarik Wareh.
        p.   cm. — (Hellenic studies ; 54)
    Includes bibliographical references (p.   ) and index.
    ISBN 978-0-674-06713-4 (alk. paper)
1. Isocrates—Criticism and interpretation. I. Title.

    PA4218.W36 2012
    885'.01—dc22   2012029958

Contents

Acknowledgments

Anthony A. Long, Giovanni R. F. Ferrari, and Mark Griffith supervised my first work on this topic in Berkeley. I am grateful for their continuing support. That 2003 dissertation did not yet discuss Aristotle's *Nicomachean Ethics*, Plato's *Phaedrus*, the biographical genre, or Isocrates' *Philip* (whereas it gave significant attention to the *Crito* and the *Euthyphro*), so it was a long process of development that has led to the present book. Also at Berkeley, sociologists Robert Bellah, Ann Swidler, and Loïc Wacquant, to whom I was introduced by fellow classicist Håkan Tell, advanced my thinking about the kind of questions and answers it was worth seeking in my work; though this book is coy in its devotion to the sociological muse, it has been encouraged and changed by their teaching.

Dustin Gish of the Society for Greek Political Thought stimulated the birth of this book in its present form by inviting me to contribute to a panel at the meetings of the Northeastern Political Science Association in 2006. This presentation was the germ of chapter 1. Chapter 2 was first presented to the West Coast Plato Workshop in San Diego in the spring of 2010. I am grateful for the invitation to share my work there with an impressive assembly of open-minded philosophers. In particular, D. S. Hutchinson and Monte Ransome Johnson warmly encouraged my labors at a crucial point and generously shared with me their important ongoing work on Aristotle's *Protrepticus*.

I am grateful for the assistance of a 2009 summer stipend from the National Endowment for the Humanities.

This work was supported in the most generous way imaginable by the Center for Hellenic Studies in Washington, DC, where I enjoyed the privilege of residency with my family for ten months in 2009–2010. Adequate thanks are impossible and would only begin with the names of every Fellow, Senior Fellow, and member of the staff and administration. Still I must mention in particular the friendly camaraderie of Sarah Ferrario and Josh Reynolds. I also thank James Clauss for believing, before I got to the CHS, in the importance of my work on literary culture in the "lost years" between Plato and Callimachus.

Most of all I thank Greg Nagy. I have benefited not only from his devoted leadership of the CHS but from his inspired teaching and wise counsel.

My work from 2005 until the completion of this book was sponsored by Union College under its mission to foster the liberal arts. The college has generously provided grants (from the Humanities Research Fund) and leaves that have allowed me to pursue this work. I have also enjoyed great support from Marianne Snowden and the rest of the college's staff. The students are the heart of the college, and this book could not have been written without their vital curiosity and willingness to confront difficult questions about everything from Aristotle's metaphysics, Pindar's Greek, and Medieval Latin love lyric to Ruskin, *Beowulf*, and *King Lear*. I also express my deepest thanks to my colleagues throughout the college whose unfailing support and friendship have sustained me. I have been inspired by their commitment, creativity, and integrity as scholar-teachers.

It was a pleasure to work with the expert publishing team of Jill Curry Robbins, Casey Dué, Lenny Muellner, and Kerri Cox Sullivan, and to receive the insightful comments of the press's reader. Andrew Ford was kind enough to criticize a draft of the book's introduction.

I am grateful for the support I have received from all my family. My parents, Faiz and Laura Wareh, first opened up the world to me as an object of love and study, and my children, Faiz and Cora, are immeasurably enriching my knowledge of art, life, and nature.

Pattie Wareh's suggestion that I consider the appearance of Plato and Aristotle as perfect courtiers in Castiglione's *Cortegiano* can be counted only the least of her graces. In an echo of the introduction's epigraph, she may fitly be hymned as Proclus did Athena Polymetis, ἣ βίοτον κόσμησας ὅλον πολυειδέσι τέχναις.

This book owes much to these teachers and friends, but I am sure I am responsible for its remaining faults.

Introduction

αἱ δὲ βίον σοφίῃσιν ἐκόσμεον.

And some gave life the ornament of their wise arts.

Orphic *Catabasis*, P. Bon. 4, fol. 3ʳ, line 7

THIS BOOK IS A STUDY of the professional, literary, political, and theoretical links between the school of Isocrates and the schools and careers of recognized philosophers such as Plato and Aristotle. It argues that the positions of the Isocrateans—their "rhetorical" mode of training, of performing, and of constructing social value, and the account they gave of it—were not just a challenging provocation to the "philosophical" project but also a creative inspiration, directly digested and reworked in such major works of practical philosophy as Aristotle's *Nicomachean Ethics* and Plato's *Phaedrus*. These surprisingly close theoretical interconnections between rhetoric and philosophy, discoverable through careful readings of the texts, are further supported by a new history of the school movement of the fourth century, bringing together for the first time the range of evidence needed to tell the story of major and minor philosophical and rhetorical students' ambitions, concerns, and audiences—their interactions (polemical and otherwise) and their "politics" (in relation both to each other and to the field of power).

The extent and significance of these phenomena have not been properly appreciated because of two obstacles the book seeks to overcome. First, although both Isocrates and the recognized philosophers grappled with the difficulties facing the student of the practical sphere of human life (the unknowable, the need to act, human nature), nonetheless, due to a prejudice against rhetoric, the recognition of these difficulties in works such as the *Nicomachean Ethics* and the *Phaedrus* is taken as a sign of philosophical sophistication and even daring, while in the pages of Isocrates this has seemed an all-too-expected "low" and "productive" concern. This study helps us see how tenuous these differentiating labels can often be, and how they derive from a shared struggle for ownership over mutually developed ideas. In fact, the attempt to theorize a way of working with practical uncertainties is not narrowly rhetorical or philosophical but comes from a distinguished tradition of argument over the theory of practice, also recoverable in medical treatises such as *On Ancient Medicine*.[1]

The second barrier to rendering the scene of fourth-century scholastic competition from this new perspective is simply that its participants, and the historical traditions that provide evidence for their careers, have never been completely assembled in a single scholarly account. By illuminating the significance and committed lives of such fragmentarily known figures as Theodectes, Theopompus, Cephisodorus, and Isocrates of Apollonia, we are able to recover several neglected strands that belong to this history of philosophy. These include examples both of recognized philosophers doing the "unphilosophical" (Aristotle's competitive engagement with Isocrates, or Speusippus' *Letter to King Philip*) and of "outsiders" doing what has to be called "philosophy" (Theopompus critiquing the Theory of Forms in a manner deemed worth citing by Simplicius in his commentary on Aristotle's *Categories*).

The book, then, is divided into two parts. The first concentrates on reading the texts of Isocrates, Plato, and Aristotle to bring out the theoretical affinities between them. The second more fully constructs the perspective from which we may understand these links, through a study of the historical evidence, not only for the careers of Isocrates and his major contemporaries, but extending into the generation of Isocrates' students. Among its other contributions, this story of a wider and previously unexamined scholastic milieu sheds light on the "lost years," so poorly attested in many genres of literature, that connect the literary and intellectual culture of Classical Athens to the period of Hellenistic authors and schools.

---

[1] Medicine remains in the background of the present study. In chap. 2, I give reasons for my confidence that the connection in Plato's *Phaedrus* between rational medicine and philosophical rhetoric is not accidental at all, but shows the special preeminence of these two arts in the area of epistemological self-reflection. The counterexample of harmonic theory is meant to show how uniquely this province belonged to rhetoric/medicine. When Plato and Aristotle admit the practical arts into their thinking—the physicians of the *Phaedrus* and also the homely carpenters of the *Nicomachean Ethics*'s craft analogy—these are not mere illustrations but gestures towards the prestige and influence of a methodological problematic staked out by such disciplines as medicine and, in no small part, the Isocratean theory of education and performance. Neither medicine nor rhetoric had clear priority or an exclusive claim to the major theory-of-practice topics, and (at least in the texts under consideration here) rhetoric offers a more complete and relevant competing treatment of the same philosophical issues.

The Lost Years: Literary Competition, Philosophy, and Politics in the Generation after Plato and Isocrates

The decades after the mid-350s BC are a crucial, but little understood, transitional period in Greek literary and intellectual history. On the far side of these years are the famous works of Plato (d. 348/7); on the near side, in the third century, the familiar movements of Hellenistic philosophy and imaginative literature. Surviving from the period in between are important works of Athenian political oratory, but otherwise only the most fragmentary glimpses of the process by which the interests, motivations, habits, and career-profiles of early-fourth-century intellectuals altered and gave way to a new cultural and political order under Macedonian and Ptolemaic patronage, the Hellenistic world of Callimachus and Epicurus. Scholars of Hellenistic Greek literature and culture (in addition to historians of philosophy) know that this period's developments must have formed much of the essential background to the texts they study,[2] but it remains an untold chapter in intellectual history.

The present book helps fill this gap through a historical and textual study of the politics and the educational character of the philosophical schools founded by Plato and his contemporary Isocrates. My work aims to clarify the complexities of the period, in which conventional generic oppositions (philosopher, orator) are not always adequate. I thus describe a "politics" of intellectuals without reducing it to conventional political factions and give due emphasis to the (not always successful) efforts of philosophers to create politically meaningful work that would be evaluated by the specific standards and values of scholastic circles.

Aristotle, Isocrates, and Plato

The opening section of the book, entitled "Isocrates and Aristotle: An Entanglement," is a challenge to the assumption that the essential ideas of Aristotle's *Nicomachean Ethics* can be fully understood without reference to the system of rhetorical education which we can know through Isocrates' surviving works. This argument is supported by an important similarity between the two teachers' theoretical accounts, which has not been adequately studied: Aristotle and Isocrates both express a theory of how an actor (the virtuous man for Aristotle, the politically active orator for Isocrates), through rigorous training or habituation, achieves a state of readiness to act "just the right way" in a crucial moment's unscripted performance. I adduce terminological and structural echoes between the two accounts to argue that this resemblance

---

[2] See chap. 4, n1.

cannot be coincidental, but most likely reflects direct influence (and at the least a shared reliance on the topics and terminology of the political-rhetorical mode of education). While I do not debate the consensus of modern philosophers that Isocrates was not one of them, I present the evidence to conclude that Aristotle's well-known "less precise" framework for ethics should be studied alongside the Isocratean approach, to which it is conceptually akin. Our increasing understanding of Aristotle's *Protrepticus* (and Isocrates' important role in it) provides an exciting laboratory in which to test ideas about the connections between the two thinkers' public commitments to the exalted claims and practical value of "philosophy."

Existing studies, when they have considered Aristotle and Isocrates together, have proceeded along entirely different lines[3] and have not yet led to a revision of the standard view that Isocrates (for all his use of the word *philosophia*) lived and died without any remarkable effect on the history of philosophy. My argument for the relationship between the *Nicomachean Ethics* and Isocratean theory aims to provide a dramatic justification for the attention the book goes on to pay to the more historical evidence (rarely granted much consequence) of the contact between Isocrates and Aristotle's careers and schools. If a work as familiar as Aristotle's *Ethics* can be rendered newly meaningful through its connection to the disfavored Isocratean milieu, then it is imperative to review what can be understood about that milieu as part of the wider terrain that includes Plato and Aristotle. And if the theoretical elements Aristotle borrowed from political life and the rhetorical tradition have been ascribed serious philosophical value with almost universal agreement (with the telling exception of some ancient polemics from sources who recognized and protested these overtures to rhetoric), then surely we owe it to ourselves to renew questions about the full extent of the audience to which Aristotle and other philosophers of his period spoke—to redraw the lines that define the field of intellectuals mutually interested in each other's doctrines and prestige (while, at their best, approaching a stance of theoretical disinterestedness).[4]

Sometimes the topicality of rhetorical thinkers such as Isocrates for Plato and Aristotle has been granted, without any follow-up interpretative claims, so that we are not asked to *read* any differently the commitments and considerations we see Aristotle and Plato taking up in their texts. I therefore begin immediately with such claims. In particular, the two chapters immediately following this introduction establish Isocrates' teachings as an important theoretical and technical background to Aristotle's *Nicomachean Ethics* and *Protrepticus* and Plato's *Phaedrus*. Once we are persuaded that such texts come into better focus

---

[3] See chap. 3, n1.

[4] This notion of a "field" is loosely derived from Bourdieu: see e.g. Bourdieu 1991.

from this point of view—that a sympathetic engagement with Isocrates' project makes us better observers of how Aristotle and Plato work out and position their philosophical arguments and ideas—we then have both the motivation to take up a more historical study of Isocrates' school and its entanglements with the philosophers, and a workable criterion of internal plausibility with which to judge and interpret the difficult evidence for the wider context of the fourth-century scholastic field.

This book argues the case for the particular importance of Isocratean thinking in making possible and influencing Aristotle and Plato's works of practical philosophy. I do not, however, see the literary activities of Isocrates and his school as the only possible defining parameters for a project to recover and flesh out new sources of Academic and Aristotelian problems and thinking. For example, I have to believe, despite the loss of so much of the literary record, that there is still much to be said about how everything ventured intellectually and practically by the fifth-century sophists informed, provoked, and challenged all the fourth-century writers considered in this book.[5] Still, in this book I have chosen to study this tradition as exemplified in Isocrates' thinking and activities, because these are explorable and contemporary: we have the corpus of Isocratean works (and a wide variety of ancillary literary sources), and there can be little doubt about the central importance of Isocrates as an exponent of the empiricist approach to the theory and practice of life *during the lifetimes* of Plato and Aristotle. Moreover, Isocrates' longevity and numerous students (if not a lasting and organized school) give us the opportunity to pursue the study forward into time and to compare the varied courses of the scholastic projects set in motion by Isocrates, Plato, and Aristotle.

A focus on Isocrates' special role reveals his participation in a shared framework of protreptic and inquiry. This (and not an awkward and confused effort to ape the terminology of another discipline) is the proper explanation for his deploying concepts such as *phronēsis* ("intelligence"), *ideai* ("forms"), *philosophia* ("love of wisdom"), and discourses of virtue and the good life (self-cultivation and care of the soul, the place of external goods in our value scheme, etc.). If we consider there to have been an open conversation, the result is not that we will confuse or identify Isocratean and Aristotelian accounts of deliberation, individual nature, and other topics. Rather, the result is a more complete picture of a complex space and arena within which Isocrates and Aristotle were among

---

5 See the instructive (and very different) recent approaches of Tell (2011) and Tindale (2010). See also the thoughts of Halliwell (1997:120f.) on the limitations of the notion that Isocrates continued the Sophists' intellectual project. This is, nonetheless, only to mention one tradition relatively close to the one this book considers; I suspect that future studies will eventually show that we are only at the beginning of following all the cultural and intellectual strands that provided material for the thinking of an Aristotle.

those intervening to contest and refine such notions. When we approach a less familiar and more obviously hybrid text such as Aristotle's *Protrepticus*, we will be better able to appreciate how and why, before a wider audience that certainly would have included Isocrateans, the key philosophical values are at the same time exalted to the heavens and given deep practical-life resonance.

It is a testament to Plato's intellectual courage that he builds such a shaky bridge in the *Phaedrus* from rhetoric to philosophy, with a construct of "Hippocratic" medicine serving to support the span. If Plato had more strictly denied these connections instead of exploring them, it would be much more difficult work to place him in our story. As it is, by admitting a prestigious practical-arts model (medicine) into a discussion of genuinely philosophical practice, he takes up a position in the methodological debates of the practical arts more broadly. If we reanimate this debate with the evidence of the rationalist and empiricist voices of the Hippocratic Corpus, then we quickly find how inevitably *every* position in this arena admits and grapples with the same core problem that entangled Isocrates and Aristotle with one another—the ultimate impossibility of a practical art that is completely rationally formulable. No extreme of "rationalistic" practical art escapes this problem, and we are forced to concede that when "empiricist" critics (physicians, Isocrates, Aristotle, and even Plato at times) abandon rationalism's totalizing claims, they do so not out of a distaste for reason or an ignorant faith in some counterfeit form of truth-authority, but precisely because they hope to save the wider scientific project of producing *some* methodology responsive to the uncertainties and imprecisions of life as experienced and dealt with by human beings. Reason, knowledge, and truth retain great importance under such an approach. Indeed, Aristotle took up the balanced empiricist approach against Plato's rationalism precisely because he believed it was a more philosophically sophisticated method for ethics and politics. The *Phaedrus*, while it suppresses any fair defense of the empiricist position, shows us that this discussion, with its attendant philosophical possibilities, was already seriously underway in Plato's Academy.

Moreover, the fundamental disagreements between Phaedrus's Socrates and Isocrates should not blind us to their important agreement on some questions of rhetoric. For example, both have taken up positions as staunch defenders of flexible *logos* against any *tekhnē* (art) that claims to offer written prescriptions adequate to the demands of action. They also share some strikingly similar rhetorical conceptions, such as how "forms of speech" are to be applied according to *kairos* (the opportune moment).

Thus, the complex marriage Isocrates effects in his theory between *doxa* (appearance or belief) and *epistēmē* (knowledge) is not an evasion of the demands of reason. Rather, this synthesis tells us, in a nutshell, of an ongoing methodological struggle, with an interesting philosophical past, present, and future. Physicians, sophists, and practical philosophers alike faced the problem of how to combine an aspiration to effective mastery with the admitted fact that the world of their experience is full of unknowns and imprecisions. Arguably the more sophisticated responses to this problem are those that honestly and seriously take up both sides of the tension. Isocrates, like Plato and Aristotle, was led by these reflections to reject any approach whose "rationalized" appeal was so shallow and uncritical as to aim at a complete and ordered rulebook (*tetagmenē tekhnē*) that would obviate the need for a living and breathing intelligent faculty. The disagreements and opposing stances between Plato, Isocrates, and Aristotle proceed from this basic shared problematic. Under the sway of Plato, it can be easy to forget how exceptional his radical solution was, tending more often than not to exalt abstract truth and deductive reason, while diminishing the practical arts' claim to arrive at the good through reflection on experience. Time spent with Aristotle's practical philosophy, however, is always enough to remind us of the powerful stream of empiricist thinking against which Plato often fought.

Justified and guided by the demonstrated place of Isocrates in the philosophical conversation about the practice of life, we must try to make something of the historical evidence for Aristotle's engagement in his career with the political and rhetorical slogans, theories, and audience-effects of Isocrates' teaching (as in the traditions about Aristotle's rhetorical teaching, considered in chapter 3). The difficulty, and often unreliability, of our sources make this difficult. Still, it is possible to draw suggestive and plausible conclusions, and it is better to sift for bits worthy of consideration than to allow ourselves the false purism and blind-flying of an approach that abandons this effort of contextualization.

School Creatures: Literary Competition, Philosophy, and Politics

What we can begin to recover through such evidence is the "politics" of scholastic activity in the fourth century. This is the task of the book's second part. The term "politics" helps us to see the individuals we are studying as interconnected, interested, and interdependent actors in a social space defined by their community, competition, and mutual effects on each other's self-fashioning and careers, rather than as vehicles of pure intellectual effort. This is an attractively complicated undertaking, in part because the very interest (capital, social currency) at stake in this space (a Bourdieusian "field") is the disinterested commitment to the loftiest version of the projects that defined their schools. These people can and should be taken seriously as intellectuals, because they did struggle to realize achievements meaningful in purely intellectual terms, not only in appearance, but in reality; that does not mean, however, that such achievements were valued exclusively for their internal characteristics and theoretical effects.

While due attention must be paid to the destructive and political aspects of intellectual controversies, their intellectual substance cannot be dismissed. Misclassifying the field's participants either as pure littérateurs or as purely political animals only causes us to mistake their proper connections. For example, neither a focus on literary style nor an analysis of pro- and anti-Macedonian political sympathies reveals how the "historians" Theopompus and Ephorus can be meaningfully understood as Isocrateans, but attention to the full range of their intellectual interests and interventions makes the Isocratean label fit—unmistakably, in Theopompus' case. Likewise, to understand how and why the origin of prose encomia for deceased powerful individuals took place within Isocrates' school, we must keep in mind not only the pressures and enticements of the Hellenic and Macedonian political situation but also the opportunities afforded by this genre and its occasions to promote philosophical protreptic by exploring its topics, staking out positions of interscholastic import (e.g. the intersection of virtue, power, and the course of human life), and establishing in a dramatically public way the speaker's claim to didactic ("philosophical") authority. The genre's suitability to these purposes explains why it was quickly and widely appropriated in scholastic circles. It was topical for Xenophon and Aristotle and became the object of scholastic literary rivalry.

The evidence for Isocrates' school brings to light a number of figures who made undoubted contact with the schools of Plato and Aristotle, whose intellectual pretensions are recoverable through references in sources ranging from the titles of Aristotle's lost works to the surviving fragments of Middle Comic humor. Moreover, we find that a single individual's participation in multiple scholastic milieus was not extraordinary. Not only did fourth-century intellectuals find it natural to pass between the school of Isocrates and those of Plato and Aristotle, but even texts from Academic circles can assign a nonpolemical significance to such cross-contacts. The schools thus constructed a common professional space, or field of mutual effects.

In the context of a critical study of school culture, a text such as Speusippus' *Letter to Philip* (addressed by Plato's nephew and successor to the Macedonian king in 343/2), with its poisonous attack on Isocrates and his school, has much to say about the mixed motivations and methods with which school adherents received, digested, and responded to each other's work. This allows us to return to the Isocratean texts and more reliably assess in retrospect how Isocrates replies to such competitive confrontations with his characteristic desire to hold himself above the fray and to defend the purity of his own scholastic program's objectives.

Looking Beyond: Fourth-Century Scholastic Politics as a Case Study

The various details and episodes of this history add up to a coherent picture of an intellectual playing field, as it existed over a difficult and fairly brief transitional time between the Classical and Hellenistic periods. This picture problematizes the boundary between rhetoric and philosophy, challenges some common views on the history of philosophy, and revises some of the terms in which Aristotle is to be interpreted. The specific insights of this account, considered from a more general perspective, also have exemplary value for literary and intellectual historians who look beyond antiquity. The basic methodological problem is not without parallels in better-documented historical periods: a group of forgotten writers who have never been constituted as a group worth studying because they are located at the intersection of what were soon to become (and eternally to be studied as) different disciplines. Also of general interest are the conflicts and crises that arise when intellectuals attempt to draw borders around the space in which their work can be pursued for "pure" and "disinterested" motivations, under the pressure of reconfigurations in the field of political power (in my study, the end of the Classical *polis* and the rise of Macedonian power). Indeed, much as the artists Michael Baxandall studied in *The Limewood Sculptors of Renaissance Germany* expressed a distinctive kind of cultural creativity and differentiation into schools or styles in response to a threat to their autonomy as craft workers, so too was there, in the relations I describe, a remarkable change in the atmosphere of scholastic competition, and in the very nature of intellectual prestige.[6]

Several elements of the thematic complex under study here figure in later problems of cultural history. For example, in Early Modern literature, an intense interest in "self-fashioning" often led to involved negotiations among virtue, interest, address to princes, and rhetorical/social performance. The story told in these pages may, I hope, help readers who study such phenomena to understand how the social concerns of their period led to a renewal of interest in Isocrates (alongside such key texts in the Isocratean reception as Cicero's *De oratore*), who became more topical and popular with its authors than with those of any later time. The book's conclusion returns to this period in order to address these issues.

---

[6] Baxandall 1980. Baxandall's study is also paradigmatic in its attention to factors that explain the succession of a "great" generation by an obscure one.

Part I

Isocrates and Aristotle
An Entanglement

The Influence of Rhetorical Education on Aristotelian Ethics

Knowledge, Training, and Performance

THE *NICOMACHEAN ETHICS* gives an account of a virtuous agent's formation and practice. To appreciate this text fully, it is natural to want to know as much as possible about all the theoretical and technical discourses and ideas that informed Aristotle's seminal work. This project of contextualization, while it will always be held back by our profound ignorance of almost everything similar and relevant that had been said before Aristotle, nonetheless still offers the possibility of new insights into Aristotelian thought. This chapter considers the hypothesis that several of Aristotle's familiar and characteristic ways of thinking about ethics are indebted to a multidisciplinary[1] tradition that confronted the peculiar problems involved in establishing and defending an art (*tekhnē*) creative, responsible, and flexible enough to answer to the uncertainties of lived practice. In particular, we are only beginning to understand the resonance Aristotelian ethical theory would have had for that portion of the ancient audience steeped in the methods and ambitions, the intellectual inheritance and preoccupations, of a contemporary rhetorical school such as that of Isocrates.

Isocrates' school was flourishing in Athens during the twenty years (ca. 367–347 BC) that Aristotle spent as a student in that other, more famous, school of *philosophia*, Plato's Academy. Isocrates' *philosophia*, squarely focused on the best and most practical preparations for public life, is so much more pedestrian than Plato's philosophy, and so difficult to fit within our own genre of philosophy, that few modern readers have hesitated to exclude Isocrates' ideas from comparison with any really philosophical doctrines. The definition of

---

[1] Some of the ramifications through medical theory will be considered in connection with Plato's *Phaedrus* in chap. 2. Other "empiricist" practical-arts methodologies turn out to be less relevant than they might at first appear (see the end of chap. 2 for the counterexample of harmonic theory).

his *philosophia* as rhetoric (which it certainly is *inter alia*) has set the limits of inquiry. Yet Isocrates is reflective about his role as an educator, and about the process through which his students have progressed, to the point that he has a *theory* of education and practice (the formation of a person towards the best ends), albeit one we have to reconstruct from unsystematic texts whose many aims do not include theoretical exposition.[2]

One single statement of Isocrates' has been more influential than any other on modern opinion: his profession that his students, having received their training from him, cannot hope to handle the situations in which they must perform through systematic knowledge (*epistēmē*) but must rely instead on beliefs or appearances (*doxai*).[3] In the wake of Plato, what is less "philosophical" than substituting *doxa* for *epistēmē*? But a fair picture of Isocrates' ideas is more complex. He does assign a definite value and role to *epistēmē*, but he denies that its prescriptions can ever be adequate preparation for meeting the contingencies and complexities of a life of action. In actuality, these practical concerns are closely related to Aristotle's practical philosophy and even—as we will consider in the next chapter—to a strand in Plato's thinking.

In Isocrates' very parsing of science's limits, and of the less exact means that must be adopted toward the end of the best actions, his concerns are nearer to those of Aristotelian ethics than to any other point of comparison. His notion of a thoroughly cultivated orator whose readiness and proficiency are displayed in a crucial moment's unscripted performance may be compared to Aristotle's discussion of virtue as a habitually strengthened state of character, in which an agent is ready to perform good acts.

I will consider the relation of several overlapping basic notions that occur in both Isocrates and Aristotle's *Nicomachean Ethics*. While the questions of influence that such an investigation raises are not easy to decide, we can immediately discern how unjustly we have neglected Isocrates' *Against the Sophists* and *Antidosis* as necessary and fruitful points of reference against which to understand Aristotelian ethics.

If significant parts of Aristotle's orientation and terminology are appropriately understood in connection with such a milieu, and the connection shows signs of lying fairly near the surface for Aristotle's contemporaries, the immediate result will be not necessarily a revision in our reading of Aristotle on any single matter of doctrine, but a new perspective on Aristotle's audience, on the lines of affiliation and difference between him and others, and on the import

---

[2] Halliwell 1997 is a thoughtful meditation on these issues, arguing that "Isocrates ought to be regarded as a much more problematic thinker than most historians of ideas currently take him to be" (p. 108).

[3] Isocrates *Against the Sophists* 8, *Antidosis* 184, 271, discussed below.

his own positions may have held among the other entrants in a wider scientific (or even political) arena,[4] and, from this added vantage point, a possible avenue towards grasping certain of Aristotle's nuances or resolving some of the myriad confusions, contradictions, and difficulties that his interpreters face. The most important result, however, will be an awareness of another context, besides the history of philosophy narrowly construed, in which we can make a legitimate claim for the significance of Aristotle's intervention, and of another discourse to which the cast of his ethical thinking also belongs.

An Art of Practice

Aristotle's serious engagement with the "craft analogy" in the *Nicomachean Ethics* is widely appreciated, although perhaps an unfamiliarity with the range of evidence for ancient discussions of the various arts' natures and methodologies sometimes tempts us to regard the insights derived from this analogy more as testimony to Aristotle's homespun good sense[5] than as an indication of his self-positioning in relation to other intellectuals. When we look at the kind of *tekhnē* that interests Aristotle and Isocrates and earns their esteem, we find substantial similarities. In the brief text *Against the Sophists*, Isocrates rejects the handbook-writers' regimentation of *tekhnē*: he complains it cannot possibly do justice to the art of oratory, a "creative affair,"[6] in which a truly skilled speaker (*tekhnikōtatos*, 12) produces *logoi* that "partake of the circumstances of the moment" (*kairoi*). Aristotle, too, when he discusses the methodology of ethics, appeals to an art such as medicine to illustrate how there is "nothing fixed" (*hestēkos*) in such

---

[4] One salutary result—to be pursued in the following chapter—is a correction of our naïve tendency to see Aristotle as being in competition and dialogue with Plato more than with any other thinker, so that we may in turn see Plato's exceptionalism in sharper relief and feel more keenly the tensions in his confrontations and compromises with the practical arts.

[5] For example, Hardie (1980:136) sees the application of the analogy to the doctrine of the mean in *Nicomachean Ethics* II 6 as "a popular illustration, a lecturer's aside, rather than an essential part of the exposition." Even when the analogy is accorded a fundamental importance, the *tekhnai* are still usually seen as features of everyday life rather than as disciplines that have elaborated their own methodological problems and solutions.

[6] Isocrates *Against the Sophists* 12: ποιητικοῦ πράγματος τεταγμένην τέχνην παράδειγμα φέροντες λελήθασιν σφᾶς αὐτούς (see Vallozza 2003:22–25 for an effort to find "dialogic" elements in the Isocratean corpus that fit this description). For Aristotle's acknowledgment of the value of written *sungrammata* alongside his insistence on the necessary and complementary role of experience, see e.g. *Nicomachean Ethics* X 9, 1181b1–6; cf. *Politics* 1286a10–22, where the king's relationship to the law (and address to "circumstances," or *prospiptonta*: cf. Isocrates *Panathenaicus* 30, *Epistle* 5.4, Steidle 1952:276; of actual leaders in *Antidosis* 131, *Evagoras* 43; of Isocrates' own rhetorical performance in *Antidosis* 140; a counterexample where *to prospipton* is not the circumstance for action but the inept response, *Epistle* 6.10) takes the place of the normal distinction between law and decree (*Politics* 1291a36f., *Nicomachean Ethics* 1137b27ff., *Rhetoric* 1354a32ff.).

matters, and precision (*takribes*) is not attained.[7] In ethics, it is only "in outline" (*tupōi*) that we can determine knowledge of the highest good, give an account of the actions that must be performed, or describe the individual virtues as means.[8] From this imprecise feature of "the general account," Aristotle turns immediately to the fact that in particular cases (*ta kath' hekasta*) even less exactness is possible: particulars "do not fall under any *tekhnē* or precept, and the agents themselves must consider the things that relate to the *kairos*, as in the arts of medicine and helmsmanship" (1104a6–10).[9] In any case, even if the product produced is the same, a real craftsman (analogously to the virtuous person) produces not by following another person's instructions but in accordance with the *tekhnē* within himself (II 4, 1105a21–26). Finding and keeping to the mean, a defining part of Aristotle's ethical theory, is also paralleled in the arts and crafts. "Good craftsmen [*tekhnitai*] look to the intermediate when they produce" (II 6, 1106b13f.). The trainer (*aleiptēs*, 1106b1f.)—who is also a particularly important analogue for Isocrates (*Antidosis* 180–185[10])—exemplifies how this is not a matter of mere arithmetic. And medicine, too, illustrates how *orthos logos* prescribes the intermediate (*Nicomachean Ethics* VI 1, 1138b26–29), not only in virtue, but "in all other pursuits which are objects of knowledge" (*peri hosas estin epistēmē*).[11] So while Aristotle insists that virtue is not a *tekhnē* (*Nicomachean Ethics*

---

[7] *Nicomachean Ethics* II 2, 1104a3–7. *Akribeia* is an interesting common thread to pursue in methodological discussions ranging from Thucydides to Aristotle. See e.g. Hirsch 1993, which comments on the importance of this term in the methodological engagement of Plato's *Phaedrus* with Hippocratic medicine (a subject I explore at length in the following chapter). Arnim (1898:14) discusses the scholastic split between Gorgias' students Isocrates and Alcidamas in these terms: Isocrates "one-sidedly" devoted himself to a new oratorical ideal of *akribeia*, to the point of cutting himself off from the old sophistic tradition of extemporizing to which Alcidamas adhered (a split which continued to the day of Aristides and beyond), adopting an incompatible method with different limitations and capacities dictated by the changing demands on speech. On *akribeia* in Isocrates, see further Usher 1990 on *Panegyricus* 11, Too 1995:183, Abernathy 2003, and Innes 2007:161.

[8] *Nicomachean Ethics* 1094a25, 1104a1f., and 1117b20–22, respectively, laid out more fully below.

[9] Note the narrower sense of (formalized) *tekhnē* alongside *iatrikē* and *kubernētikē* (sc. *tekhnē*) referring to the skilled practice in particular cases that cannot be covered by universal laws.

[10] In this context note the reference to *kairoi* in the description of the learnt practice of both gymnastics and philosophy students (*Antidosis* 184; cf. *Panathenaicus* 30, *Against the Sophists* 8, 16).

[11] To Broadie (1991:187), *Eudemian Ethics* II 5, 1222a6–14, "suggests that the good ethical agent is like familiar craftsmen, except that he works with pleasures and pains, actions and emotions, whereas they work with leather or stone or the hot and cold humours of the body"; this way of putting the distinction doesn't work as well if we are thinking of *rhētorikē tekhnē*. *Eudemian Ethics* II 3, 1220b21–27, extends the doctrine of the mean further in two directions, to cover unskilled action (*praxis atekhnos*) and scientific action (*praxis epistēmonikē*), though all the examples are of *tekhnai*. "Scientific" here is presumably used in the same loose sense (to be discussed further below) as evidently applies in the quotation I have made from *Nicomachean Ethics* VI 1, and perhaps *praxis epistēmonikē* is nearly synonymous with *praxis tekhnikē*.

VI 5), he has nevertheless openly modeled many of its important features on the *tekhnai*.

While for Aristotle practical life is not governed by a productive *tekhnē*, neither is it a "science" in his strictest usage of the word *epistēmē*. Yet we will be concerned to see how both Aristotle and Isocrates make some approach to a knowable "science of practical life," and in Aristotle the term *epistēmē* can be used loosely enough to embrace this at times, not carefully distinguished from *tekhnē* and applied, for example, to medicine. The many connections between the discourses of the *tekhnai* and the terms of Aristotle's ethical theory involve all of these polyvalent terms. There was significant discussion in many disciplines about the grounds of knowledge, the limits of knowledge, and what could be accomplished in theory and in practice despite these limits; if the ancient writers who defended experience (*empeiria*) as a reliable foundation for skill and performance[12] are not building up the kind of demonstrative science described in the *Posterior Analytics*, their aspirations and habits of thought are no further removed from what we would recognize as "science" than those of their rationalist rivals. For example, the more empiricist author of *On Ancient Medicine* is every bit as interested in setting the knowledge of human physiology on a solid epistemological foundation as the more rationalist and deductive Hippocratic writers; it is, in fact, scientific honesty that leads him to probe more attentively the weaknesses of that foundation. Indeed, even in Aristotle's treatises on nature, there is little of the pure deduction he describes in the *Posterior Analytics*, not to mention in the ethical writings with which we are concerned—so this scientific ideal of theoretical knowledge, though it arises in philosophical polemics, is also not a real obstacle to comparative study of Isocratean and Aristotelian "practical philosophy."

Aristotle's insistence on the differences between *tekhnē* and *phronēsis* (the intellectual virtue operative in virtuous action) demands more careful consideration. Does it definitively separate the Aristotelian and Isocratean approaches? After all, Isocrates lacks any urge to declare a distinction between his concerns and *tekhnē*. He retains the general framework of *tekhnē*, despite all his ambitions to raise the art of oratory to the more sophisticated level of preparation for

---

[12]   See esp. Hutchinson 1988, the most important contribution to date to understanding the connections I explore in this chapter. Hutchinson brings together the empiricism of the Hippocratic treatise *On Ancient Medicine* (on which now see Schiefsky 2005), of Isocrates, and of Aristotle's ethics. The basic issues of method and practice were raised in other fields; for example, while I treat harmonic theory below as a counterexample, Barker makes several suggestive connections between this field and other disciplines (2007:66, 88f., 104). It is dangerous to assume that any fourth-century discourse about practice is not "scientific" and taking a considered epistemological position of some kind, empiricist or rationalist; once we trace the overlapping ideas and influences, we have to do with a circle of scientific discourse that includes Aristotle.

creative improvisation in response to the world's fluid circumstances. Aristotle, as we have seen, credits the *tekhnitēs* with many practical abilities (e.g. acting in the *kairos* when precept fails; a disposition to choose the mean) that correspond closely to the most impressive aspects of the state maintained by the agent habituated to virtuous action. In fact, Aristotle explicitly compares the acquisition of *tekhnai* and *aretai* through habituation (*Nicomachean Ethics* II 1, 1103a31–b2, b6ff.).[13] Thus when Aristotle grounds his doctrine that virtue is not a *tekhnē* in a strict distinction between production (*poiēsis*) and *praxis* (VI 4–5), we must admit that even Isocrates' lofty "creative affair" (*poiētikon pragma*) of *Against the Sophists* 12 can be fully contained within the Aristotelian notion of craft production; the need to *produce* something better for a worthy end is reason enough to move decisively beyond the rote knowledge of the cookbook blunderer.

It is precisely a consideration of the ends of action and production that leads Aristotle to insist on his distinction, which means that my attempt to show how naturally Aristotle's theory of virtuous action fits the Isocratean model of training and performance will depend on challenging the correctness and the necessity of Aristotle's claim that artful production, being for the sake of the product, must always be clearly distinguished from virtuous action, which according to Aristotle is for its own sake (*Nicomachean Ethics* VI 5, 1140b6f.).

In this passage Aristotle carefully distinguishes action (the realm of *phronēsis*) both from production and from the realm of more scientific theoretical knowledge.[14] In both Aristotle and Isocrates, practical intelligence, or *phronēsis,* is used not just to distinguish the sophisticated and deliberative stance that befits action in the world from the principles of lower, more rote, labors, but also to define a practical sphere outside the scope of *epistēmē*.[15] Where Aristotle draws his emphatic contrast between *epistēmē* and *phronēsis,* he cites diagnostically the deliberation over particulars (1141b8–23, 1142a20–27), a larger issue whose importance we will consider more closely below. For Isocrates, the *phronēsis* sought by his students (built upon well-formed *doxai* and immediately useful for action) is to be clearly distinguished from *epistēmē* (*Antidosis* 271).[16]

---

[13] Aristotle is very careful, however, to say that we become virtuous through our just actions (*prattontes*), whereas we learn crafts *poiountes* ("by producing"). For him, "playing the cithara well or badly" is an issue of production.

[14] On this triple distinction see also Nightingale 2004:202–204.

[15] Our future examinations will complicate this formulation: in Aristotle's protreptic language, *phronēsis* also includes the highest levels of philosophical contemplation, and a fuller account of Isocratean *epistēmē* shows that it has an important role, serving as the necessary foundation for the orator's performative readiness.

[16] For the importance and significance of *phronēsis* in Isocrates, see Alexiou 2010:130, with complete bibliography.

In Aristotelian terms, the more problematic of the two boundaries is the one between production (where craft operates) and action (where practical intelligence operates). While we have seen that some regard the entire craft analogy as somewhat extraneous and an ill fit for Aristotle's ethical theory, it is significant that others have felt that the apparent exclusion of craft activity from the category of "action" performed with the end of "*eupraxia* itself" (1140b7) is awkward on purely internal grounds. For Sarah Broadie, it is problematic for Aristotle's theory of rational choice that the self-contained end of such a choice is "devoid of empirical content," and Aristotle over the course of the sixth book of the *Nicomachean Ethics* finds himself "straining to show how rational choice and decisions of craft are fundamentally different."[17] Eugene Garver takes the opposite approach, claiming that Aristotelian *tekhnai* (and most notably the art of rhetoric as Aristotle himself describes it) have the very feature of Aristotelian *praxis* that troubles Broadie; in this reading, Aristotle does not deny internal ends to the arts but merely posits that they are subordinate to the external ends.[18] Terence Irwin has likewise commented that Aristotle "will face serious difficulties if he does not allow the same event to be both an action (in so far as it is done for its own sake) and a production (in so far as it is done for the sake of some end external to it),"[19] and he accordingly translates the ambiguous text of *Nicomachean Ethics* X 7, 1177b16–18, "Hence among actions expressing the virtues those in politics and war are pre-eminently fine and great; but they require trouble, aim at some [further] end, and *are choiceworthy for something other than themselves.*"[20]

Isocrates could accept all aspects of this last pronouncement. Political life, practiced through *politikoi logoi*, is more than an instrumental game. Isocrates charges the sophistical writers of *tekhnai* with teaching the worst kind of external ends (*polupragmosunē, pleonexia*) while neglecting the true benefits (*agatha*) of *politikoi logoi* (*Against the Sophists* 20). In contrast, Isocrates cautions those who

---

[17] Broadie 1991:185.
[18] Garver 2006:15–46. I have not done justice to the subtlety of Garver's interpretation: the orator's productive aim includes the practice of rational persuasion (not any persuasion, not sophistry), and rationality has aspects that "can be achieved *in* action and not merely *by* action"—the orator's decisions and fund of knowledge are oriented toward this kind of end (38). Perhaps, then, we can judge the orator as a *tekhnitēs* strictly by the quality of his product (his speech), while acknowledging that the speech itself may demonstrate a standard of *eupraxia*. An error (cf. *Nicomachean Ethics* VI 5, 1140b21–25) that caused a departure from *eupraxia* would vitiate the product.
[19] Irwin 1985:342.
[20] εἰ δὴ τῶν μὲν κατὰ τὰς ἀρετὰς πράξεων αἱ πολιτικαὶ καὶ πολεμικαὶ κάλλει καὶ μεγέθει προέχουσιν, αὗται δ' ἄσχολοι καὶ τέλους τινὸς ἐφίενται καὶ οὐ δι' αὑτὰς αἱρεταί εἰσιν. Irwin takes pains to avoid the simpler translation "not choiceworthy for themselves," which would seem to exclude the *praxis* dimension of productive activities.

pursue such empty ends that his *philosophia* (the word itself is a reminder that he had appropriated this term for his project from his rivals' conception of what is pursued for its own sake[21]) much sooner confers on its adherents the benefit of goodness (*epieikeia*) than its presumed technical objective, *rhētoreia* (21).[22] In Isocratean theory, the Aristotelian virtues of moderation (*sōphrosunē*) and justice (*dikaiosunē*) are present from birth according to an individual's nature,[23] but the study of *politikoi logoi* provides those virtues with the greatest encouragement and exercise they can receive (ibid.). The secondariness (in sequence and in likeliness of achievement, at least) of narrowly professional and instrumental goals in Isocratean education[24] is reinforced by Isocrates' insistence upon the benefits of "philosophical" study for those students who can never become orators (*agōnistai*), who despite their deficiency of natural talent can become "more intelligent" (*phronimōteroi*, echoing Aristotle's term for practical wisdom).[25] At times, Isocrates promotes the ethical results of proper rhetorical training so ardently that they appear to be the most essential proof of education's power; it can make human beings "braver, gentler, more intelligent" (to quote *Antidosis* 211, a passage in which Isocrates defies anyone who doubts the existence of a *paideia* for the human soul).[26]

---

[21] Comparable is Isocrates' programmatic use of "care for the soul" (*To Demonicus* 6, *Against the Sophists* 8, 17, *Evagoras* 41, 80, *Areopagiticus* 43, *Antidosis* 304), discussed further below in connection with Aristotle's *Protrepticus*.

[22] The compatibility of this goal of *epieikeia* with Aristotle's *Nicomachean Ethics* is discussed in more detail below ("The Individual's Nature").

[23] For the relation between Isocratean and Aristotelian virtues, see also Alexiou 2010:104f.

[24] An interesting comparison for "general ethics" as a preparatory stage of "philosophical" *paideia* is the use of Isocrates' protreptic and ethical writings in the later Neoplatonic curriculum. What we would think of as Platonic studies were preceded by a propaedeutic cycle of the trivium and quadrivium, and "then a set of preparatory ethical studies and prologues involved recourse to three hortatory discourses by Isocrates" (*To Demonicus*, *To Nicocles*, and *Nicocles*) (Hoffmann 2006:605). I will discuss this further as an example of interscholastic borrowing in chap. 3.

[25] Isocrates *Against the Sophists* 15, on which see further below ("The Individual's Nature"). In *Antidosis* 201, Isocrates says that only a few students from *any* of the schools (ἐξ ἁπάντων τῶν διδασκαλείων) become *agōnistai*, whereas the vast majority of students continue life as laymen (*idiōtai*). Isocrates proceeds to note the improved qualifications of these *idiōtai* both in social life (ἔν τε ταῖς ὁμιλίαις χαριεστέρους ὄντας ἢ πρότερον ἦσαν) and in political life (τῶν τε λόγων κριτὰς καὶ συμβούλους ἀκριβεστέρους τῶν πλείστων, 204). The former description echoes Aristotle's description of the nameless virtue "most like friendship," even if it tends a bit away from Aristotle's mean towards the ingratiating extreme (*Nicomachean Ethics* IV 6, 1126b11–19); it is perhaps even closer to the Aristotelian virtue of wit (IV 8, 1127b33–1128a1) and not totally irrelevant to Aristotle's discussions of friendship.

[26] For all the seeming universality of this passage, Isocrates makes clear (*Antidosis* 274) that no *paideia* or *tekhnē* can make virtue in those with inferior natures (τοῖς κακῶς πεφυκόσιν). Note the repetition of *pros epieikeian* (212). Elsewhere, it is true, the importance of the orator's virtuous reputation appears in a more instrumental light (278).

Practical Deliberations

Deliberation is another element of Aristotle's ethical theory that suggests parallels to the methods whereby the orator approaches performance, though when Aristotle connects deliberation with *phronēsis*, he takes pains to reiterate the exclusive boundary that separates *phronēsis* from *tekhnē*:

> Regarding *practical wisdom* we shall get at the truth by considering who are the persons we credit with it. Now it is thought to be a mark of a man of practical wisdom to be able to deliberate well about what is good and expedient for himself, not in some particular respect, e.g. about what sorts of thing conduce to health or to strength, but about what sorts of thing conduce to the good life in general. This is shown by the fact that we credit men with practical wisdom in some particular respect when they have calculated well with a view to some good end which is one of those that are not the object of any art. Thus in general the man who is capable of deliberating has practical wisdom.
>
> *Nicomachean Ethics* VI 5, 1140a24–31
> (Revised Oxford Translation)

The laboriousness of the qualification "which is one of those..." testifies to the essential similarity of calculation (*logismos*) in production and action,[27] and we have perhaps already begun to suggest the problems that lie in determining the relationship between Isocrates' *tekhnē* of *politikoi logoi* and "the good life." It is possible to remain somewhat within the Aristotelian theory and to make such a difficult case more tractable by analyzing, again, the *praxis* and *poiēsis* dimensions of a rhetorical performance. A schematic account might be as follows. A craftsman *qua* craftsman works as an instrument to achieve an end external to himself *qua* craftsman. It is for the craftsman's employer to deliberate about the *praxis* dimension of what the craftsman does: whether it should be done or left undone, and how it is to be done apart from productive

---

[27] We must understand the famous dictum in *Physics* II 8 that "*tekhnē* does not deliberate" (199b28) in its heuristic context: Aristotle is refuting the conclusion that nature lacks purpose because it does not deliberate. Nature is always already engaged in the masterful and purposeful fulfillment of its craftsmanlike ends, which do not require selection or decision. In any case, Aristotle speaks explicitly of the art-practitioner's deliberation at *Nicomachean Ethics* III 3, 1112a34–b17, with discussion of arts that call for more (medicine, money-making) or less (gymnastics) deliberation. Broadie (1991:203f.) distinguishes well between "deliberative craft" and "the more mechanical exercise of craft" (under principles, like nature's, that "need no monitoring"), but it is not so evident to me that Aristotle's virtue/craft comparison involves only "habitual skills automatically applied" and not deliberative craft (which surely can better parallel the operation of deliberation as described in Aristotle's account of decision, *Nicomachean Ethics* III 2–3).

considerations. But if the craftsman and his employer are not defined in the same way ("one in account"), they may well be one in number—and the true orator takes responsibility for both of these roles.

In this light we can turn to Isocrates' own account of deliberation. In first introducing his *philosophia* as the discipline that makes the soul (*psukhē*) more intelligent (*phronimos*), Isocrates defines the function (*ergon*) of the soul as deliberation (*Antidosis* 180–182). The scope of this deliberation includes both public and private or personal matters (180). In a related passage (*Nicocles* 8 = *Antidosis* 256),[28] which extols *logos* and justifies Isocrates' paramount emphasis on its cultivation, Isocrates offers an analogy between the *rhētōr*'s persuasive arguments (the *poiēsis* dimension, as it were) and the deliberations that take place in one's own mind for our own purposes (*pros hautous*), which would seem to be part of Aristotle's "good life."[29]

Isocrates and Aristotle are both concerned to understand how an agent, performing amid all the contingencies of life, and equipped with imprecise knowledge but the strength of well-trained dispositions, chooses the best course of action. The analogy of *tekhnē* continues to exert a living influence on Aristotle's ethical theory when it has ostensibly been left behind, and this is especially meaningful if we consider the art of oratory. Aristotle's ultimate motivation for insisting that *phronēsis* lies apart from *tekhnē*, employs a special kind of calculation ("deliberation"), and devotes its operation to a different order of ends may be, in large part, to assert the privileged and prestigious position of the kind of human actions he wishes to designate as done for their own sake. (And Isocrates is clearly no less driven to stake such a claim.) It may be more economical to emphasize the non-productive dimensions of the actions performed under the guidance of a "*tekhnē* of practical life" such as Isocrates', and to ask if Aristotle might well respond to Isocrates by saying, "What you claim to teach the orator is what I call practical wisdom, and if the style of political oratory and self-cultivation you call *philosophia* lives up to your promises, then it cannot be summed up with the part of my theory intended to explain a craft like shipbuilding or even medicine." Now in actuality, we would not need to surprise Aristotle with Isocrates' presumptuous aspirations, since in fact the account of "the good life" retailed in Isocrates' school was prestigious and familiar,[30] so that some of the problems raised by philosophical readers of the

---

[28] For Isocrates' self-citations and the attendant textual issues, see Pinto 2003.

[29] This passage's assertion of the value of producing a privately deliberate (*euboulos*) person (together with the distinction *rhētorikoi* vs. *eubouloi*) thus recalls the passages we have already discussed in which Isocrates considers the important ethical progress his education offers to students who cannot become *agōnistai*. Cf. Natali 1994:379f.

[30] There is extensive historical evidence for contact and competition between Isocrates, Aristotle, and their schools—not least in the tradition of Aristotle's afternoon rhetoric lectures. I will

Nicomachean Ethics may in fact betoken the external pressures exerted by the alternative model we find in Isocrates. In particular, Aristotle's use of analogies of unclear scope, and of examples that don't fully test and define his theory, may reflect how authoritatively the empiricist intellectual inheritance was being applied to the theory of training for practical life. Aristotle's own *Rhetoric* states that "the duty of rhetoric is to deal with such matters as we deliberate upon without arts or systems [*tekhnai*] to guide us"[31] and has been rightly understood as describing a *tekhnē* without the narrowly productive focus based upon which the *Nicomachean Ethics* distinguishes craft from *phronēsis*.[32]

Yet in *Nicomachean Ethics* Aristotle insists that "the orator does not deliberate whether he shall persuade"; in other words, it is always ethics and not rhetoric when we are deliberating over the *ends* of life's *praxis*, and the productive pursuit of the orator is but one of the many means (requiring their own deliberation) we apply towards those ends. Clearly Isocrates would not accept this and would insist that his domain is "ethical" by Aristotle's definitions. Granted, he arrives at this insistence not only out of a desire to emulate a philosopher like Aristotle, but also through another set of distinctions he wants to establish between himself and other rhetorical practitioners. Below we will consider Isocrates' rejection of an inflexible and "ordered art" (*tetagmenē tekhnē*) of rhetoric—a programmatic stance taken up in the rhetorical and not the philosophical arena—to discover where it leaves Isocrates in relation to Aristotle. Yet Isocrates also owes his claim that orators can and should be educated to show flexibility—and his attempt to develop a sophisticated way of defending it as rooted in sound knowledge but not limited by procrustean formulas—to the need to place himself above not only those who promised results from the cookbook-*tekhnai* (equally scorned by Aristotle), but also those like Alcidamas, whose polemic against confining persuasion to the fixed written word sought to undermine the very literary authority Isocrates (and the philosophers) might use to theorize the agent's free and responsive well-trained actions.[33] However sterile it may seem in the pages of Alcidamas, the

---

consider this evidence in later chapters; my purpose here is to test the plausibility of a theory of influence using only the evidence in each author's extant exposition of his doctrines.

[31] *Rhetoric* I 2, 1357a1–4 (Revised Oxford Translation).

[32] See e.g. Shields 2007:377: "Aristotle does not suppose it appropriate to persuade for the sake of persuasion, or even to persuade for the sake of winning. Interestingly, when he approaches rhetoric as a productive craft, Aristotle assumes that persuasion is its goal, but then credits his audience with the intelligence to sort out reasonable sorts of persuasive appeals from the banal, fatuous, and manipulative." Balla (2004:56f.) has drawn several connections between Aristotle's *Rhetoric* and Isocratean thought, including the preference for deliberative oratory, a pragmatic and empirical conception of knowledge, and the reliance on the audience's *endoxa*.

[33] Compare n7 above.

oralist's challenge and extemporizing ideal reflect a debate whose philosophical productivity is evident in Plato's *Phaedrus*, and which must be given significant credit for spurring Isocrates (and by extension Aristotle) into taking up the challenging paradoxes of practical "philosophy." In the following chapter, we will consider more fully how Plato inherits the terms of this debate, joining Isocrates in dismissing a mere "written *tekhnē*" (e.g. *Phaedrus* 275c5), while being forced to come up with a more complex response to the greater sophistication and philosophical authority of the practical-arts methodology and debate that ran from the Hippocratics to Isocrates (and whose heir Aristotle made himself in many respects, wielding its empiricism against the authority of Platonic idealism).

In the final section of this chapter, we will more fully consider Isocrates' theoretical and protreptic insistence that his education is founded on ethical self-cultivation and rejects any valuation based on possessions and other externals. In this light, it should be all the clearer how he presented his methods as completely satisfying the kind of criteria laid down by Aristotle as distinguishing the realm of virtuous action from the world of *tekhnē*—that acts are done for their own sake, and "proceed from a firm and unchangeable character."[34] Rather than resisting this basic commonality, we may more profitably ask whether these kinds of professions on Isocrates' part are the authentic starting point of his educational philosophy and conception of *politikoi logoi*, or whether they are rather defensive counterblasts against rivals who painted him as a maker of technicians more than a maker of men. The first is probably closer to the truth. The idea of public speech unguided by the good is thoroughly foreign to Isocrates' approach. The terminology of intelligence, "philosophy," and care of the soul are woven everywhere into his works. Yes, he saw and spoke of the heights of lofty human aspirations in decidedly political-rhetorical terms, but his claims for the nobility, wisdom, and disinterested goodness possible within this arena are a pure and sincere statement of the highest human good, one he hoped would prevail against others that did not draw equally from conventional and intellectualist values (this explains Isocrates' powerful impression as an example to Cicero). The language of philosophical protreptic he took up existed before him and carried him in its stream. It may seem to us that Isocrates was out of the mainstream, but this impression would not have been so likely for his contemporaries, as it was not in antiquity for Cicero or for the Neoplatonist schools that thought his works could serve as a valuable ethical introduction to philosophical study,[35] the first step of a *gradus ad Parnassum*, but with all the

---

[34] *Nicomachean Ethics* II 4, 1105b27–33 (trans. Ross 1925).
[35] See n24 above.

importance of the first step, turning away from the false path of the world's vulgar scheme of values.

We may, then, best seek commonalities between Isocrates and Aristotle in the realm of those affairs that are not susceptible to the direct application of systematic knowledge, but which require a more practical and deliberative approach, sensitive to the particularities of changing circumstances. As we have already begun to see and will see more fully, both thinkers have set out to explore just this realm. Both define it against matters in which *epistēmē* is authoritative and adequate, even using a common example (*grammata*) to make this contrast. Aristotle observes that the science of *grammata* admits no room for doubt, decision, or deliberation (καὶ περὶ μὲν τὰς ἀκριβεῖς καὶ αὐτάρκεις τῶν ἐπιστημῶν οὐκ ἔστι βουλή, οἷον περὶ γραμμάτων, 1112a34–b2). Isocrates defines the difference between *logoi* and *grammata* in the latter's complete non-involvement in the moments that call for fitting action (*kairoi, Against the Sophists* 12f.), and we have seen the connection between Isocrates' and Aristotle's language of deliberation when speaking of the production of actions.

Indeed, this connection is natural enough, as no Classical Athenian would have disputed the necessary connection between deliberation (*bouleu-*) and action (*prag-*). Yet the multiple connections between the two theories of practice on this point are underscored by the fact that Isocrates, despite his overriding focus on political action, makes it clear that the deliberative process at the heart of his educational program also applies to highly individual decisions of the kind considered in Aristotelian ethics.

The Crucible of Action

Given the inexactitude that must reign over our actions, how, finally, does the actor synthesize the available (provisional and extra-scientific) particulars in the performance demanded by the crucial moment? Strangely, what remains largely absent both from Aristotle's ethical treatises and from Isocrates' writings is a more closely observed account of how everything actually gets put together on the playing field of life. We hear of the *kairos* but lack the case studies (or a more detailed theoretical analysis) in either author of how the ablest agents respond to its challenges. Isocrates suggests the basis of an answer in *Antidosis* 184,[36] saying that after learning and habituation are complete, the speaker faces the *kairoi* in reliance upon *doxai*. We look for more detail than this in vain, and Aristotle does not seem any more interested in giving a detailed and analytical description. In both theories, the very fluidity of ultimate circumstances dictates

---

[36]   Closely related passages are *Against the Sophists* 8, 16.

that any exposition of method must focus on defining the kinds of preparation that enable us to confront such a world.

Perhaps neither author is as concerned to offer useful insights into the rigors of action, as to defend an account of action beginning from the basically empiricist assumption that the knowledge[37] on which we depend for action is imprecise and not firmly in our grasp.[38] Of course, for Aristotle, defending this theoretical orientation entailed a philosophical labor and achievement of a kind Isocrates could not have contemplated. Some of what most clearly shows Aristotle's openness to practicing rhetoricians' and empiricists' models of knowledge—as his critical use of reputable opinion (*endoxa*)—would nonetheless figure prominently in any philosopher's account of his distinctive contributions to ethical theory. Aristotle is returning to pre-Platonic technical methodology— to the mainstream of real-world thought about how competent actors master their materials and circumstances to make some progress despite unresolvable uncertainty and ignorance—in the conviction that Plato's radical rationalism was not a necessary or even desirable condition for a philosophically rigorous approach to the actions of life. This perspective can thus sharpen our perception of Aristotle's philosophical difference from Plato, keeping clearly in view the less appreciated background on which Aristotle relied: the claims being put forward for the sophisticated capabilities of empirically grounded practical *tekhnai*.[39]

Despite the Isocratean and Aristotelian theories' apparent deficiency in analysis of the final action's mechanics, some Aristotelian passages do address how action is conditioned by *doxa* and *kairos*, two terms of crucial importance to Isocrates. Aristotle's discussion of belief (*doxa*) concludes that "*doxa* precedes decision or is inseparably connected to it" (προγίνεται δόξα τῆς προαιρέσεως ἢ παρακολουθεῖ, 1112a11f.).[40] Something more of the improvisatory basis of action is conveyed in general terms when Aristotle allows that some important determinations can only be reached "in outline" (τύπῳ). In a programmatic

---

[37] Isocrates' dramatic statements about the importance of the *doxai* the orator relies upon in action should not blind us to the role he accords to *epistēmē* in the orator's education.

[38] Hutchinson (1988:39) has also arrived at the conclusion that "Aristotle rejects characteristically Platonic views on practical skills in favour of their Isocratean alternatives."

[39] To give a small example: Aristotle's discussion of the relationship between virtue and *tekhnē* can no longer be seen as primarily made with reference to the Socratic doctrine (see the references in Irwin 1985:342, note on *Nicomachean Ethics* 1140b21–25).

[40] In discussing that practical sense (*nous*) with which we orient ourselves to particulars, Aristotle says we must give our attention to the undemonstrated *doxai* of those who have more experience, because of their "possession of an eye [*omma*] as a result of their experience" (1143b11–14). The eye analogy interestingly evokes a complex but instantaneous synthesis of particulars, but here the *doxai* are simply "opinions" whose use is prescribed together with rigorously settled demonstrations.

statement at the beginning of the *Nicomachean Ethics*, Aristotle announces the importance of knowledge (*gnōsis*) of the highest good, "at least in outline" (τύπῳ γε, 1094a25). Thus it is with a provisional grasp on this good that we aim for it. Here Aristotle's criterion of importance "for our lives" (*pros ton bion*) repeats exactly those words used by Isocrates to announce his criterion (not met by excessive study of philosophical theories of being), by which all study must be preparatory for speech and deliberation (*pros ton bion*, *Antidosis* 269).

Again, in stressing the practical aim of ethics, which is not to know (*eidōmen*) what virtue is but to become good (1103b27–29), Aristotle declares up front that any account of actions to be performed has to be given in outline (πᾶς ὁ περὶ τῶν πρακτῶν λόγος τύπῳ καὶ οὐκ ἀκριβῶς ὀφείλει λέγεσθαι, 1104a1f.), and this would seem to apply to our accounting and deliberation in process when actions must actually be performed. In this same passage, Aristotle uses Isocrates' preferred term, *kairos*, for the moment and urgency that must be confronted on this basis of inexactitude (δεῖ δ' αὐτοὺς ἀεὶ τοὺς πράττοντας τὰ πρὸς τὸν καιρὸν σκοπεῖν, 1104a8f.). Later, as Aristotle turns to a more detailed account of what the virtuous person aims for—that is, the definition of the mean state between extremes that makes us good in some particular way—we are again faced with the need to recognize a target inexactly for the practical purposes of aiming at it in our actions (e.g. "So much for bravery. It is easy to grasp what it is, in outline at least [τύπῳ γε], from what we have said," 1117b20–22 [trans. Irwin 1985]).

The Individual's Nature

The nature (*phusis*) of an individual is a factor that works at the margins of both Isocrates' and Aristotle's theories, excluded from the influence of training or habituation, though frequently mentioned by Isocrates, given his ambition to develop premier-league oratorical talent. It nonetheless plays a role in both writers' accounts of individual formation, as the substantively irrational germ around which the formally rationalized system[41] of self-fashioning operates.

For the most part, Aristotle's ethical teachings are not concerned with those individual natures incapable of virtue in the first place—these would, in his view, only be diseased or properly subhuman natures, to whose crippled possessors the categories of virtue and vice can hardly apply (1148b15–49a24).[42] Rather, Aristotle is interested in those whose natures enable them to acquire the virtues,[43] and for these creatures, endowed as they are with correct natures

---

[41] I borrow the terms from Max Weber.

[42] Aristotle's examples regrettably include the extremes of non-Greek humanity, who he says lack reason, and homosexuals.

[43] These would seem to be, at least, all those men whose virtuous development is sufficient to realize the good legislator's aims. They are often clubbily referred to in the first-person plural.

capable of virtue, the main point is that virtue is purely a matter of habituation, a process which neither depends on nature nor involves a struggle against nature (1103a18ff.). When considering the material the educator or legislator has to deal with, Aristotle is ready to call those with natural gifts "fortunate," but as he goes on immediately to speak of a preexisting readiness for virtue, it is clear that he has early habituation in mind as the crucial factor in making a subject susceptible to the influence of *logoi* and instruction (δεῖ <u>προδιειργάσθαι</u> <u>τοῖς ἔθεσι</u> τὴν τοῦ ἀκροατοῦ ψυχήν ... δεῖ δὴ τὸ <u>ἦθος</u> προϋπάρχειν πως οἰκεῖον τῆς ἀρετῆς, 1179b24–30).

The term *ēthos,* or "character," while in this passage clearly associated with *ethos,* or "habit," does allow some room for ambiguity. In book VI of the *Nicomachean Ethics* (1144b1–17), Aristotle acknowledges the evidence showing that virtues of character, in some way, can exist in us by nature from birth.[44] Yet this recognition serves Aristotle mainly as a foil for stating how incomplete, unworthy of our highest nature, and even dangerous such endowments remain without the contributions of *phronēsis.* In comparison to natural virtue, "full virtue" and its associated *ēthē,* the subject of the *Ethics,* are a different object of human efforts and are pursued in a different way (ἕτερόν τι τὸ κυρίως ἀγαθὸν καὶ τὰ τοιαῦτα ἄλλον τρόπον ὑπάρχειν, 1144b7f.). Notably, throughout this passage, Aristotle not only stresses the incompleteness of natural virtue (ἡ φυσικὴ ἀρετή) in comparison to full virtue (ἡ κυρίως) but also avoids the implication that strong natural endowments are of any advantage whatsoever.[45] Irwin seems justified in concluding that Aristotle does not consider inborn qualities or aptitudes to be "genuine virtues."[46] Nor are weak natures to blame for vice: in discussing the individual virtues, Aristotle makes clear his view that character defects are states arising from choices made (and the importance of choice, or *proairesis,* in Aristotle's overall account of ethics can hardly be overestimated), rather than expressions of *dunamis,* or "capacity" (e.g. 1127b14f., cf. more generally 1106a6–10). Ultimately, in any case, "all who are not maimed ... may win [happiness] by a certain kind of study and care" (1099b18–21).

---

[44] πᾶσι γὰρ δοκεῖ ἕκαστα τῶν ἠθῶν ὑπάρχειν φύσει πως· καὶ γὰρ δίκαιοι καὶ σωφρονικοὶ καὶ ἀνδρεῖοι καὶ τἄλλα ἔχομεν εὐθὺς ἐκ γενετῆς, 1144b4–6.

[45] Perhaps Aristotle's strongest recognition of natural virtue's power comes at 1151a18f., when he allows that either it or habituated virtue may teach the agent correct belief about the first principle of virtuous action, i.e. provide a right orientation toward the ends for which we act. It seems clear that the continence and judgment needed to realize these aims must come through habituation and cultivation of practical wisdom. We may be fortunate enough to have some natural inclination toward the aims ordained for us by nature, but the practical science of action derives little of value from this.

[46] Irwin 1985:349 *ad loc.*

In contrast to Aristotle, Isocrates is quite emphatic about his students' need to possess the right individual *phusis* if they are to realize the highest aims of his education and become consummate political actors (*agōnistai*).[47] This point is closely tied to Isocrates' rejection of the sophists' cookbook-like approaches that claim to reduce the highest accomplishments to the level of mere ABC's (the *epistēmē* of *grammata*). Isocrates instead offers his own much more advanced[48] and versatile brand of education, which he claims is adequate to the complex realities in which his students hope to act effectively. What fatal omissions by the authors of rote methods does Isocrates claim to repair? Those factors in education to which the rules of a technique can never answer: nature (*phusis*) and experience (*empeiriai*).[49] On this point, despite the differences, the two have in common a view of education for action that requires due attention to the determinative practical constraints within which progress must be made towards the right kind of actions. Aristotle's circumstantialism—his interest in making the best choice within the bounds of circumstances, which underlies his analysis of ethical and political *aporiai*—brings him closer to Isocrates. Both claim that the right experiences (for Aristotle, habituation) are required more than *logoi*. Both would strenuously oppose the claim of a written treatise to fashion *aretē* out of a bad nature (Isocrates *Antidosis* 274), with their agreement also taking in the limitation of systematic procedures in this domain.

Isocrates' regard for *phusis* seems to indicate a pessimism in comparison to Aristotle about the adequacy of practical training, or certainly about its wide role in determining the virtues attained by humanity (or at least Greek citizenry) in general. The student's inborn *phusis* is, of course, beyond the educator's influence in both theories; while Aristotle and Isocrates are certainly differently attentive to the issue and the ethico-political consequences of such facts, it is still worthwhile to construct the properly comparable case, in which each theory is allowed to have its say about the same natures (say, "good civic material").

A closer look into Isocrates' views shows—to a reader looking for that comparable case—that the person of undistinguished *phusis* is not in fact excluded from Isocratean educational theory, and indeed that this person's prospects under the regime of a practical education are the object of some theoretical

---

[47] For this term, see n25 above, and cf. "Demosthenes" 61.44 (a text that shows an unmistakable Isocratean influence), Plato *Phaedrus* 269d2.

[48] The orientation of Isocrates' school to the highest levels of professional oratory is a crucial point, forcing us to examine his occasional remarks about the value and effect of his education for students who cannot reach that level in order to make an apples-to-apples theoretical comparison with Aristotle's ethics.

[49] Isocrates *Against the Sophists* 10. Other passages that recognize the importance of *phusis* in education are *Against the Sophists* 17f. and *Antidosis* 185–188.

interest to Isocrates. In *Against the Sophists*, Isocrates considers the value of *paid-eusis* for the orator in building up the resources upon which he may draw in his performances, and he then insists that it is not without value for the person whose deficient *phusis* disqualifies him from becoming an *agonistēs* or maker of *logoi*[50] (τοὺς δὲ καταδεεστέραν τὴν φύσιν ἔχοντας ἀγωνιστὰς μὲν ἀγαθοὺς ἢ λόγων ποιητὰς οὐκ ἂν ἀποτελέσειεν, αὐτοὺς δ' ἂν αὑτῶν προαγάγοι καὶ πρὸς πολλὰ φρονιμωτέρως διακεῖσθαι ποιήσειεν, 15). Training can "advance them and bring them into a more *phronimos* state." *Phronēsis*, of course, is an essential part of Aristotelian virtue, but here it is not yet made clear what actions, if any, a sharpened *phronēsis* would enable. However, on the last page before *Against the Sophists* comes to an end,[51] Isocrates suggests that the most general progressive tendency of students under his *philosophia* is specifically ethical. This striking claim clarifies his doctrine of *phusis* and provides us with a sounder basis on which to make the comparison to Aristotle's general conception of progress towards virtue:

> καίτοι τοὺς βουλομένους πειθαρχεῖν τοῖς ὑπὸ τῆς φιλοσοφίας ταύτης προσταττομένοις πολὺ ἂν θᾶττον πρὸς ἐπιείκειαν ἢ πρὸς ῥητορείαν ὠφελήσειεν. καὶ μηδεὶς οἰέσθω με λέγειν ὡς ἔστιν δικαιοσύνη διδακτόν· ὅλως μὲν γὰρ οὐδὲ μίαν ἡγοῦμαι τοιαύτην εἶναι τέχνην, ἥτις τοῖς κακῶς πεφυκόσιν πρὸς ἀρετὴν σωφροσύνην ἂν καὶ δικαιοσύνην ἐμποιήσειεν· οὐ μὴν ἀλλὰ συμπαρακελεύσασθαί γε καὶ συνασκῆσαι μάλιστ' ἂν οἶμαι τὴν τῶν λόγων τῶν πολιτικῶν ἐπιμέλειαν.

Nevertheless, those who wish to follow the prescriptions of my philosophy may be helped more quickly to fair-mindedness than to speech-making. Let no one think that I mean that a sense of justice is teachable; I contend that there is no sort of art that can convert those who by nature lack virtue to soundness of mind and a sense of justice. But I certainly do think that the study of political speeches can assist in encouraging and training these faculties.

Against the Sophists 21 (trans. Mirhady and Too 2000)

---

[50] If we shift our attention to Aristotle's *Politics*, we find in the description of the "statesman" (*politikos*) little direct mention of *phusis* (as we do in, for example, the discussion of what makes conspirators tick: 1312a17f.); the general account is based on the idea of a generically human political capacity, and the three requirements enumerated in Politics V 9, 1309a33–39 (*philia, dunamis, aretē kai dikaiosunē*) all correspond to the variable conditions of a given *politeia*, which seems to stress the social, as opposed to natural, context of their acquisition. Furthermore, Aristotle's first example of a quality that is essential and rare (τίνος ἔλαττον μετέχουσι πάντες, 1309b2f.), and thus to be given especial weight, is the general's experience (*empeiria*: διὸ ἐν στρατηγίᾳ μὲν εἰς τὴν ἐμπειρίαν μᾶλλον τῆς ἀρετῆς, 1309b4f.).

[51] For the discourse's problematic closure see Too 1995:161ff., 194ff.

Granted, the highest goal of training under Isocrates is *rhētoreia*. But another benefit accrues "much more quickly," which implies progress made in meaningful and immediately beneficial increments each step of the way—a secure improvement even for the student who never fully acquires the powers of the complete *rhētōr*. And this beneficial result is *epieikeia*, that "decency" which Aristotle takes as often simply denoting the good (ἀντὶ τοῦ ἀγαθοῦ, *Nicomachean Ethics* 1137b1, a sense Aristotle employs alongside its technical use for a supererogatory form of *dikaiosunē*).[52] It may seem puzzling that Isocrates concludes by specifying the work that leads his students to Aristotelian virtues of character such as *sōphrosunē* and *dikaiosunē* as "the *epimeleia* of *politikoi logoi*." But this phrase (like Isocrates' more programmatic favorite, *tēs psukhēs epimeleia*, or "care for the soul"[53]) indicates the highest end (political life as a *rhētōr*) for which the training aims,[54] and our discussion has suggested that if we were to define the regime by what Isocrates indicates as its most regular, general, and secure effects, we could well call it instead the cultivation of virtue (*epieikeia* as opposed to *rhētoreia*).

A passage in *Antidosis* resoundingly confirms Isocrates' view that the most generally produced result of his school's training is improvement in *epieikeia* and *phronēsis*. Here Isocrates, aware that his claims for his program of rhetorical education are challenged by a basic skepticism towards all "philosophical" exhorters and professors of human excellence, defends the principle of moral improvement of the soul through purposeful training:

[209] οὐ μόνον δ' ἐκ τούτων, ἀλλὰ καὶ τῶν λοιπῶν εἰκότως ἂν ἅπαντες τὴν ἄγνοιαν θαυμάσειαν τῶν τολμώντων οὕτως εἰκῇ καταφρονεῖν τῆς φιλοσοφίας, πρῶτον μὲν εἰ πάσας τὰς πράξεις καὶ τὰς τέχνας εἰδότες ταῖς μελέταις καὶ ταῖς φιλοπονίαις ἁλισκομένας πρὸς τὴν τῆς φρονήσεως ἄσκησιν ταῦτα μηδεμίαν ἡγοῦνται δύναμιν ἔχειν, [210] ἔπειτ' εἰ τῶν μὲν σωμάτων μηδὲν οὕτως ἂν φήσειαν εἶναι φαῦλον, ὅ τι γυμνασθὲν καὶ πονῆσαν οὐκ ἂν εἴη βέλτιον, <u>τὰς δὲ ψυχὰς τὰς ἄμεινον</u>

---

52 Despite Isocrates' insistence, in what follows, that (contrary to the sophists) the virtues are not a simple matter of teachable *tekhnē*, it is clear that the obstacles thrown up by *phusis* in the way of ethical improvement are nothing like those that limit the number of those who can become masterful orators. Thus, when Isocrates is discussing the right method for developing virtue, the student's *phusis* is a secondary concern. Likewise, Aristotle distinguishes *mathētos* "learnable" from *ethistos* "habituable" (1099b9), and moral education (while indeed, like the Isocratean training, a species of education) deals in the latter.

53 See n21 above.

54 I believe that it is precisely because Isocrates has so elevated the end of *logoi* that he feels compelled in such a passage as this one, by introducing the discussion of *epieikeia* and *aretē* and the distinction from *tekhnē*, to try to make it clear that his methods and results do not produce the (contemptible and empty, in his view) situation of chasing after *logoi* purely by means of *logoi*.

πεφυκυίας τῶν σωμάτων μηδὲν ἂν νομίζουσιν γενέσθαι σπουδαιοτέρας παιδευθείσας καὶ τυχούσας τῆς προσηκούσης ἐπιμελείας, [211] ἔτι δ' εἰ περὶ τοὺς ἵππους καὶ τοὺς κύνας καὶ τὰ πλεῖστα τῶν ζῴων ὁρῶντες τέχνας ἔχοντάς τινας, αἷς τὰ μὲν ἀνδρειότερα, τὰ δὲ πραότερα, τὰ δὲ φρονιμώτερα ποιοῦσιν, περὶ τὴν τῶν ἀνθρώπων φύσιν μηδεμίαν οἴονται τοιαύτην εὑρῆσθαι παιδείαν, ἥτις ἂν αὐτοὺς ἐπί τι τούτων ὧνπερ καὶ τὰ θηρία δυνηθείη προαγαγεῖν, [212] ἀλλὰ τοσαύτην ἁπάντων ἡμῶν ἀτυχίαν κατεγνώκασιν ὥσθ' ὁμολογήσειαν μὲν ἂν ταῖς ἡμετέραις διανοίαις ἕκαστον τῶν ὄντων βέλτιον γίγνεσθαι καὶ χρησιμώτερον, αὐτοὺς δ' ἡμᾶς τοὺς ἔχοντας τὴν ταύτην, ᾗ πάντα πλείονος ἄξια ποιοῦμεν, τολμῶσιν λέγειν ὡς οὐδὲν ἂν ἀλλήλους πρὸς ἐπιείκειαν εὐεργετήσαιμεν.

[209] In addition to these, there are other reasons why everyone would naturally be surprised at the ignorance of those who so casually dare to despise philosophy. First, although they know that all pursuits and arts are acquired by practice and hard work, they think that these have no power where the training of intellect is concerned. [210] Then, although they agree that no body is so weak that it cannot be improved by exercise and labor, they do not think the soul, by nature superior to the body, can become finer [*spoudaioteras*] as a result of education and the proper training. [211] Furthermore, although they see that some individuals are skilled at [*tekhnas ekhontas...hais*] making horses, dogs, and most other animals braver [*andreiotera*], or gentler [*praotera*], or cleverer [*phronimōtera*], they think that no such education [*paideian*] has been discovered to develop these same qualities in human beings. [212] Instead, they condemn us all to such misfortune that they would agree that every other being becomes better and more useful through our intellect, but they dare to declare that we who have this intellect by which we make everything else more valuable could not help each other at all to become better.

(Trans. Mirhady and Too 2000)

Both in the account of how students of *philosophia* progress and in the physical analogies to this process, Isocrates emphasizes the language of hard work (*meletai, philoponiai, askēsis, gumnazō*, etc.).[55] The sustained discipline of this method may be compared to Aristotelian habituation. In the last lines

---

[55] Many of these same terms are used in the *Nicomachean Ethics* (e.g. δι' ἀγυμνασίαν καὶ ἀμέλειαν, 1114a24f.; πολλοὺς πόνους ὑπομένειν, 1104a31f., analogically; ἄσκησίς τις τῆς ἀρετῆς, 1170a11f.). For the triad nature/practice/knowledge see the following chapter and Shorey 1909. Cf. *Rhetoric*

quoted, Isocrates again chooses *epieikeia* as the word to sum up the benefits of the rigorous self-cultivation in which he believes. This is an indication of the remarkably universal level on which Isocrates speaks in order to defend his *philosophia*'s most basic principles.[56] In this passage the care of the soul has the set goal of *epieikeia* (not *rhētoreia*). The *phronēsis* by which we are to achieve this goal is the same faculty ordinary people apply to other practical goals, so that phrase "we ourselves who possess this *phronēsis*" seems supremely inclusive. Even the language of *phusis* is used in a manner that lacks the faintest suggestion that any of "us" might lack the natural gifts necessary to answer Isocrates' call to self-improvement.[57] Isocrates dwells not on the possible deficiencies of our *psukhai* but on the fact that nature has endowed them with capacities superior to our bodies (τὰς δὲ ψυχὰς τὰς ἄμεινον πεφυκυίας τῶν σωμάτων, 210). When Isocrates clearly rejects the view of any who think that no known *paideia* is applicable to human nature (περὶ τὴν τῶν ἀνθρώπων φύσιν μηδεμίαν οἴονται τοιαύτην εὑρῆσθαι παιδείαν, 211), he encourages a wide view of what may be made of "our" common and undistinguished natures. As Isocrates continues this plea to develop the capacities of our moral nature, he ends with the complaint that people have not grasped the power of *paideia* and *epimeleia* (diligent pursuit) to benefit our nature far more readily than the nature of animals, who we see can be taught outlandish tricks and skills beyond the scope of what we would consider their ordinary nature (ἐκ τούτων δύνανται γνῶναι τὴν παιδείαν καὶ τὴν ἐπιμέλειαν, ὅσην ἔχει δύναμιν, οὐδ' ὅτι ταῦτα πολὺ ἂν θᾶττον τὴν ἡμετέραν φύσιν ἢ τὴν ἐκείνων ὠφελήσειεν, 214). By making "our nature" (τὴν ἡμετέραν φύσιν) the direct object of "benefit" (ὠφελεῖν), Isocrates suggests that, in this general context, our nature, so far from being an obstacle, is expandable and improvable.[58]

1410b8, in which "invention can only come through natural talent or long practice; but this treatise may indicate the way it is done."

[56] Azoulay (2010) studies the distinctions through which Isocrates defines an elite in cultural, social, and intellectual terms (the changing notion of *epieikeis* as traced by Brun [2007] alongside *phronimoi, spoudaioi, kharientes, eugeneis*, etc.); cf. Azoulay 2007:194f.

[57] This is, indeed, no more than we would expect on the basis of our interpretation of *Against the Sophists* 15, which it does much to confirm.

[58] Cf. Isocrates' statement in *Antidosis* 181 that by means of *philosophia* we get more intelligent souls (*phronimōterai psukhai*). To save Isocrates from inconsistency, perhaps it would be more appropriate to say that the true potential of our individual natures is rarely understood or developed, and that *epieikeia* at least is well within the range of the ordinary human nature of the wide civic audience Isocrates aims to impress. Note the close similarity of wording to *Against the Sophists* 21, πολὺ ἂν θᾶττον πρὸς ἐπιείκειαν ἢ πρὸς ῥητορείαν ὠφελήσειεν, discussed above. The comparison is different, but in both passages it is the benefit of *epieikeia* (implying quite Aristotelian character virtues, I have argued) that is "much more readily" available to even the ungifted through Isocratean training.

Phronēsis for Aristotle is not only a principle of ethics, but also a general intelligence that serves philosophy and life. Some remarks near the end of *Topics* illustrate this and show the role Aristotle concedes to individual nature at the point when dialectical training culminates in decision and performance. Aristotle has been speaking of the importance in dialectic of accumulating and laying out a range of possible lines of argument and states:

> Moreover, as contributing to knowledge [*gnōsis*] and to philosophic wisdom [*tēn kata philosophian phronēsin*] the power of discerning and holding in one view the results of either of two hypotheses is no mean instrument; for it then only remains to make a right choice of one of them. For a task of this kind a certain natural ability is required [*dei ... huparchein euphua*]: in fact real natural ability [*euphuïa*] just is the power rightly to choose the true and shun the false. Men of natural ability [*hoi pephukotes eu*] can do this; for by a right liking or disliking for whatever is proposed to them they rightly select what is best. It is best to know by heart arguments [*logoi*] upon those questions which are of most frequent occurrence ...
>
> Aristotle Topics VIII 14, 163b9–18
(trans. Pickard-Cambridge 1928)

This is connected to the Isocratean form of practical thinking. In both, a store of preparatory knowledge and training—arguments, points of view, common conceptions, and the like—puts the student well on the road to *phronēsis* and *philosophia*, though individual *phusis* is a further requirement that enables the most talented students to marshal and select the arguments in the moment so as to succeed in the *agōn*.

In this chapter, Aristotle uses a variety of key terms for the foundational knowledge in which the dialectician should be well versed: for example, "familiar and primary ideas" (*endoxa, prōta*). He also draws an analogy to the geometer's training and exercise in the elements (*to peri ta stoikheia gegumnasthai*). The verb, analogizing the disputant's training to the gymnast's, is Isocratean (*Antidosis* 180–185) and rhetorical.[59] True, the noun, "elements" (*stoikheia*), also brings to mind Isocrates' disdain for an art of rhetoric no more creative than the science (*epistēmē*) of basic literacy (*grammata*, *Against the Sophists* 10), and his preference for such loftier terms as *ideai* (or, in his gymnastics analogy, *skhēmata*).[60] Yet his

---

[59] Note the opposition between the well-trained orator (*gugumnasmenos*) and the naturally talented one (*euphuēs*, the same word Aristotle has used in the passage just discussed) at Aristotle *Rhetoric* 1410b8.

[60] The *ideai* of Isocrates *Against the Sophists* 16 will be considered in the following chapter.

caution in *Antidosis* 266—that intellectual pursuits such as geometry are merely "gymnastics of the soul and a preparation for philosophy" (γυμνασίαν μέντοι τῆς ψυχῆς καὶ παρασκευὴν φιλοσοφίας)—closely parallels what Aristotle says here.

Aristotle and Isocrates share and contest the language in which they describe how practical performance both depends on ordered elementary building blocks (*stoikheia*, etc.) and yet ultimately reaches a loftier level that transcends them (*euphuïa*, etc.). I have just mentioned how Isocrates in *Against the Sophists* refutes his rivals who try to systematize ("offering the model of an ordered art," *tetagmenēn tekhnēn paradeigma pherontes, Against the Sophists* 12) the art of speaking on the level of the art of letters (*grammata*). It is very striking, then, that Aristotle in his *Protrepticus* defends a theoretical orientation that elevates to the top of the value scale the rigorous philosophical pursuits that Isocrates wants to keep in a preparatory and instrumental role, in terms that sound as if they were taken from Isocrates' description of his pedantic and ineffective rivals:

> For prior things are always more familiar [*gnōrimōtera*[61]] than posterior things, and what is better in nature than what is worse, for there is more knowledge of what is determinate and <u>orderly</u> [*tōn gar hōrismenōn kai <u>tetagmenōn</u> epistēmē*] than of their opposites, and again of the causes than of the effects. And good things are more determinate and organized than bad things, just as a fair person is more determinate and organized than a foul person; for they necessarily have the same mutual difference. And prior things are causes more than posterior things, for if they are taken away, then so are the things that take their being from them (if numbers <are taken away>, then so are lines, if lines then surfaces, and if surfaces then solids), and elementary letters [*stoikheia*] are causes more than what are named "syllables."
>
> Aristotle *Protrepticus*, in Iamblichus *Protrepticus* VI 38.3–14 Pistelli (5a W, B33 D)[62]
> (trans. Hutchinson and Johnson 2009)

Aristotle's *Protrepticus* is a text rich in Isocratean connections (to be explored further below) and, as Hutchinson and Johnson will argue in their forthcoming

---

61 Or, "more known": this is the familiar Aristotelian distinction between what is "by nature" better known (i.e. higher in the explanatory analysis) and what is better known *to us*.

62 In citing Aristotle's *Protrepticus*, I refer to the source text and also to the fragment numbers of Walzer 1934 (taken over by Ross [1955]) and Düring 1961 (with A, B, C prefixed, showing classification as testimonia, fragments, and related texts).

edition, was likely a dialogue with a role for Isocrates.[63] If we consider the echo in this passage of Isocrates' provocative rejection of the most inert and useless kind of handbook *epistēmē* (*tetagmenē tekhnē*), it appears that Aristotle may be purposefully and boldly throwing Isocrates' language back at him. Lowly *stoikheia*[64] (cf. Isocrates' *grammata*) can serve as a model of how the philosopher's most important and "prior things" are knowable in a rationally ordered way (in contrast to the always somewhat intractable and unknowable principles of worldly action).[65] In other words, Aristotle may intend a riposte to Isocrates in this subtext: "No, we in the Academy, when we pursue the causes of something, do not simply and mistakenly try to express the principles of a 'creative affair' [Isocrates' *poiētikon pragma*] in the reductive, incommensurate, and mistakenly technical terms of whatever simplified principles are more easily tractable by reason and theory."[66]

---

[63] Despite the influential argument against the dialogue form by Jaeger (1948:55f.), according to which a speech marked by "imitation of the Isocratean exhortation or παραίνεσις" was only recast as a dialogue by Cicero in *Hortensius*, a conclusion defended by Düring (1961:29–32), the plausibility of the dialogue form has been recognized by e.g. Allan (1953:249f.), who regretted Ross's failure to indicate where we might feel "some doubt whether the sentiments were those of Aristotle himself, since readers without experience of sources of this kind will probably assume that they are," and stopped just short of seeing Isocrates as a likely character, conjecturing that "Aristotle may easily have supposed himself addressing the royal personage, to whom the work is inscribed, in rivalry with a representative of the Isocratean school, who would maintain that a mathematical and scientific training such as the Platonists offer is useless for practical life." Compare, later in the fourth century, Praxiphanes' dialogue between Isocrates and Plato *On Poets* (Diogenes Laertius 3.8).

[64] It is to be expected, if we give due weight again to the complex interlacement of terms with which Isocrates and Aristotle contest both theoretical and practical values, that *stoikheion* is a congenial word for Isocrates. It can mean the principles of a sound constitution (στοιχεῖα πρῶτα καὶ μέγιστα χρηστῆς πολιτείας, *To Nicocles* 16). More interesting still is the only other Isocratean usage of the word, an important theoretical passage (*Epistle* 6.8) where Isocrates says that his *philosophia* teaches how *ideai* are used in speaking (*logoi*), but also that they are a basic principle (*stoikheion*) "in all other things and in your *pragmata*." Note, however, the practical and political orientation of both passages. In their forthcoming *Protrepticus* commentary, Hutchinson and Johnson argue (in their note on Iamblichus *Protrepticus* VI 38.14 Pistelli) that the literary-critical use of *stoikheia* (i.e. in educational traditions allied to Isocrates) is, contrary to a mistaken view of Diels and Düring, the source of its usage for "elements"; several passages in Plato and Aristotle deal quite explicitly with "the familiar metaphor of letter, syllable, word, and phrase to stand for various levels of analysis of reality, from primitive elements up to complex wholes."

[65] In Aristotle's *Rhetoric* I 6, 1362a20f., though, the *stoikheia* of the good and the expedient (that is, their definitional principles as subjects of forensic and deliberative oratory) are to be investigated. Xenocrates wrote four books of *Stoikheia on Kingship to Alexander* (Diogenes Laertius 4.14).

[66] I do not pretend to exhaust every topic treated in common by Isocrates and Aristotle's *Nicomachean Ethics*. For example, *akrasia* is an important consideration for both thinkers, an account of which in Isocrates would take in *Antidosis* 221, *To Demonicus* 21, *Nicocles* 21.

From Preparation to Performance

A discussion of *phusis* has already necessarily led us to consider Isocratean training and the habituation so fundamental to Aristotelian ethical theory, and to identify general similarities between these two disciplines. On this basis, we are not surprised to find Isocrates comparing the teacher of philosophy to gymnastic trainers who "train them and habituate [ἐθίζουσι, Aristotle's regular term] them to hard work" (*Antidosis* 184). It remains to examine both authors' methods in greater detail to understand how each conceives that which is preparatory to action. Knowledge (*epistēmē*), while rejected by both Isocrates and Aristotle as an inappropriate way to speak of the aimed-for state that enables the right and best kind of actions, nevertheless plays an important preparatory role in both theories. It is by considering together these steps which an agent takes towards action (another, as we have seen, is deliberation) that we may achieve some insight into how, after the actor's habits have been trained under each of the two regimes, action actually comes about in the moment of necessity. This transformation of education into life is an ultimate aim for both Isocrates and Aristotle, and in each of their conceptions there is a distinctly performative synthesis of theory and practice, scientific and unscientific, deliberation and reason, provisional particular and established universal.

The Place of Knowledge

Since Isocrates was Plato's contemporary and competitor, his depreciation in some passages of *epistēmē* in favor of *doxa*, reversing as it does Plato's most important priority, has served many modern interpreters as ready proof of Isocrates' supremely "unphilosophical" character. In drawing a comparison between Isocrates' *philosophia* and Aristotle's ethical teachings, we must be more careful. Aristotle maintains very clearly that neither ethical action nor moral philosophy is a scientific undertaking, and he endeavors to find the right language to describe what ethics is instead. We should explore, therefore, any overlap between the two ways of thinking about the limitations of knowledge in practical matters. Moreover, there are grounds for revising the common belief that Isocrates' belittlement of *epistēmē* is absolute and *per se*, in favor of a more nuanced account of what Isocrates did and did not consider *epistēmē* to be good for. The precise manner in which *epistēmē* fits into the two theories involves some important and irreconcilable differences in perspective, but the several points of contact again demonstrate the value of counterposing Isocrates' project with Aristotle's.

Systematic knowledge does play a definite role in Isocratean education. Its function is essentially preparatory—something to be acquired before action is taken or a speech delivered. The passages depreciating *epistēmē* are concerned rather with action; like Aristotle, Isocrates denies the existence of a science of action, though science may be ancillary to action. Thus in *Antidosis* 271, Isocrates speaks of how *a* knowledge (indefinite) to inform our actions is unavailable, much as in *Against the Sophists* he scorns the sophists' cookbook approach to *logoi* (as if the *epistēmē* of *grammata* would be worth anything, 10—again, not ruling out another *epistēmē*). Likewise, the uselessness of *epistēmē* in *Antidosis* 184 is also limited to its direct application in the crucial moments (*kairoi*) of political life, which cannot be brought under the control of systematic knowledge.[67] In less notorious passages, Isocrates can be found plainly asserting knowledge's significant place in education. These include *Against the Sophists* 16 (ἐπιστήμην ... εἰδόσι), *Antidosis* 187 (λαβεῖν τὴν ἐπιστήμην: the definiteness and preparatory role of the knowledge), and *Antidosis* 201 (the acquisition of definite plural *epistēmai* as preliminary and complementary to practice).[68]

In book X of the *Nicomachean Ethics*, Aristotle states that the discussion so far has fallen short of its aim, which is not knowledge[69] about virtue, but virtuous actions—the actual possession and use of virtue, by whatever means is effective (1179a34–b4). If we restrict ourselves to familiarizing the would-be virtuous individual with the nature of virtue by means of arguments (*logoi*), we are gathering in only the low-hanging fruit among all potential virtuous actions. Aristotle describes the character so preeminently susceptible to virtue as "well-born" (ἦθος ... εὐγενὲς, 1179b8). While it seems most likely that, on the theoretical level, Aristotle means those persons who have been gradually habituated to virtuous dispositions (ὁ δὲ λόγος καὶ ἡ διδαχὴ μή ποτ' οὐκ ἐν ἅπασιν ἰσχύει, ἀλλὰ δεῖ προδιειργάσθαι τοῖς ἔθεσι τὴν τοῦ ἀκροατοῦ ψυχήν, 1179b23–25), his

---

67 These two passages will be reconsidered in the context of the following chapter.

68 The branches of knowledge with which the student-*rhētōr* is concerned may to some extent be identified with the *ideai* Isocrates likens to gymnastic *skhēmata* (see *Against the Sophists* 16). Thus Natali (2001), as part of an argument that the material in Aristotle's rhetorical writings has ethical import (taking up von Arnim's suggestion that Aristotle's early ethical thought could be reconstructed on the basis of the ethical examples in the *Topics*, p. 1), states, "There is, in fact, no reason why τόποι of this kind, collected and elaborated to be used in dialectical discussions on ethics, cannot be used also by those who deliberate and debate with themselves about how to act. This same possibility of twofold use of the τόποι is found in many orators of the time" (91). In a note, Natali (2001:212n97) specifies: "For example, in the series of rhetorical ἰδέαι taught by Isocrates to his disciples. Cf. *Antid.* 180–185." A relationship between Isocrates and Aristotle's *Rhetoric* (stressing the distance between ethics and rhetoric) is also posited by Garver (1994:195), reflecting an interesting view that Isocrates in the rhetorical domain is not more practical than Aristotle, but less (interested in the production of discourse rather than the production of actions).

69 The terms are γνῶναι and εἰδέναι, not ἐπίστασθαι.

formulation here is closer to the Isocratean view of who constitutes the (naturally) well-suited audience for educative discourse.[70]

But Aristotle's concern in these final pages of the *Nicomachean Ethics* is to realize the project of ethics more fully by expanding the pool of human subjects, and this means a way of educating those who can only be reached by compulsion, not argument. Here (somewhat surprisingly, since we are moving on beyond the means of *logoi*) is the first situation where Aristotle prescribes the direct pursuit of an *epistēmē*, namely that legislative science necessary to anyone who hopes to instill moral virtue in another. Unlike any *epistēmē* recommended by Isocrates to his students, this one is reserved to the ethically and intellectually mature helper of others and is not part of the self's resources which all agents must cultivate in order to be virtuous. It is thus, for its possessor, an extra attainment built upon a foundation that includes complete virtue, but, for its beneficiaries, an external means to virtue.

No too close comparison is to be made with any Isocratean *epistēmē*. One might imagine that Aristotle would recognize the contribution of various sciences, in an ancillary role, to character development (as Isocrates does), but he seems nowhere to do so. Perhaps, however, the discrepancy is somewhat smoothed if we consider the advanced nature of Isocratean training, intended for older students who have conceived a desire to develop new excellences by attaching themselves to a school of *philosophia*.[71] Aristotelian habituation must begin in childhood; progress towards a more ambitious and public role (*nomothetikos* for Aristotle, *rhētōr* for Isocrates) can only begin once one's adult character is already well formed. Yet we must acknowledge that, for Isocrates, the acquisition of *epistēmē* is not merely of use in fostering others' progress, but is an indispensable preparation for any life of action[72]; if Isocrates' reputation

---

[70] In the same sentence (1179b8), Aristotle also identifies the elect audience as "the liberal ones of the youth" (τῶν νέων τοὺς ἐλευθερίους), which certainly seems consistent with the student demographic of the fourth-century Athenian schools' *philosophia*.

[71] This point can be pressed to narrow further the gap between Aristotle and Isocrates' notions of *phusis*. When Isocrates complains repeatedly that his methods cannot make *agōnistai* of those candidates he receives already deficient in nature, we must recall that, in Aristotelian terms, his students begin their training with their habits (and more loosely, their "nature") already decisively formed. If Isocrates had not couched his more universal theory of virtuous self-formation with such constant reference to the goals of the would-be *agōnistēs*, this propaedeutic stage would be clearer to us. As it is, this counts as another aspect of Isocrates' theory obscured by his presentation of his educational ideas in polemical, epidictic, and apologetic discourses rather than in treatises.

[72] As noted above, even the Isocratean *idiōtēs* participates in political decision-making (τῶν τε λόγων κριτὰς καὶ συμβούλους ἀκριβεστέρους τῶν πλείστων, *Antidosis* 204), but he is no Aristotelian legislator. The Aristotelian virtues are also not private, but rather social and (in the widest sense) political, as they had been for Plato (e.g. *Symposium* 209a, *Gorgias* 464b).

as the enemy of *epistēmē* were better deserved, his theory would more closely approximate Aristotle's.

Aristotle's concluding remarks on the legislative science deserve our closer attention. Two interesting points emerge. First, Aristotle takes great pains to make clear that, while he does have a universal *epistēmē* in mind (1180b13–28), legislative science is not something done on the scale of the polis,[73] but rather, realistically speaking, part of the duty of every individual in their capacity as *philos* to any other (ἑκάστῳ δόξειεν ἂν προσήκειν τοῖς σφετέροις τέκνοις καὶ φίλοις εἰς ἀρετὴν συμβάλλεσθαι καὶ δρᾶν αὐτὸ δύνασθαι, ἢ προαιρεῖσθαί γε, 1180a31f.). Indeed, Aristotle holds that individually tailored *paideia* is superior to a generalized regime (ἔτι δὲ καὶ διαφέρουσιν αἱ καθ᾽ ἕκαστον παιδεῖαι τῶν κοινῶν, 1180b7f.). Insofar as it treats the individual case, the legislative science is even partially substitutable by experience (1180b16–20). The science itself in this discussion is never spoken of as *nomothetikē*; instead, Aristotle prefers the personal expression "to become *nomothetikos*" (1180a33f., 1180b24f., 1180b29, 1181b1), putting us again in mind of the advanced studies of the individual to whom all the *Nicomachean Ethics* is addressed, and of the analogous advanced studies undertaken in Isocrates' school. Second, the Aristotelian legislator, trying as he does to compel virtuous behavior out of the illiberal, faces limitations to his success somewhat reminiscent of Isocrates' insistence on the ultimate intractability of nature ("not just anyone can improve the condition of just anyone, or the person presented to him; but if anyone can it is the person with knowledge [*tou eidotos*]," 1180b25–27, trans. Irwin 1985).

Despite a fundamental difference in their valuation of impractical sciences,[74] Isocrates and Aristotle both draw a contrast between mathematics, as a discipline in which young people can profitably seek mastery, and the completion of training for action, which requires a fuller engagement in life's experiences. Isocrates, like Callicles in *Gorgias*, approves geometry for the young (*tois neōterois*, *Antidosis* 268) as "a training of the soul and a preparation for *philosophia*" (γυμνασίαν μέντοι τῆς ψυχῆς καὶ παρασκευὴν φιλοσοφίας, 266). Aristotle observes that the young may quickly pick up the universal science of mathematics,[75] whereas more mature experience is necessary to acquire the

---

73 At least not necessarily or theoretically: whether the laws are "for the education of one or of many, seems unimportant," 1180b1f., trans. Irwin (1985).

74 It must be borne in mind that we are comparing only the conception of moral education in *Nicomachean Ethics* to Isocratean *philosophia*, which wants nothing to do with anything approaching Aristotelian "first philosophy."

75 Mathematics is of course an *epistēmē* for Aristotle (e.g. *Metaphysics* 1061b28–33, *Eudemian Ethics* 1219a17), though he here uses the personal expression *mathēmatikos genesthai*, as we have seen him do in speaking of legislative science.

practical wisdom concerned with particulars (1142a11–20). These views show some common ground in their authors' attitudes towards *epistēmē* as preparation for, and a more universal concern than, the immediate requirements for the performance of the best actions.

Isocratean and Aristotelian Protreptics

It will be reserved for chapter 3 to consider the historical tradition that suggests a polemical competition between Aristotle and Isocrates—for example, the evidence that Aristotle developed a public form of rhetoric instruction as a response to the success of Isocrates' school in capturing the audience of lofty-minded and "philosophical" youth in Athens. The purpose of this chapter (and analogously of the one that follows) is to suggest the theoretical and intellectual links between the two thinkers, as a background against which to interpret the historical evidence for contact and influence between them. Too often, the testimonia for the polemic have been brought up, only to be dismissed on the basis of the unexamined and apparently obvious ground that Isocrates is a light-weight and therefore cannot be a serious adversary or interlocutor.

Aristotle's *Protrepticus*, or exhortation to philosophy,[76] offers intriguing evidence that spans both of these dimensions of his entanglement with Isocrates: the theoretical and the polemical. I treat it here because its importance for my purposes lies especially in how it shows Aristotle thinking through the intellectual analogies between his own ideas and Isocratean ones. Several issues that would allow us to interpret these analogies more specifically—for example, those attending the reconstruction of the fragmentary text and its generic classification (in particular, the question of whether it is a dialogue, and if so of the assignment of speech)—must remain uncertain, though we may expect significant illumination of them in Hutchinson and Johnson's forthcoming edition, translation, and commentary.[77] For my present purposes, it is not absolutely essential that the reader accept their reconstruction of a dialogue in which Isocrates was one of the speakers. What is crucial is that Aristotle in this exoteric protreptic articulates the case, and the reasoning, for a "practical philosophy" with recognizable theoretical affinities to Isocrates, alongside a higher order of philosophical

---

[76] For the genre of philosophical protreptic, see Slings 1999:67–95.

[77] D. S. Hutchinson and Monte Ransome Johnson, *Aristotle: Protrepticus*, Cambridge Classical Texts and Commentaries, forthcoming. I am grateful to these scholars for discussing their work in progress with me. While a close connection between the *Protrepticus* and Isocrates had already been suggested by others (see below), I believe that the value of the Aristotelian text for understanding the aspects of Isocrates' thought under study here will emerge much more clearly from Hutchinson and Johnson's work than from previous studies, not least through a defense of Aristotle's authorship of important passages that were excluded by scholars whose critical assumption was a uniform discourse in the persona of Aristotle.

contemplation that outranks it without supplanting it entirely (much as in the *Nicomachean Ethics*, book X). In other words, this is material that can and should be approached with the same method we have applied to Aristotle's *Nicomachean Ethics*, but in which it should not be surprising if we discover closer connections to Isocrateanism in its specific focuses, with Aristotle thinking through the links and parallels, constructing no mere straw man, but rather an Isocrates who meets him halfway as a theorist. This is not simply Isocrates through the eyes of Aristotle, or in Aristotle's hostile sights, but an "Isocrates" sympathetically fleshed out in a mixture of Isocratean and Aristotelian discourse, a character whose dialogic contributions best serve to develop the protreptic value of Aristotelian moral and practical philosophy. In short, Aristotle has included a rival version, and not an inverted travesty, of his own claims for the philosophical life. It would be analytically useful to label the voice of "Isocrates" in the *Protrepticus* even without the latest editors' conclusion that Isocrates is in fact a named speaker.

We cannot discover much about the formal frame of the *Protrepticus*, but the testimony of a royal Cypriot addressee, given by Stobaeus, is a suggestive connection to Isocrates' own didactic Cyprian orations, which reflect not only his maneuvering for patronage, but his confidence that educated and powerful rulers represented a unique opportunity for his own *philosophia* to bring about some real good. Stobaeus mentions "the *Protrepticus* of Aristotle, which he wrote to Themiso (king of Cyprus), saying that no one has more good things going for him to help him do philosophy, since, as he has great wealth, he can spend it on these things, and he has a reputation [*doxa*] as well."[78] This idea recurs in the Isocratean *To Demonicus*,[79] as the ill use base deceivers make of their fortune is

---

[78] Stobaeus 4.32.21 (1 W, A1 D), trans. after Hutchinson and Johnson 2009. τὸν Ἀριστοτέλους Προτρεπτικόν, ὃν ἔγραψε πρὸς Θεμίσωνα τὸν Κυπρίων βασιλέα λέγων ὅτι οὐδενὶ πλείω ἀγαθὰ ὑπάρχει πρὸς τὸ φιλοσοφῆσαι· πλοῦτόν τε γὰρ πλεῖστον αὐτὸν ἔχειν ὥστε δαπανᾶν εἰς ταῦτα, ἔτι δὲ δόξαν ὑπάρχειν αὐτῷ. See further Chroust 1966 for an answer (in terms of the temporal and scholastic politics impinging on Isocrates and Aristotle) to the question, "What prompted Aristotle to address the *Protrepticus* to Themison?" Cf. Ostwald and Lynch 1994:619: "Aristotle's *Protrepticus*, or 'Exhortation to Philosophy,' may be read as a challenge to Isocrates' political influence, patronage, and intellectual following on the island of Cyprus. Having befriended and memorialized Eudemus, a political exile from Cyprus, Aristotle seems to have taken it upon himself to try to counteract Isocrates' standing among the Cypriot Evagorids by offering to Themison, a prince or minor Cypriot king, a vision of *paideia* and the philosophical life different from that presented by Isocrates in his *Antidosis* of 353 by emphasizing the primacy of the 'theoretical' over the 'active' life, the possibility of precise knowledge about human values analogous to mathematical knowledge, and the pleasure of devoting one's energy and life to intellection (*phronesis*)." I would suggest, however, that it is precisely the high role Isocrates also grants to *epistēmē* and *phronēsis* (whatever the differences) that justifies the whole engagement on Aristotle's part. See also Weil 1980, Berti 1997.

[79] In this section I make my own suggestions for connections to the works of Isocrates worth exploring in order to understand the content and context of the *Protrepticus*. For previous suggestions,

lamented in contrast to the life driven by the higher pleasures of virtue: "Good fortune has handed them money, a good reputation [*doxa*], and friends, but they have made themselves unworthy of the prosperity they possess" (49, trans. Mirhady and Too 2000). Isocrates' own praise of Evagoras concludes with words encouraging his surviving son Nicocles in his zeal for virtue, exhorting him to the discipline of his soul (*epimeleisthai kai tēn psukhēn askein*) in order be worthy (*axios esei*) of his royal inheritance, and continuing the language of philosophical cultivation of the intellect, claiming that while it befits all to value *phronēsis* highly,[80] "you [pl.] especially, because you hold power over very many and very important affairs" (80). From this point Isocrates rapidly brings his discourse to an end, culminating with the word *philosophia* itself: it is to philosophy that Nicocles must stay true in order to become the kind of man it befits him to become.[81] Thus Aristotle's reported introduction of the *Protrepticus* along these lines is entirely within the topics of protreptic he shared with his rival.

The very same combination of themes (ethical cultivation, worthiness of royal position, immortal reputation versus perishable outward ornament) is repeated in Isocrates' *To Nicocles* (31f.). When we hear in *To Demonicus* that we are to despise those who cannot make proper use (*khrēsthai*) of the goods they possess, the thought is developed with a comparison to the owner of a fine horse who lacks the knowledge of horsemanship,[82] and we may think of the association, in the Oxyrhynchus fragment of Aristotle's *Protrepticus*, between the worthless man (*mēdenos axios*) splendidly and abundantly furnished with external goods (*tois ektos lamprōs kekhorēgēmenos*), and the horse whose golden trappings disguise its poor nature (*phaulos*).[83] This association is confirmed as

---

see Einarson 1936: esp. 264–269 and 273–278, Nix 1969: esp. 75ff., and Bertelli 1977b:23–27 (with further bibliography, 24n19). Jaeger (1948:57) connects the *Protrepticus*'s exhortatory formulae with Isocrates' (the statement is vague, but he seems to have in mind a connection between e.g. *nomizein* at POxy 666, lines 65, 102f., and 131 [3 W, B2–3 D], and the imperatives *hēgou* and *nomize* in *To Nicocles* [8×] and *To Demonicus* [10×]). These studies are already adequate to establish that the voice of Isocrates is present in some sense in the remains of the *Protrepticus*. On the contested authenticity of *To Demonicus*, cf. Too 1995:58n53 and Jebb 1893:82. It is Isocratean enough (perhaps a production of his school, so Burk 1923:56, and hardly a sophistic work, *pace* Drerup 1906) and so obviously remote from the climate of Aristotle that its affinities to Aristotelian protreptic are part of the phenomena we have to explain here.

80   Reading ὡς with the MSS and editors (Benseler-Blass, Drerup, Norlin); the Budé edition's ὧν, given without any note in the apparatus or effect on the French translation, seems to be a lapse, though this is also the reading in Wilhelm Lange's 1803 edition (on the basis of a Munich MS of no value and a Latin version) and was wrongly attributed to Codex Vaticanus 65 by Coray (according to Drerup 1906).

81   *Evagoras* 81: ἂν γὰρ ἐμμένῃς τῇ φιλοσοφίᾳ καὶ τοσοῦτον ἐπιδιδῷς ὅσονπερ νῦν, ταχέως γενήσει τοιοῦτος οἷόν σε προσήκει.

82   *To Demonicus* 27: ὥσπερ ἂν εἴ τις ἵππον κτήσαιτο καλὸν κακῶς ἱππεύειν ἐπιστάμενος.

83   POxy 666, lines 92–100 (3 W, B2 D), ed. Grenfell and Hunt = Stobaeus 3.3.25 (with the reading *kekosmēmenos*).

Aristotle goes on immediately to consider the man inferior to his own domestics (*oiketai*, line 121), which more precisely matches the thought of the fine horse's ignorant owner in *To Demonicus*. Thus, at this stage of his argument, and especially in this "rhetorically charged conclusion,"[84] "Aristotle" continues to use Isocrates' terms and values, hoping to persuade those who accept the Isocratean notion of the benefits *philosophia* bring to the statesman that his school confers those same benefits (with further studies leading to additional and more solidly grounded benefits). In consonance with Isocrates, "Aristotle" here promotes living well (*zēn eu*) over living (*zēn*) and admonishes us, "nor should one sail to the Pillars of Heracles and run many risks for the sake of property [*khrēmatōn heneka*]" while neglecting intelligence (*phronēsis*). At this point Aristotle is still at pains to keep his protreptic relevant to the conventional *topoi* shared by Isocrates, and he even adds an Isocratean touch by suggesting that *phronēsis* is manifested in our *doxai*, so that if we pursue philosophy and intelligence, we will substitute our own *doxai* (*tais hautou [doxais]*) for those of the majority as a more proper guide to follow. The break with Isocrates only becomes more sharply defined a bit later, when "Aristotle" turns to "precision about the truth" and more mathematical forms of knowledge.[85] I stress the importance of his having first strongly assured us that his vision is inclusive of everything moral and intelligent that would have been generally credited to the Isocratean approach.

More important are the Aristotelian touches that show how "Isocratean" topics are being engaged seriously for their affinities to Aristotle's own philosophical principles. The orientation defined by these topics may not be the best one, in Aristotle's view, but it is a properly philosophical orientation and not a mere foil: at the least, a position whose principled adherents are worth addressing persuasively in their own terms. Hutchinson and Johnson's reconstruction identifies "Isocrates" as the speaker in a text from POxy 666 and sees a passage from Iamblichus *Protrepticus* VI as taking up this discussion, if not in the voice of Isocrates, then with the character "Aristotle" at least "agree[ing] to a limited extent with the line of argument."[86] Either way, we have an intriguingly

---

[84] Iamblichus *Protrepticus* VI 40.1–11 Pistelli (5a W, B53 D), translation and comment in Hutchinson and Johnson 2009:7.

[85] Iamblichus *On General Mathematical Science* XXVI 83.6ff. Festa (8 W, C55:2 D). This passage thus culminates the value scale announced by "Aristotle" in pitting "prior things" against "posterior things" in Iamblichus *Protrepticus* VI 37.26ff. Pistelli (5a W, B32 D).

[86] POxy 666 cols. ii–iii (3 W, B2–5 D), assigned to "Isocrates" in Hutchinson and Johnson 2009 and 2010; Iamblichus *Protrepticus* VI 37.3–22 Pistelli (4 W, B8–9 D), assigned to "Isocrates" in Hutchinson and Johnson 2009 but to Aristotle in idem 2010:2, where this Aristotelian response is also supplemented with texts from Philoponus' *Commentary on Nicomachus of Gerasa's Introduction to Arithmetic I* (1.14–49 Hoche 1864), Proclus' *Commentary on Euclid's Elements I* (second prologue, ch. 4, 64.8–68.4 Friedlein), and Iamblichus *On General Mathematical Science* (better known in Latin as *De communi mathematica scientia* and never translated into English) XXI–XXVII. The fact that

Aristotelian digestion of unmistakably Isocratean principles. Following on these two sections, the editors' preliminary work consistently posits a set of objections to abstract studies in the persona of Isocrates.[87] After this point, of course, Aristotle goes on to answer Isocrates' objections; our interest here is not to claim that Aristotle lets Isocrates win in the *Protrepticus*, but that he lets him speak[88] in terms that mingle the two thinkers' principles and establish certain *topoi* that remain recognizable in the complete and final Aristotelian protreptic to philosophy.

The POxy 666 fragment of the *Protrepticus* (3 W, B2–5 D) lays a foundation, and issues a general invitation to the love of wisdom, by expressing the nobility and loftiness of adherence to "philosophy" in value terms shared between Isocrates and Aristotle. Faced with the evidence of misfortune, we should "consider success in life [*eudaimonia*] as in fact not consisting in the possession of lots of things as much as in the condition of the soul" and be unimpressed with the man who "is splendidly furnished with the externals but is himself worth nothing." Without the proper concern for our nature and the condition of our souls, those other things cannot be good and are turned to harmful ends like the proverbial "knife for a child."

At this level of generality, the exhortation to care for the soul more than the body and external goods is indeed perhaps as Isocratean as Aristotelian. The Isocratean *To Demonicus* announces a similarly lofty—while resolutely practical[89]—protreptic perspective. Other rhetorical discourses may provide encouragement or exhortation (3–5), but the speaker of this address will actually illuminate the educational path to virtue (*aretē*, 5) and shift the focus from cleverness in speech to ethical self-cultivation (*ta tōn tropōn ēthē*), which is the heart of philosophy (*to kratiston tēs philosophias*, 4). From here the speech moves immediately to the same "knife for a child" caution employed by "Isocrates" in Aristotle's work: "Strength is a benefit when it is joined with practical wisdom [*phronēsis*],[90] but without this, it does more harm to those who have it: it embel-

---

arguments could be entertained for attributing a single passage either to Isocrates or to an Aristotle who "agrees to a limited extent" is a convenient illustration of the very point I wish to argue here.

87   Iamblichus *On General Mathematical Science* XXVI (79.5–24, 80.5–81.4 Festa; 5b W; C32:2, B52, C41 D), assigned to "Isocrates" in Hutchinson and Johnson 2009 and 2010.

88   Again, an alternative reconstruction of the *Protrepticus* in which all these affinities occur in the voice of Aristotle himself (e.g. speaking in a unified discourse) would show no less striking an engagement and cooptation.

89   For Isocrates' practical test of cultivation of the soul—not empty professions of knowledge, but scrutiny of actions and an ability to work from *doxai*—cf. *Against the Sophists* 7f.

90   The same term used in Isocrates, *Evagoras* 80 (quoted above). We should be cautious about the translation "practical wisdom," even in Isocrates; the plainer "intelligence" may be more suitable. In Aristotle's *Protrepticus*, *phronēsis* is the general term for philosophical wisdom or intelligence, and not confined to the practical sphere as in the *Nicomachean Ethics*.

lishes the bodies of those who exercise, but it obscures their care for the soul" (6, trans. Mirhady and Too 2000).

The Isocratean *To Demonicus* applies philosophical and even Platonic scales of value in its protreptic. The revaluation of pleasure is an important example: industry (*philoponia*) applied to virtue and to education (*paideia*, 45) is the source of the most genuinely (*malista gnēsiōs*, 46), purely, and securely (*bebaioteras*) possessed pleasures (*hēdonai, terpseis*).[91] There are two rival loves for the direction of our life: reason and the passions as typified by drunkenness. The drunk man's mind (*nous*) is like a chariot (*harmata*) that has thrown its drivers (*hēniokhoi*), and the proper driver is the thinking faculty (*dianoia*).[92] In both these passages reason and study are the only firm basis for the conduct of life. Against this background, the discourse states a fundamental principle of Isocratean oratory in its precept that the only occasion for speaking, apart from absolute necessity, is when the speaker possesses clear knowledge (*oistha saphōs*, 41).

In Isocrates, these topics are tied to the majesty of *logos* and, by extension, to the specifically intellectual powers. Despite the characteristically Isocratean atmosphere of discussion—with its royal-didactic and political contexts—no one denies Isocrates' evident concern to insist that his approach to *politikoi logoi* is a high form of intellectual self-cultivation, leading to a perspective (on practical affairs, at least) that is more theoretical, oriented to a higher good and not to narrow interests or the petty concerns of *tekhnē*. Still, even with a strong reading of Isocrates' philosophical self-fashioning, it is striking that Aristotle has "Isocrates" move to the concluding protreptic exhortation ("we should do philosophy," *philosophēteon*) by way of the claim "that wisdom [*phronēsis*] comes from learning or searching [*zētein*]."[93]

The emphasis on the investigative spirit (*zētein*) in this last step of Aristotle's "Isocrates" strikes the modern reader at first as a likely point at which the specifically Aristotelian conception of philosophy has taken over. However, several

---

91. In *Nicocles* 59, the idea of virtue's higher pleasure (with a *psukhē* of unencumbered conscience life is lived most pleasantly, *hēdista*) is directly opposed to the false value attaching to great possessions, which we have discussed above (*tous pleista kektēmenous*). I do not deny the essential conventionality of this moralism (cf. *Areopagiticus* 43, where the traditional education of the citizenry—the taming of their souls—proceeds alike by the cares bestowed on fine practices [*epimeleiais tōn epitēdeumatōn*] and by toils leavened with pleasures [*ponois hēdonas ekhousin*]) but wish to stress Isocrates' concern to advance it into the unmistakable language of philosophical protreptic.

92. Cf. Plato *Phaedrus* 246ff.

93. τὴν δὲ φρόνησιν ἅπαντες ἂν ὁμολογήσειαν ἐκ τοῦ (Wilamowitz: εἰς τὸ pap.) μανθάνειν γίγνεσθαι <καὶ> ζητεῖν ὧν τὰς δυνάμεις φιλοσοφία περιείληφεν, ὥστε πῶς οὐκ ἀπροφασίστως φιλοσοφητέον καὶ ..., POxy 666, lines 161–170, the end of the papyrus fragment (3 W, B5 D); for the expression *tēn dunamin tinos perilambanein*, cf. Isocrates, *To Nicocles* 9.

Isocratean passages show that this is also an important element of Isocrates' *philosophia*. In *Busiris*, Isocrates spins a legend about the Egyptian priests' invention of *philosophia* as a training (*askēsis*) for their souls, whose scope included not only legislation (*nomothetēsai*) but also "to investigate the nature of reality" (*tēn phusin tōn ontōn zētēsai*, 22). Elsewhere the idea of investigative examination in Isocrates, while occurring in connection with practical and political matters (*pragmata*), is part of an effort to cluster as many intellectual and philosophical terms of praise as possible. When Evagoras is praised for his intellectual (*tēn gnōmēn*) endowments, Isocrates' point is that the success of his practical plans depended on a foundation of investigation and thoughtful reflection (*zētein kai phrontizein*, *Evagoras* 41).[94] According to a parallel passage in *To Nicocles* (46), those who wallow in shallow pleasures envy sensible people (*eu phronountes*), resist truths (*alētheiai*) and knowledge about what concerns themselves, and above all are unwilling "to labor and trouble their soul by examining [*skepsasthai*] the necessary facts of life" (trans. Mirhady and Too 2000).

The programmatic opening chapters of Aristotle's *Metaphysics* take on similar problems concerning knowledge, learning, and experience and are rich in connections with these portions of the *Protrepticus*.[95] Take, for example, the definition of the wise man (*sophos*) as "he who can learn things that are difficult, and not easy for man to know" (τὸν τὰ χαλεπὰ γνῶναι δυνάμενον καὶ μὴ ῥᾴδια ἀνθρώπῳ γιγνώσκειν, *Metaphysics* I 2, 982a10f.). Besides the shared equation between wisdom and the activity of effectively gaining knowledge, both passages define a wise man who can and should make executive use of his knowledge. The wise man of the *Protrepticus*'s "Isocrates" will be able in action to exercise the power and use the resources that would be like a "knife for a child" to the uninquisitive person, and the *Metaphysics*' man who can gain knowledge of causes should command and be obeyed, "for the wise man must not be ordered but must order [*epitattein*], and he must not obey another, but the less wise must obey *him*" (982a17–19). The idea of a rightfully commanding science (compare also the *eleuthera epistēmē* of *Metaphysics* 982b27) recurs in the *Protrepticus* passage hesitantly assigned to "Aristotle" but showing some connections to the voice of "Isocrates": "In these as it were more commanding kinds of knowledge exists what is good in the strict sense ... one ought to do philosophy, since only philosophy includes within itself this correct judgment and

---

[94] Other philosophical vocabulary in this passage includes *phronēsis* and care for the soul (*tēs psukhēs ... epimeleian*, for which collocation cf. also *To Nicocles* 12, 51).

[95] For the appropriateness of this text as a comparison to the *Protrepticus*, compare also the remarks of "Aristotle" "on the comparative value of sight, perception, opinion, and knowledge" (in the summary of Hutchinson and Johnson 2009:10) at Iamblichus *Protrepticus* VII 43.25 ff. Pistelli (7 W, B72 D).

this intelligence to issue orders without errors."[96] And "Aristotle" returns to the criterion of the wise man[97] in a passage emphasizing that this knowledge will inform *choice* of what is good in the practice of life: "What norm do we have or what more precise standard of good things, than the wise man? For all things that this man will choose, if the choice is based on knowledge, are good things."[98]

The common thread in these passages is a learning- and knowledge-based form of wisdom, espoused by "Isocrates" and "Aristotle," that certainly has loftier theoretical aspirations in Aristotle's theory (knowledge of causes for its own sake), but which nonetheless (protreptically) keeps in its sights the test of life's choices and actions. If we are to distinguish the two accounts more carefully, we are fortunate to have parallel texts from *Metaphysics* and the "Isocrates" of *Protrepticus* that directly, and differently, frame the question of applying purely theoretical insight in the crucible of productive action. "Isocrates"—echoing the painstakingly qualified reservations expressed about abstract pursuits by the real Isocrates in *Antidosis* 261–269—declares not only that practical training and facility (*gegumnasmenoi kai doxazontes orthōs*, Iamblichus, *On General Mathematical Science* XXVI 80.22 Festa, 5b W, C41 D) are the proper determinants of competent performance of actions, but even that an admixture of demonstrative science tends to spoil the practical competence:

> [80.5] For we have the greatest example in the sciences that are similar to it, and the opinions that fall under them, for we see none of the things which the geometers are able to observe by means of proofs as being something that they themselves are capable of doing, but the land-surveyors are capable, by experience, to divide an estate and all the other variables in quantities as well as places, whereas those who know about the mathematical subjects and the discourses about them know how they should act, but are not capable of acting. [80.13] The case is similar with music and the other sciences in which there is a division separating the cognitive aspect from the empirical. [80.15] For those who determine the proofs and the arguments about harmony and other suchlike things, just as in philosophy, are accustomed to enquiring, but take no part in activities. [80.19] In fact, even if they happen to be capable of crafting any of them, when they learn the proofs, they immediately do them worse, as if on purpose, whereas those who have no knowledge of the arguments, if they are trained and have correct

---

[96] Iamblichus *Protrepticus* VI 37.14–22 Pistelli (4 W, B9 D), trans. Hutchinson and Johnson 2009:3.
[97] This echoes, again, the examination of the "wise man" to determine which knowledge is wisdom in *Metaphysics* I 2.
[98] Iamblichus *Protrepticus* VI 39.18ff. Pistelli (5a W, B39 D).

opinions, are altogether superior for practical purposes. [80.23] So too with the subject matter of astronomy, such as sun and moon and the other stars: those who have practiced knowledge of the reasons and arguments have no knowledge of what is useful for humans, whereas those who have what is called navigational knowledge about them are capable of predicting for us storms and winds and many of these phenomena. [81.1] Hence for practical activities such sciences will be entirely useless, and, if they miss out on the correct activities, the love of learning misses out on the greatest of goods.

Iamblichus *On General Mathematical Science* XXVI 80.5–
81.4 Festa (8b W, C41 D)
(trans. Hutchinson and Johnson 2010:10)

This would seem a very unpromising passage in which to discern Aristotelian parallels. Yet the opening of *Metaphysics* is in dialogue with it, for Aristotle considers, if not the detriment of universal or theoretical knowledge for practical performance, at least the frequent inutility of art (*tekhnē*), which is being considered as a species of universal judgment: "With a view to action experience seems in no respect inferior to art, and men of experience succeed even better than those who have theory without experience" (I 1, 981a12–15).[99] Here the framing implies that theory could well be an enhancement to what experience provides, while interestingly avoiding a direct statement about whether this is so. The sentence clearly addresses the same general issue Aristotle makes "Isocrates" address in the *Protrepticus*, seeing the possibility of the Isocratean view yet failing to rebut the Isocratean rationale for positively avoiding the introduction of demonstrative science into the arts of practical life. Aristotle acknowledges the inferiority of the straw man, "theory without experience," while leaving us to wonder about the perhaps unpredictable interference effects generated by theory *added to* experience. When and how, exactly, do we apply our knowledge of universals to the individual, with which our actions and productions are concerned, and with which we are otherwise acquainted by experience? In the real world, we often do find experience outdoing theory; what are the conditions under which its foundational contribution to good practice is supplemented or even supplanted?[100]

---

[99] Compare the parallel formulation in Isocrates *Against the Sophists* 8 (*doxa* a more consistent basis for success than *epistēmē*).

[100] Compare also Isocrates' praise in *Nicocles* of long and wide expertise among officials in monarchies, in contrast to the limited experience of democratic officeholders. The former have more experience (*tais empeiriais proekhousin*, 18), which even compensates for any deficiency in their individual nature (*phusis*). Crucially (*to de megiston*, 21), the monarchical officials choose the most

Later in the *Protrepticus*, well after Isocrates has finished speaking, "Aristotle" is free to develop a "properly philosophical" account (indeed, it is strikingly Platonizing) of how theory should properly ground the empirical arts by which we live our lives.[101] "Aristotle" argues here that, because the *tekhnai* seek what has advantage for life by reference to (mere) experience of what is, it is only the "philosopher's vision ... of these things themselves, not of imitations" that can deliver life's true advantage. Matthew Walker has analyzed this argument for the utility of contemplation for practical life (as providing more proper standards of reference), seeking to reconcile it with the more familiar strand of Aristotelian thought, equally present in the *Protrepticus*, that defends contemplation as for-its-own-sake and in no need of any utilitarian defense. The philosopher, by "looking toward nature and toward the divine ... goes forth and lives according to himself,"[102] gaining precise knowledge of "boundary markers" (*horous*, 55.1) that are useful guides to practical life and the human good; according to Walker, this is because these *horoi* allow the philosopher to make comparative judgments between, on the one hand, the majesty of the cosmos and the divine intellect, and, on the other hand, human nature—both how we are "miserable and difficult" (*athlios ... kai khalepos*) and also our intellect as the "god in us" (*Protrepticus* VIII 47.5–48.21 Pistelli, 10a–c W, B104–110 D).[103]

The principle of reference to "things themselves" is extended into legislation: a good lawgiver will not look at and imitate existing *politeiai* "whether of Sparta or Crete or of any other such state" but will follow "what is eternal and unchanging."[104] Essentially, the statesman will need an ultimate grounding in knowledge of the Form of the Good in order to do his job. Bertelli suggests that *Antidosis* 80–83 is Isocrates' reply to this,[105] in particular his clear limitation of the legislator's work to compiling and selecting from existing "well regarded" laws (83). Aristotle's reply to this in turn would have been in the programmatic conclusion of *Nicomachean Ethics* X, where the proof that "sophists" teach their subjects despite lacking knowledge of them is that they thought legislation

---

intelligent persons (*phronimōtatoi*) as their advisors: those who have actual knowledge (*epistamenous*) in practical affairs. This kind of passage reminds us that, whatever the Isocratean prejudice against branches of knowledge whose connection to *pragmata* he found to be weak, he never forgets to insist on the decisive importance of intellectual qualifications within the realm of practice (here even setting aside his concern with the limitations of *phusis*).

[101] Iamblichus *Protrepticus* X 54.12–56.2 Pistelli (13 W, B46–50 D, trans. Hutchinson and Johnson 2009:17 and Ross 1952:47–49).

[102] *Protrepticus* X 55.26–56.2 Pistelli (13 W, B50 D).

[103] Walker 2010.

[104] Iamblichus *Protrepticus* X 55.17–25 Pistelli (13 W, B49 D).

[105] Bertelli 1977b:22–25; it is likely, however, that the *Protrepticus* followed the *Antidosis*.

could easily be accomplished by collecting reputed laws (with Aristotle's *suna-gagonti tous eudokimountas*, 1181a16, clearly echoing Isocrates' *eudokimountas ... sunagagein*, 83).

Note that the originality of the orator stands in contrast to this task for Isocrates, so that Aristotle's polemic is somewhat specious insofar as it takes legislation and not oratory as the diagnostic case to determine the role of general-ized knowledge for Isocrates. Aristotle elides this by castigating the "soph-ists" for making legislation inferior to rhetoric, without considering the point of making rhetoric—the art that has to respond to the political life that proceeds once the laws are set—superior to legislation.

The evidence here for an Isocrates–Aristotle polemic is indisputable, and Bertelli valuably adds to our knowledge of it by showing that the opening words of Aristotle's *Politics* II again directly echo this passage of *Antidosis*. Here Aristotle sounds a defensive note about his decision to go beyond the existing laws and constitutions:

> Our purpose is to consider what form of political community is best of all for those who are most able to realize their ideal of life. We must therefore examine not only this but other constitutions, both such as actually exist in well-governed states, and any theoretical forms which are held in esteem [*dokousai kalōs* = *Antidosis* 83, *eudokimountas*]; that what is good and useful may be brought to light. And let no one sup-pose that in seeking for something beyond them [*to zētein ti par' autas heteron* = *Antidosis* 83, *zētein heterous*] we are anxious to make a sophisti-cal display at any cost; we only undertake this inquiry because all the constitutions with which we are acquainted are faulty.

> 1260b27–37 (trans. Jowett 1921)

Here we must note Aristotle's defensiveness about departing from the empirical *methodos*: such a departure could seem "sophistical." This fits with his admission in the *Nicomachean Ethics* X passage of the additional importance of experience (e.g. *prosdein ... empeirias*, 1181a12). It seems Aristotle wishes to reassure his reader that he understands the empirical nature of the inquiry into human laws and will endeavor to avoid the mistaken principles that have hindered the "sophists" from proceeding properly in this largely empirical subject. Bertelli sees here the possibility of a move in an Isocratean direction but resists it, claiming that "Aristotle's insistence on the *empeiria* necessary to the true legislator should not suggest ... a concession to his adversary."

I agree that Aristotle remains committed to the value of universal knowl-edge (*to katholou eidenai*) in subjects that also require experience, but I propose that we *do* see some concession to Isocrates[106] (and the other exponents of the practical arts' methodology) in the tone he takes in his *Ethics* and *Politics*. A careful reading of the *Ethics* passage shows that even as Aristotle finds fault with legislation-by-collection, he has backed off entirely from the idea (which he had embraced in *Protrepticus* and *Politics*) that theoretical systems of law should be considered alongside, or instead of, extant ones. Now his argument is entirely that legislation-by-selection is being practiced incompetently by those who are not qualified to judge the best extant laws: "as though even the selection did not demand intelligence [*sunesis*] and as though right judgement [*krinai orthōs*] were not the greatest thing, as in matters of music. For ... people experienced in any department judge rightly the works produced in it" (1181a17–20, trans. Ross 1925). We should be struck by the choice of the model of the musical *tekhnē*. The sophists have not wrongly substituted *tekhnē* for *epistēmē*; they simply do not have the right *tekhnē*. The very type of those who have the authority to judge in such matters are the *experienced* practitioners of a practical art like music! If Aristotle wanted to hold to the theory-centric perspective of the *Protrepticus* passage, he has singularly failed to do so.

In the final surviving sentence of "Isocrates"' dismissal of the efficacy of knowledge-of-causes, Aristotle gives his rival a more open formula, which (taken out of context, or developed further in what is missing) matches the logic of the *Metaphysics*, where the concern is with deficiency of experience and not with the ruinous effect of abstracted theory: "*if* such sciences miss out on the correct activities [*praxeis*], the love of learning [*philomatheia*] misses out on the greatest goods" (*On General Mathematical Science* XXVI 81.2–4 Festa, 5b W, C41 D).[107] Here it sounds as if theory-with-practice could be viable, and that those who have omitted practice are securing some goods, but could have the greatest ones too with the proper attention to practice. It is worth considering why Aristotle follows up an unsparing Isocratean attack on theoretical investigation with a formula that could almost have come from Aristotle's own lips.

---

[106] The discrepancy is not lost on Jaeger (1948:266), who remarks on "the contrast between the last paragraph of the *Nicomachean Ethics* and the method of the *Protrepticus* and the *Statesman*." Jaeger goes on to call attention to the different spirit informing at least some parts the *Ethics*, e.g. 270 ("The standard there is immanent and biological. It is obtained by immersing oneself sympathetically in the manifold possible forms of the state, and not by looking to a single, fixed, ideal goal."), 395 ("The new element reveals another direction, namely the analysis of the forms of the moral life as they actually are. He abandons Plato's theory of virtue for a theory of living types, adequate to the rich variety of moral life in all conceivable manifestations"). A further indication of Aristotle's concession to Isocrates may be found in the fact that Philodemus later considered Aristotle open to the charge of traducing philosophy precisely by joining the law-collectors: see chap. 3 below.

[107] εἰ δὲ τῶν πράξεων τῶν ὀρθῶν ἀπολείπονται [sc. αἱ τοιαῦται ἐπιστῆμαι], τῶν μεγίστων ἀγαθῶν ἀπολείπεται ἡ φιλομάθεια.

These subtle affinities show Aristotle's concern to do some justice to the Isocratean school's claim to "love of wisdom," "care of the soul," and so forth, if only to reach the audience of those whose interest in philosophy and in moral and intellectual self-cultivation generally had been inspired through Isocrates' doctrine and ideals. Perhaps the ultimate hope is to expose some contradiction between Isocrateanism and reasoned theoretical argument, but by acknowledging the two strands in tension within Isocrates' project (charitably enough to provoke our recognition of Isocrates' own slogans), Aristotle effectively credits Isocrates with the status of a rival who promotes at least an alloy with a philosophical element. Despite Isocrates' resolute method of experience and emphasis on the performative and imprecise *doxa* that guides practice, he also consistently pleads for learning, philosophy, and a cultivation of that knowledge which does *not* strike him as foolishly recondite and irrelevant to the world of practice. Aristotle must bring this point of connection into focus in order to develop not only the lustrous distinction that attaches to a certain lofty philosophical vantage point on reality which Isocrates has failed to appreciate, but also the adequacy of his own practical philosophy to combine theoretical and practical understanding as effectively and usefully as his rival was widely credit -ed to have done. In short, a sentence for "Isocrates" such as this one, dangling everything desired before the student in love with intellectual and practical mastery of self and of the environment, makes Isocrates a properly protreptic speaker in the dialogue, charting a philosophical course forward for anyone who chooses to follow him.

In support of this, we may note that the motto "Isocrates" proffers here, *philomatheia*, is not a usual Isocratean or Aristotelian expression for the method and object of their philosophies,[108] but it does have a discernible flavor of philosophical protreptic.[109] In the *Protrepticus* itself, an Academic speaker[110] employs it to speak of the basic, universal, and positive human urge towards knowledge and clarity, and away from obscurity and ignorance: "And the fact that most

---

[108] Compare, however, the many occurrences in Plato's *Republic*, where *philomath-* is generally paired with, and synonymous with, *philosoph-* (apart from Glaucon's reservation at 475d–e). Its protreptic flavor is appropriate to the topic of education (development of human natures and desires in a philosophical direction).

[109] I was grateful to learn, after developing these thoughts, of Norman Sandridge's work on this term ("*Philomatheia* and the Knowledge of Leadership in Xenophon's *Education of Cyrus*," unpublished paper), which highlights its applicability in Xenophon (with related expressions of desire or eagerness for learning and inquiry) to the range of pursuits undertaken by the honor-seeking Persian nobles. Protreptic marries philosophy with worldly success and utility, and this is an interesting demonstration of how the term can apply in the latter domain with only a light suggestion of the philosophical (albeit a very pregnant suggestion, if we read Xenophon through the lens of many of his recent critics).

[110] Identified by Hutchinson and Johnson as Heraclides Ponticus.

people avoid death also shows the soul's love of learning [*philomatheian*]; for it avoids what it does not recognize [*gignōskei*], what is dark and not clear, and naturally seeks what is evident and recognizable [*to gnōston*]."[111] Similarly protreptic is the Isocratean aphorism in *To Demonicus* 18: "If you are a lover of learning (*philomathēs*), you will be a polymath (*polumathēs*)." In the *Nicomachean Ethics*, the same word appropriately occurs in book X, in a discussion that explains pleasure in terms of the universal human attraction to the various activities that make up life itself, the natural object of our desires: "Living is a type of activity, and each of us is active towards the objects he likes most and in the ways he likes most. The musician, for example, activates his hearing in hearing melodies; the lover of learning [*philomathēs*] activates his thought in thinking about objects of study [*tēi dianoiāi peri ta theōrēmata*]; and so on for each of the others."[112] The context and subject matter are strongly protreptic. This whole part of the *Nicomachean Ethics* culminates a discussion of practical and moral philosophy with a gesture towards the supreme happiness of the contemplative life. In the remainder of *Nicomachean Ethics* X 5–6, Aristotle relates the degrees of goodness of various activities to the degrees of goodness of their corresponding pleasures, and then establishes the life of theoretical study as the pleasantest human activity. Again the *philomath-* stem stands for the basic creditable human urge, activity, and pleasure—learning—before the discussion is refined into a technical consideration of what theoretical study is. The subject of pleasure in particular is a major protreptic *topos*. The passage about the soul's natural *philomatheia* quoted from *Protrepticus* VIII follows on a dismissal of the unchoiceworthy pleasure of sleep (45.25–46.1 Pistelli, 9 W, B101 D) and anticipates the dialogue's climactic revelation, that activating intelligence in the philosophical life is life in the highest degree, so that "living pleasantly and feeling true enjoyment belong only to philosophers, or to them most of all."[113]

---

[111] Iamblichus *Protrepticus* VIII 46.8–11 Pistelli (9W, B102 D), trans. Hutchinson and Johnson 2009:11.
[112] X 5, 1175a12–15, trans. Irwin (1985).
[113] Iamblichus *Protrepticus* XI 59.11–13 Pistelli (14 W, B91 D), trans. Hutchinson and Johnson 2009:19f.

2

Plato's Concession to the Practical Arts in the *Phaedrus*

O NE OF THE MOST IMPORTANT THREADS running through the intellectual history of the fifth and fourth centuries was the multidisciplinary attack on the question of what kind of art or science could hope to master the complexities of human experience. This was a question of theology, of history, of physiology, of politics, of rhetoric, and of ethics. The practitioners and theorizers of the arts contended to show that they could reduce the myriad factors governing practical outcomes to some kind of reasoned order, and that they relied on a foundation of critically scrutinized general principles—knowledge of what was knowable.

Plato confidently asserted that the rational investigation of the truth—defined in opposition to the unreasoned beliefs and knacks on which the *tekhnai* relied—was the proper foundation for virtue and (as we read in the *Phaedrus*) for proper rhetoric. Yet, on the basis of the previous chapter's Aristotle–Isocrates comparison, we can see more clearly that Plato was completely and acutely aware of the rival claims of the practical and empirical arts, finding himself forced to use their terms and take a position in their internal debates. Thus Socrates in the *Phaedrus* tells orators to think like physicians—in particular, like the "Hippocrates" who founded all medicine on a complete and systematic theory of nature, or in other words a rationalist who turned out the kind of Presocratically flavored speculations we find in the treatise *Regimen*.[1] Yet he cannot have been unaware of the sophistication with which a rival text like *On Ancient Medicine* defended the superiority of a medical science, and a practice of medical treatment, based on the same complex of experience, imprecise knowledge, and so on, that we have been discussing. Some of the methodological similarities between *On Ancient Medicine*, Isocrates, and Aristotle have been

---

[1] Hutchinson 1988: esp. 22ff.

previously adumbrated[2]; what I would like to emphasize is that the empiricist physicians had worked out no less a "conception of medicine as a systematic body of knowledge."[3] We are forced to recognize that Plato deliberately caricatures and silences the vigorous ongoing discussion of how the *tekhnai* can be made adequate to the reality of *praxis* and described adequately by and for the truly intelligent practitioner. He must ally himself with one school of medicine over another, when an informed reader would know that the caricatured physicians equaled Socrates' "Hippocrates" in scientific spirit and methodological seriousness.[4] It can be no accident that it is against rhetoric that Plato deploys this sleight of hand.

Plato aspired to exalt the empery of accountable knowledge and reason but strictly maintained the distinction between the practical arts and his own philosophical enterprise. In light of this tendency, the *Phaedrus* has long interested Plato's readers for the seriousness of its engagement with the rival art of rhetoric, for in the *Phaedrus* we learn that persuasive rhetoric can indeed be a proper art or *tekhnē*, something better than the artless *empeiria* attacked in the *Gorgias* or the poetic technique without knowledge ridiculed in the *Ion*, and indeed something that, in this elevated form, is an inescapable part of philosophy. Readers who are sympathetic to the intellectual aspirations of rhetoric in its own right, or who are intrigued by the appearance that Plato is flirting in this dialogue with the illicit powers of Eros and rhetoric, will inevitably ask, upon learning that philosophy cannot be separated from "true" rhetoric: can philosophical rhetoric, in turn, be completely and convincingly disentangled from "popular" rhetoric?

While the dialogue certainly means to hold the line between the two, it equally aims at a complicated picture of the relationship between them, so that there is still much to learn by studying the analogies and compromises by means of which Plato is able to claim rhetoric for philosophy. Rhetoric modified by an adjective is still rhetoric, and Plato has allied philosophy to a beast that lived in the outside world and had its own natural limits and capacities. A particularly instructive way to diagnose the effects of this is to examine the analogy of "Hippocratic" medicine adduced by Socrates for true rhetoric:

> Soc. [270b] Well, isn't the method of medicine [*tropos tekhnēs iatrikēs*] in a way the same as the method of rhetoric?

[2] Hutchinson 1988:26–50.
[3] Schiefsky 2005:52, quoted more fully on p. 72.
[4] Indeed, from the point of view of modern medical science *On Ancient Medicine* has a much sounder methodological philosophy. A text such as *Regimen* is important in the history of ideas for insisting that reasoned principles *could* exist, not for the highly implausible principles it rashly puts forth.

Phdr. How so?

Soc. In both cases we need to determine the nature [*dielesthai phusin*] of something—of the body in medicine, of the soul in rhetoric. Otherwise, all we'll have will be an empirical and artless practice [*tribē kai empeiria*]. We won't be able to supply, on the basis of an art, a body with the medicines and diet that will make it healthy and strong, or a soul with the reasons and customary rules for conduct [*logous te kai epitēdeuseis nomimous*] that will impart to it the convictions and virtues we want. ...

Soc. [270c] Do you think, then, that it is possible to reach a serious understanding of the nature of the soul without understanding the nature of the [world as a] whole [*aneu tēs tou holou phuseōs*]?

Phdr. Well, if we're to listen to Hippocrates, Asclepius' descendant, we won't even understand the body if we don't follow that method.

Plato *Phaedrus* 270b1–9 and c1–5
(trans. Nehamas and Woodruff 1995)

The import of this analogy is *not*, we will see, that medicine had a unique and distinct kind of claim to scientific rationality (as the least "popular" of the arts, to use a term from the *Phaedrus*). Rather, for Plato's contemporary audience, who would have been better informed than we are about the methodological debates of the practical arts, the medical analogy involved Socrates in a host of issues that applied in common to multiple practical arts, including rhetoric as well as medicine. It is largely "the result of chance" that the first general epistemological critique in our literary record (the Hippocratic *Art*) is medical and not rhetorical, and it can be difficult to determine which of the two disciplines pioneered a given line of attack on their shared problems.[5]

Within this context, the rationalist medical principles to which Socrates appeals are in constant dialogue with a more empiricist, but no less rigorous, strain of medical methodology that wants to achieve the very same goal as Socrates—a well-founded claim to reasoned systematicity—but to do so with greater confidence by taking into full account the challenges of harmonizing rational order with practical circumstances. In fact, as we will see, there is no such thing, whatever Plato may lead us to believe, as a purely empiricist medical methodology, and we may admire those Hippocratic authors who are the least inclined to attempt a tidy divorce between the two paths, having studied the

---

[5] Jouanna 1999:255f., 246–248.

attractions and limitations of both. "Knowledge" and "system" are not terms that divide the aspirations of one school from those of the other.

Not only is Socrates' Hippocratic analogy constructed purely[6] in order to elucidate the proper principles and technique of rhetoric's transactions with the soul, but the discipline of rhetoric itself was deeply involved in the same methodological dilemmas. To put it the other way around, medicine was rhetoric's near neighbor and could serve as a useful analogy precisely because it had worked through some of the same questions of method. As I have argued in the previous chapter, Isocratean theory in particular was seeking to contribute to the reconciliation of theory and practice, an approach whose seriousness and philosophical potential is well shown by the fact that Aristotle recognizably takes it back up against Plato and develops it in the *Nicomachean Ethics*. Moreover, the *Phaedrus* itself shows signs of ironic awareness, on Socrates' part, that the rationalist tendencies expressed in a work like the Hippocratic *Regimen*[7] do in fact run the danger of failing to manage the facts of the world as they concern the agent navigating the challenges of life. So not only does the dialogue's analogy with the practical arts itself raise contradictions, but the more we flesh out the real-world nature of the models being invoked, the more we may also suspect that Plato himself is conscious of the compromises involved, determined to take them seriously and to confront the strengths and attractions of a very prestigious rival intellectual tradition.

Knowledge and Performance in the *Phaedrus* and in Isocrates

The idea of a rhetorical *tekhnē* developed in the *Phaedrus* is not without its contradictions. It is philosophical and grounded in dialectical knowledge of the truth, and yet at the same time the dialogue's argument repeatedly admires its purely practical advantages over unphilosophical rhetoric and recognizes that it is and must be an art suited to use in real circumstances. We could explain these two sides of Socrates' true rhetoric by crediting him with an original synthesis of empirical technique and scientific purity, but a closer look at rhetorical and medical writers suggests that it is simpler to see a basis for both sides in the internal debates of the *tekhnē*-practitioners, who on their own were busy trying to reconcile the same two approaches to a sound method.

---

[6] See Joly 1994:43f.

[7] Here I take *Regimen* only as the treatise most evidently allied to rationalist Presocratic cosmology and thus of particular help in understanding the kind of medicine described in the *Phaedrus*; for the moment I gloss over the legitimate objections to identifying it with the "Hippocrates" of the *Phaedrus* (e.g. Mansfeld 1980:342 and 361n65, whose argument that Socrates has in mind *Airs, Waters, Places* is in turn rejected by Joly [1994]).

Rather than acknowledging that rhetoric as generally encountered is a *tekhnē* with all that entails, so that philosophical rhetoric is distinguished by being not merely an art but something more,[8] Socrates takes the opposite approach and argues that a foundation in true knowledge is a requisite for every art, so that rhetoricians working without such a foundation are practicing an *atekhnos tribē* (260de). It is important to note that when Socrates allows rhetoric to speak in her own defense, rhetoric does not defend the idea of a *tekhnē* that requires no knowledge, as we might expect from the conventional interpretation of passages in Isocrates that seem to say that the orator relies on *doxai* (notions, opinions, judgments) and not on *epistēmē* (knowledge).[9] Rather, rhetoric insists that knowledge of the truth is an *expected* prerequisite for speaking and persuading in accordance with the art of rhetoric:

> *Soc.* [260d3] But could it be, my friend, that we have mocked the art of speaking more rudely than it deserves? For it might perhaps reply, "What bizarre nonsense! Look, I am not forcing anyone to learn how to make speeches without knowing the truth [*agnoounta talēthes*]; on the contrary, my advice, for what it is worth, is to take me up only after mastering the truth. But I do make this boast: even someone who knows the truth [*tōi ta onta eidoti*] couldn't produce conviction on the basis of a systematic art [*tekhnēi*] without me."
>
> *Phdr.* [260e] Well, is that a fair reply?
>
> *Soc.* Yes, it is—if, that is, the arguments now advancing on rhetoric testify that it is an art [*tekhnē*].

Plato Phaedrus 260d3–e3

While introducing uncertainty about rhetoric's status as a *tekhnē*, Socrates nonetheless considers that rhetoric's defense *may* be satisfactory and admits that the better sort of existing rhetoric could have pretensions quite near to those he will advance for true rhetoric: not that it is an *epistēmē*, but that it depends on sound knowledge as a preliminary.

Within this broad similarity, we can recognize the role Isocrates assigned to *epistēmē* in his system of oratorical education, but only if we first recover his discussion of knowledge from the obscurity in which it has lain. What has covered over the importance of knowledge in Isocratean education is the fact

---

8 Compare how Aristotle in the *Nicomachean Ethics* insists (VI 5, 1140b1–7) that *phronēsis*, which operates in *praxis* and thus in ethics, is not the same as *tekhnē*, although the distinction is not always perfectly clear (as discussed in the previous chapter), so that Aristotle too finds himself compromising his distinction and coming nearer to the *tekhnai* in his model.

9 These passages and their interpretation will be discussed more fully below.

that Isocrates has more impressively stressed its limitations—that it cannot precisely and effectively master the onrush of circumstances in which the orator must decide and speak. Never mind that Aristotle felt the need to stress these same limitations for the purpose of laying out a theoretical and practical basis for the virtuous actor in the *Nicomachean Ethics*: these passages are nonetheless the first reached for to demonstrate the gulf separating Isocrates from the philosophical way of conceiving things. While we must and will admit the shortcomings, from a Platonic point of view, of the role knowledge plays in Isocrates' system, we must first study that role positively.

In *Against the Sophists* 16,[10] in which Isocrates polemizes against "sophists" who share many points in common with the sophistical and rhetorical opponents we meet in Plato, Isocrates insists on the achievability of knowledge in education:

> Now that I have gone this far, I wish to speak more clearly about these things. I contend that it is not all that difficult to gain a knowledge of the forms [*ideai*] that we use in speaking and composing all speeches, if a person surrenders himself not to those who make easy promises but to those who know something about them.

Isocrates, *Against the Sophists* 16
(trans. Mirhady and Too 2000)

In this emphatic assertion (βούλομαι ... ἔτι σαφέστερον εἰπεῖν ... φημὶ γὰρ ἐγὼ ...), Isocrates specifies the object of rhetorical knowledge as the "forms" (*ideai*) used in composition. Moreover, he insists that to gain such knowledge we must put ourselves in the hands not of the charlatans with their boastful promises, but of those who already possess some knowledge in this area (*tois eidosi ti peri autōn*).

The programmatic importance of this passage is confirmed by the fact that Isocrates quotes it some thirty or forty years later at *Antidosis* 194, where it serves as evidence that no one has spoken so consistently or with greater truth and justice about *philosophia* than he (195). Here Isocrates' larger point is to take to task those critics—perhaps not very unlike Plato—who deny his pursuit the status of a *tekhnē* in the first place (202) but gloss over the uniform and consistent results of his education for all his students (203–206). These naysayers shallowly criticize the art if it does not quickly and easily transform its students (199f.), when in fact its results are to be appreciated (207) as testimony to the power of sustained effort (*epimeleia*) to effect a change in the quality of the intellect (*to phronein, phronēsis*). All of this, Isocrates says, is just as his critics know

---

[10]   Cf. Bons 1996:27ff.

happen in the *tekhnai* whose precision they recognize: our areas of knowledge are won only with hard work (μόλις μὲν ἡμῖν τὰς ἐπιστήμας παραγιγνομένας, 201).

To return to *Against the Sophists* 16, then, we seem to find a definite if limited kind of important knowledge within Isocratean education. We will consider shortly Isocrates' further indications of what these teachable and knowable *ideai* are. For now let us anticipate some of the objections to taking them seriously.[11] It helps to notice what I have already tried to suggest, which is that Isocrates brings out this claim as a crucial and distinctive feature of how he conceives the proper configuration of the basic factors of nature, diligence, and education (*paideusis*).[12] The passage concerning the *ideai* confirms that this is Isocrates' version of an already traditional triad of factors—nature, practice, and knowledge—whose history and influence have long been appreciated.[13] Socrates accepts the applicability of this same triad in *Phaedrus* 269d when he begins with the general principle that a *tekhnē* of rhetoric (*qua tekhnē*, the passage seems to imply) will be mastered if a student with natural rhetorical ability adds knowledge and practice:

> *Soc.* [269d2] Well, Phaedrus, becoming good enough to be an accomplished competitor[14] is probably—perhaps necessarily—like everything else. If you have a natural ability for rhetoric [*phusei rhētorikos*], you will become a famous rhetorician, provided you supplement your ability with knowledge and practice [*epistēmēn kai meletēn*]. To the extent that you lack any one of them, to that extent you will be less than perfect.
>
> Plato *Phaedrus* 269d2–6

Isocrates' expression describing the value of the knowable *ideai* (ἐξ ὧν τοὺς λόγους ἅπαντας καὶ λέγομεν και συντίθεμεν) could denote anything from a very mechanical to a very sophisticated process of applying knowledge in preparation and performance.[15] We should remember both the sweepingly powerful

---

[11] See also Schlatter (1972), who concludes that this word is used "in the broadest sense of general education."

[12] Isocrates *Against the Sophists* 14f., on which see Livingstone 2007:21: "Education will make the able 'more skilled' (*tekhnikoteroi*: it is not clear exactly what this means, but presumably it involves knowledge of *ideai* or *eide*)."

[13] See Shorey 1909 ("Φύσις, Μελέτη, Ἐπιστήμη").

[14] Heitsch (1993:163f. nn341 and 344) has noticed the interesting echo in ἀγωνιστὴν τέλεον (*Phaedrus* 269d2) of Isocrates' term for the successful elite performers who bring his school glory, as opposed to the larger group of students who are definitely improved by Isocratean education without achieving such success in public life, a distinction I have discussed several times in the previous chapter.

[15] As this discussion is developed in the passage following (17f.), again it is clear that the teacher's precise and complete imparting of the discipline's teachable knowledge (καὶ δεῖν ... τὸν δὲ

definition Isocrates gives to *logoi*, and also that the conclusion of Socrates and Phaedrus' discussion of the artless features of Lysias' speech (*atekhna*, 262c6) focuses on its lack of principles of rational and organic construction (264b3–c5).[16] Even if we apply a fairly technical and limited definition of Isocrates' *ideai*, it seems plausible that in this passage and others Isocrates is laying claim to a more organized compositional process that can defend itself at least against the charge of this particular kind of *atekhnia*.[17] In short, we are not entitled to be as surprised and skeptical as many would be when faced with the statement of Sextus Empiricus (*Adversus rhetoras* 62), who in a survey of various definitions of rhetoric notes that, whereas one Athenaeus defines it more conventionally as *logōn dunamis*,[18] "Isocrates asserts that the practice and pursuit of orators is no other thing than the knowledge or science [*epistēmē*] of persuasion."[19]

The more completely we review the statements in Isocrates and in the *Phaedrus* about the content and purpose of the knowledge with which the ideal orator works, the more we see that, despite the differences between the theoretical foundations of the two models, there are several common points of emphasis. In Socrates' construction, the orator's knowledge of the subject matter and of the hearer's soul allows him to adapt his speech accordingly.[20] At 271b1–5, thanks to the dialectical art of thinking, which works through division, anyone who offers a serious rhetorical *tekhnē* will have classified the "kinds," or *genē*, of *logoi*:

> *Soc.* [271b] Third, he will classify the kinds [*genē*] of speech and of soul
> there are, as well as the various ways in which they are affected, and

---

διδάσκαλον τὰ μὲν οὕτως ἀκριβῶς οἶόν τ' εἶναι διελθεῖν ὥστε μηδὲν τῶν διδακτῶν παραλιπεῖν) plays a crucial role, though this combines with aspects of performance which must be imitated from the teacher's example (*paradeigma*) rather than mastered intellectually in the full realization of the "lovers of wisdom" (τελείως ἕξουσιν οἱ φιλοσοφοῦντες).

16   Cf. Bons 1996:50–55.

17   For further discussion of Isocratean *ideai*, see Sullivan 2001, Bons 1996:19–64, and the works cited in Gaines 1990:165nn2f.

18   See Reinhardt and Winterbottom 2006:258f., on Quintilian *Training in Oratory* 2.15.23: *Athenaeus fallendi artem.*

19   See Ax 2005:151n18.

20   Besides the passage about to be quoted, compare 268bc on the judicious and selective application of effects in medicine and poetics. Isocrates' theoretical approach to the audience is a separate subject, interesting in its own right, to which I cannot do justice here. For some commonalities in Plato and Isocrates' construction of authorial independence from the audience, see Morgan 2003; for the audience–speaker dynamic in Isocrates and Aristotle, see Haskins 2004. Usener (2003), in a survey building on Usener 1994 with special reference to Isocrates' *Philip*, connects several typically Isocratean strategies (revision, reflection, looking beyond narrow circumstances of time and place, first-person plural, the dialogue with the unknown reader, etc.) to the wider literary *Adressatenkreis* that lies beyond his semi-fictive oral audiences.

explain what causes each. He will then coordinate each kind of soul with the kind of speech appropriate to it. And he will give instructions concerning the reasons why one kind of soul is necessarily convinced by one kind of speech while another necessarily remains unconvinced.

This half of the equation is quite reminiscent of Isocrates' *ideai*, which in the same passage as above he too calls the *eidē* of *logoi*:

[17] In addition to having the requisite natural ability [*phusis*], the student must learn the forms of speeches [*eidē tōn logōn*] and practice their uses [*khrēseis*]. The teacher must go through these aspects as precisely as possible, so that nothing teachable is left out, but as for the rest, he must offer himself as a model, [18] so that those who are molded by him and can imitate him will immediately appear more florid and graceful than others. When all these conditions occur together, then those who practice philosophy will achieve success. But if any of the points mentioned is left out, the students will necessarily be worse off in this regard.

Isocrates *Against the Sophists* 17–18

A closely parallel passage, Isocrates *Helen* 11, may lead us to take the intellectual level of the Isocratean *ideai* more seriously, since they are not always simple to learn but in the case of *logoi* "of general import and credibility" (*koinoi kai pistoi*, trans. Mirhady and Too 2000) are apparently hard to learn, as are the *kairoi*, and Isocrates particularly stresses the correspondingly increased difficulty of "matching" (*sunthesis*) the *logoi* with the use-circumstances, or *kairoi*.

Isocrates' emphasis on knowledge of kinds, applied in use, fits in nicely with the surprisingly practical orientation of much of the *Phaedrus*'s discussion of *tekhnē*-worthy, or "philosophical," rhetoric. The word *khrēseis* itself follows on the discussion of *eidē* in Plato (271c10–e2), just as it does in Isocrates, and the application of *aisthēsis* in this passage should be compared to the role played by *doxai* in Isocrates. It must have struck many readers of the *Phaedrus* that, despite true rhetoric's lofty pretensions, Socrates also promises that the knowledgeable possessor of a *tekhnē* will be more effective at deception (262b) and in general dwells on the persuasive power of the true orator (cf. 271b ff.), so much so that the reference to his involvement with "the truth about just or good things" (272d4–5) almost comes as a surprise. Isocrates, in contrast, perhaps more defensive about distinguishing himself from the unprincipled sophist, in the passage of the *Antidosis* introducing his defense of his "philosophy" as a *tekhnē* of painstaking intellectual self-cultivation, squarely aims this defense against impatient and shallow critics who believe oratory must consist of "deception and cheating" (199).

A deeper connection between Isocratean rhetoric and the *Phaedrus*'s true rhetoric is that they each must be flexible and are completely incompatible with the kind of fixed and specific prescriptions for action offered by the handbook-writers. This arises from the fact we have been studying, that they are both meant to be used in the complex circumstances of the real world. Though both are known to us for their writings, Isocrates and Plato are equally insistent about the inadequacy of written instruction. In *Against the Sophists* 12f.,[21] shortly after having deplored some teachers' claim that the *epistēmē* of *logoi* can be imparted in the same way as that of mere *grammata* (10),[22] Isocrates rejects the handbook-writers' regimentation of *tekhnē*: he complains it cannot possibly do justice to the art of oratory, a "creative affair" in which a truly skilled speaker (*tekhnikōtatos*, 12) produces *logoi* that "partake of the circumstances of the moment [*kairoi*]." This brings to mind at once, in general, the *Phaedrus*'s critique of written discourse, as at 275c:

> Οὐκοῦν ὁ τέχνην οἰόμενος ἐν γράμμασι καταλιπεῖν, καὶ αὖ ὁ παρα-
> δεχόμενος ὥς τι σαφὲς καὶ βέβαιον ἐκ γραμμάτων ἐσόμενον, πολλῆς
> ἂν εὐηθείας γέμοι ...

> Well, then, those who think they can leave written instructions for an art, as well as those who accept them, thinking that writing can yield results that are clear or certain, must be quite naïve ...

275c5–7

But the specific terms in which the *Phaedrus* speaks of the "use" phase of rhetoric should also be compared to Isocrates. For example, terminology of an Isocratean flavor occurs at *Phaedrus* 272a, where again the discussion is of how the relevant kinds of preparatory knowledge are actually tested in the crucible of real and present circumstances:

> ΣΩ. ὅταν δὲ εἰπεῖν τε ἱκανῶς ἔχῃ οἷος ὑφ' οἵων πείθεται, παραγιγνόμενόν
> τε δυνατὸς ᾖ διαισθανόμενος ἑαυτῷ ἐνδείκνυσθαι ὅτι οὗτός ἐστι καὶ αὕτη
> ἡ φύσις περὶ ἧς τότε ἦσαν οἱ λόγοι, νῦν ἔργῳ παροῦσά οἱ, ᾗ προσοιστέον
> τούσδε ὧδε τοὺς λόγους ἐπὶ τὴν τῶνδε πειθώ, ταῦτα δ' ἤδη πάντα
> ἔχοντι, προσλαβόντι καιροὺς τοῦ πότε λεκτέον καὶ ἐπισχετέον, βραχυ-

---

[21] This passage is considered in relation to Aristotle above.

[22] For the connections between this and the methodological polemics of the Hippocratics and the *Phaedrus*, see also Noël 2009:95f.

λογίας τε αὖ καὶ ἐλεινολογίας καὶ δεινώσεως ἑκάστων τε ὅσα ἂν εἴδη
μάθῃ λόγων, τούτων τὴν εὐκαιρίαν τε καὶ ἀκαιρίαν διαγνόντι, καλῶς
τε καὶ τελέως ἐστὶν ἡ τέχνη ἀπειργασμένη, πρότερον δ᾽ οὔ· ἀλλ᾽ ὅτι ἂν
αὐτῶν τις ἐλλείπῃ λέγων ἢ διδάσκων ἢ γράφων, φῇ δὲ τέχνῃ λέγειν, ὁ
μὴ πειθόμενος κρατεῖ.

Soc. He will now not only be able to say what kind of person is convinced by what kind of speech; on meeting someone he will be able to
discern what he is like and make clear to himself that the person actually standing in front of him is of just this particular sort of character
he had learned about in school—to that he must now apply speeches of
such-and-such a kind in this particular way in order to secure conviction about such-and-such an issue. When he has learned all this—when,
in addition, he has grasped the right occasions [*kairous*] for speaking
and holding back; and when he has also understood when the time
is right [*tēn eukairian*] for Speaking Concisely or Appealing to Pity or
Exaggeration or for any other of the kinds of speech [*eidē logōn*] he has
learned and when it is not [*tēn akairian*]—then, and only then, will he
have finally mastered the art well and completely [*kalōs te kai teleōs estin
hē tekhnē apeirgasmenē*]. But if his speaking, his teaching, or his writing
lacks any one of these elements and he still claims to be speaking with
art, you'll be better off if you don't believe him.

271e2–272b2

Socrates uses the *kairos* terms favored by Isocrates three times in close
succession,[23] clearly talks about how the speaker will apply the kinds of effects
any interpreter would include among the Isocratean *ideai*, and very significantly
finds in this performative culmination of the student's training the decisive
proof that "the *tekhnē* is well and completely produced" in him.[24]

The language with which Plato speaks of the complete assembly of the
prerequisites for artful oratory must have been very current in the circles of
rhetorical theory, for we see by now a set of echoes that can be extended:

But if his speaking, his teaching, or his writing lacks [*elleipēi*] any one
of these elements and he still claims to be speaking with art, you'll be
better off if you don't believe him.

Phaedrus 272a8–b2, quoted immediately above

---

[23] Cf. Steidle 1952:258, who numbers this among several ideas that unite Plato and Isocrates against
the general rhetoric tradition in *Phaedrus*.

[24] Compare Isocrates *Against the Sophists* 18: τελείως ἕξουσιν οἱ φιλοσοφοῦντες, cited above, n15.

To the extent that you lack [*elleipēis*] any one of them [i.e. nature, knowledge, or practice], to that extent you will be less than perfect.

Phaedrus 269d5f., quoted above

But if any of the points mentioned [again, nature, learning, or practice] is left out [*elleiphthēi*], the students will necessarily be worse off in this regard.

Against the Sophists 18, quoted above

In whatever field of endeavor one wishes to achieve the very best results, whether it be wisdom, courage, eloquence [*euglōssia*] or excellence [*aretē*], either as a whole or any part of it—he will be able to achieve this on the following conditions. First, one must possess natural ability [*phunai*], and this is a matter of good luck [*tuchē*]; the other elements, however, are in one's own hands: he must be eager for noble things and willing to work hard, beginning his studies [*manthanonta*] very early in life and seeing them through to completion over a long period of time. If even one of these factors is absent [*apestai*], it is impossible to reach the highest goal in the end [*es telos to akron exergasasthai*]; but if any human being has all these things, he will be unsurpassed in whatever he takes on [*askēi*].

Anonymus Iamblichi 95.20–23 Pistelli
(trans. Dillon and Gergel 2003:311)[25]

This last example pushes the pattern back into the fifth century, confirming that the Isocratean language that we can show was topical for Plato and Aristotle has its roots in the earlier rhetorical and *tekhnē* tradition.

Isocrates brings together prior education and the unpredictable circumstances of the *kairoi* in a comparable way in *Antidosis* 184. First the teachers have "examined the subject minutely" (*diakribōsantes*) and the students have learned (*emathon*). On this basis the students "string together" (*suneirein*) individual elements with an aim to bringing their *doxai* in closer accord with the *kairoi*. What follows are several statements often quoted to show Isocrates' enmity towards *epistēmē*—the circumstances of the moment will elude the students'

---

[25] Interestingly, Iamblichus' own protreptic goes on to use this in an *a fortiori* argument about the applicability of the principles of the practical arts to philosophy: "If this is correct even in application to the other fields of knowledge [*epistēmai*], how much more so in application to the most commanding and authoritative of all *tekhnai*, philosophy?" (*Protrepticus* XX 95.24–26 Pistelli).

epistēmai; the leap from training to performance cannot be learned by knowledge (*eidenai*); there is no *epistēmē* that can make a performance-level orator out of just anyone—but this obscures the importance of knowledge in Isocrates' system and the extent to which Isocrates' *doxai* are simply a way of talking about the *kairoi* which Plato also must address. Plato does not, as far as I am aware, claim that the *kairoi* are handled strictly through definition, division, and dialectic. It is also salutary to recall that Isocrates insists on the worth of his education for the student whose talents are not adequate for him ever to enter the arena of political oratory; such a student's education is necessarily dominated by the content of the learnable knowledge (cf. 201).

So when we return again to Isocrates' most famous statement on the limitations of knowledge, *Antidosis* 271, we can be more confident that it is proper to stress the qualifications: our nature cannot attain knowledge "*that would enable us to know what we must say or do*," so that a premium remains on those who are able to form the *doxai* that actually necessarily operate when we stand on the field of action. The words may not have sat so comfortably in Plato's mouth, but we also recognize that Plato shares Isocrates' disdain for the handbook-writers who would presume to prescribe our words and actions with minute particularity, and must also make room for new factors to operate if the insights won through dialectic are going to be brought to bear in performance through the rhetorical *tekhnē*.

Isocrates' *Antidosis*, composed in his eighties as a defense of his career before a fictional Athenian jury, notably introduces its long review of the author's educational philosophy with an appeal to the jurors that they apply the standard of knowledge and not mere *doxa*:

> Αὐτοὺς γὰρ ὑμῖν δείξω τοὺς εἰρημένους ὑπ' ἐμοῦ καὶ γεγραμμένους, ὥστ' οὐ δοξάσαντες, ἀλλὰ σαφῶς εἰδότες ὁποῖοί τινές εἰσιν, τὴν ψῆφον οἴσετε περὶ αὐτῶν.

> I shall present to you the very speeches I have spoken and written so that you will not conjecture but will know clearly what they are like when you vote on them.

> *Antidosis* 54

Ober has pointed out the Platonic and Socratic overtones of this.[26]

To sum up what we have said so far, while Isocrates did not profess Platonic dialectic as the art of thinking upon which the art of speaking must be based, he holds in common with Plato an interest in a foundation of knowledge upon

---

[26] Ober 2004:37.

which the less precisely controllable workings of discursive performance rely. Moreover, we should not accept unquestioningly Socrates' more-or-less unde-fended notion that the method of definition and division is in fact a reliable foundation for any species of rhetoric. Is it not possible that rhetoricians such as Isocrates, and practitioners of the other arts, had considered different candi-dates for the sort of knowledge from which to begin, before deciding which was of most essential value for consistently producing good outcomes on a sound basis? Isocrates was certainly well aware of the rival view that rhetorical students should spend more of their time on pursuits like geometry: indeed, he endorses a certain amount of this and proclaims himself a lover of wisdom who teaches care of the soul and so forth because he appreciates and flirts with the prestige of the philosophical way, and yet rejects the extreme explicitly as "useless."[27] Socrates' example of beginning with a definition and analysis of love (263de) makes sense, but Isocrates' *ideai* may also represent a kind of analytics. If Isocrates tends more to emphasize the limitations of knowledge, does this not inject some healthy Socratic skepticism into the discussion of whether we can indeed get to knowledge on the kinds of subjects on which we must speak? Are we allowed to act and persuade while our attainment of knowledge is still imperfect? It is difficult to have rhetoric at all if the answer is no.

When Socrates praises Isocrates at the end of the *Phaedrus*, we can suspect a serious aspect to it. I also suggest that we give due attention to the close literary similarity (unremarked, I believe) between the prophetic praise of Isocrates here, and the way Socrates and Theodorus speak about Theaetetus' potential in the *Theaetetus*. In that undoubtedly sincere tribute to Theaetetus' noble generosity, temperament, and intellect, Socrates' sums up Theodorus' just praise by saying, "You say that the man is *gennikos*" (144d5). This word is used elsewhere by Plato only in *Phaedrus* 279a4 (the praise of Isocrates), and it is a "rare and insistent doublet" of the more normal term *gennaios*.[28] The *Theaetetus* passage should have prevented ironic interpreters of the Isocrates-praise at least from claiming that this word in particular is inappropriate for Socrates' sincere admiration.[29] If Plato and Isocrates are each other's determined oppo-nents—and this is too complicated an issue to be decided easily—their rivalry

---

[27] Isocrates *Antidosis* 261–269, *Panathenaicus* 26, *Helen* 5; cf. *Busiris* 23.
[28] Pierre Chantraine, quoted in des Places 1964, s.v.
[29] Ford 1993:52n9: "Plato may be twitting Isocrates' aristocratic pretensions ... The basis for Socrates' optimistic hopes is that Isocrates is 'naturally' better at speeches than Lysias and has a more 'noble character' (*ēthei gennikōterōi*); birth and breeding thus elevate Isocrates above Lysias." Among many further commentaries on the passage may be mentioned de Vries 1971, Laplace 1988, Tulli 1990, and Erler 1993 (with a wider argument about the convergences and dif-ferences between Plato and Isocrates' critical approach to writing).

depends on some surprisingly close connections, and we should look carefully for signs in both authors of consciously moving closer still to the other's ideas: a strategy to supplant the opponent's claim, but one necessarily involving some compromises.

Adoleskhia kai meteōrologia

Before moving on to the art of medicine, we should briefly consider the lofty and showy language Socrates uses at *Phaedrus* 270a to talk about the Hippocratic method and its basis in knowledge of ultimate truths about the cosmos. Socrates asserts that "All the great arts require endless talk and ethereal speculation [*adoleskhias kai meteōrologias*] about nature" (trans. Nehamas and Woodruff 1995), and he adduces the support of Pericles' decisive encounter with Anaxagoras, from whom the great orator (*pantōn teleōtatos eis tēn rhētorikēn*) learned "the nature of mind and mindlessness."

I am interested in this particular passage because its ironic touch seems to suggest a knowingness on Socrates' part that the presumption of an absolute and all-encompassing source of truth about nature is somewhat ridiculous, especially when brought to bear on the real problems of the political world. The word *adoleskhia* means "nonsense and foolery,"[30] but a need to defend the supposed high seriousness of Plato's rationalist principles has caused LSJ and some interpreters to invent a special sense found only in this passage, "keenness or subtlety." Robert Joly, for example, is compelled to endorse the idea that Pericles fits the model of a "savant désintéressé,"[31] when anyone who has read the *Phaedo* knows that Anaxagoras is truly a "mindless"[32] basis on which to build a science. This bit of humor sharpens the problems with supposing any understanding of nature to be a reliable foundation on which to build an art that has to work in practice; at any rate, the cosmology of a work like the Hippocratic *Regimen*, despite Socrates' explicit statement that a true *tekhnē* should have such a basis, does not impress us any more, and is unlikely to have impressed Plato any more, than that of Anaxagoras. Pericles is ignorant of Socratic dialectic, anyway, and he comes off looking more like the Socrates of Aristophanes' *Clouds* than anyone else.

---

[30] Cf. the scholium to Isocrates *Against the Sophists* 8: ἀδολεσχία ἡ πάνυ φλυαρία, ἤγουν ἡ πλείστη; also Theophrastus *Characters* 3. See Diggle 2004:199 for more references ("Ἀδολεσχία is talk on matters which others perceive as unimportant. The word and its cognates are commonly applied to philosophers and sophists").

[31] Joly 1994:46f. and 51. Rowe (1986:204) mentions Hackforth and de Vries as expressing a similar view.

[32] Note, however, that while ἀνοίας (codices B, T) is probably the correct reading, Burnet read διανοίας (codex V, Aristides teste Schanz), and the other manuscripts (apographa) have ἐννοίας.

Plato seems to use the word *adoleskhia* in smiling reference to a certain kind of inspiring mystical claptrap—perhaps politically powerful or heuristically valuable, but not the product of philosophical rigor.[33] Socrates' remark to Hermogenes, at *Cratylus* 401b, that the first name-givers were *meteōrologoi kai adoleskhai tines*, is typical. Ultimately, the fact that Plato will turn to such storytelling larks at times of evident philosophical seriousness, as here in characterizing the epistemic foundation of Hippocratic medicine or rhetoric, is a subject larger than I can deal with here. As with the priests and poets of the *Meno*, or the corybantic buzzing in Socrates' ears in the *Crito*, and as with the powerful influence of Eros, Muses, and cicadas in the *Phaedrus*, sometimes Plato's Socrates signals a playful awareness of the conjectural boldness with which he paints some of the most daring and important strokes on his canvas. These free and lofty gestures are interesting to consider as an alternative to admitting the style of knowledge and phronesis cultivated in the practical arts tradition: both are ways of containing the irrational within a system.

Plato may be echoing Isocrates' *Against the Sophists* 7f., where Isocrates uses the similar phrase *adoleskhian kai mikrologian* in reference to charlatan professors who keep closer watch over discrepancies in *logoi* than in actions, and who "claim to know about future things, but concerning present things are unable to speak or advise any of the things needful." The result is that care for the soul (*tēs psukhēs epimeleian*) is brought into disrepute. This is in part a warning against handbook-precept and theorization run amok, and since we know Plato is largely sympathetic to this aspect of the critique, it is not unreasonable to think it a sympathetic borrowing. Yet Isocrates also points to the inescapable challenge of engaging with the actions taking place in the present, and this aspect of the critique is a source of more tension within the *Phaedrus*.

The Art of Medicine

The prestigious model for Socrates' true art of rhetoric in the *Phaedrus* is the medical art of "Hippocrates."[34] Although Socrates' use of this model in the first place demonstrates an acceptance that philosophical rhetoric will still be a practical art and conform to the model of some existing practical art, he also attempts to elevate the system of Hippocrates, with its concern for "the nature

---

[33] At *Parmenides* 135d, *adoleskhia* refers to the most noble and valuable method of dialectic, but in the derogatory label of *hoi polloi*; the young Socrates is told that his "fine and divine impulse" must, in order to develop into a grasp on the truth, undergo a kind of training (*gumnasai*, imperative) in something ignorantly called by this dismissive name.

[34] I drop the quotation marks henceforth and avoid the Hippocratic question altogether. My references to "Hippocrates" mean the authority cited by Socrates in the *Phaedrus*, whereas the texts in the Hippocratic Corpus will be cited by name.

of the whole" (*Phaedrus* 270c2), above the less scientific practice of other physicians, who, like the run-of-the-mill speaker, rely upon experience instead of knowledge. While I accept that this is a doctrinally crucial distinction for Plato, a look into several texts of the Hippocratic Corpus shows how hard it is to enforce, in practice, on the landscape of Classical Greek medical theory. I suggest that Plato's elision of the ambivalences to be found in the medical texts shows how powerful a claim the authority of the methodological discourses of the practical arts, considered more broadly, held over him, and how much ground he consequently had to yield to them in order to sustain his construction of any new kind of rhetoric.

The Hippocratic treatise *Regimen* may roughly exemplify the rationalist method of Socrates' Hippocrates, but it too evinces certain reservations about the scientific precision of medical practice. Hutchinson takes *Regimen* as the appropriate parallel and cites two passages (*Regimen* I 2 = VI 470–472.28-40 Littré and III 67 = VI 592.1–12 Littré) in which even that author—for whom a Presocratic-flavored cosmology is a truth, graspable by reason, from which all sound medicine can be derived—acknowledges the limitations of knowledge.[35] For all medicine had to address the frequency of the art's failure.[36] Medicine for this author is, as Hutchinson puts it, "a comprehensive body of profound and hidden truths which it is difficult to *apply* precisely." The final phase of medical therapeutics resists prescriptive knowledge: the proportion of food and exercise for each individual constitution (*pros hekastēn phusin*) is impossible to discover (*adunaton heurein*).[37] Likewise, "Concerning human regimen ... it is impossible to treat it in writing [*xungrapsai*] with precision [*es akribeian*], so as to make a due proportion of exercise in relation to the amount of food" (III 67, 1–3), and the elements of diet, "all differing from each other [*diaphora*], prevent the possibility of precise written formulation [*es akribeian xungraphēnai*]" (III 67, 11–12).

It will come as no surprise that, from my view, these citations suggest a compatibility between even this most rationalistic treatise, suggested as Plato's referent,[38] and the principal case in which Isocrates stresses knowledge's limitations. So, without disputing that a work like *Regimen* demonstrates an ardent belief in basic and universal truths that echoes Plato's faith in dialectical knowledge much better than anything in Isocrates, I have to differ with Hutchinson

---

[35] Hutchinson 1988:34.

[36] See the Hippocratic treatise *Art*, Allen 1994, and Lo Presti 2010 (on the role of errors in Hippocratic education and knowledge-discovery).

[37] *Regimen* I 2, lines 29–33 Littré.

[38] Hutchinson (1988:23) suggests that "the text which Plato was paraphrasing [in 270cd] seems to be" *Regimen* I 2.

when he goes on to cite *Antidosis* 271, in contrast, as a clear expression that only "sound opinions," and not "exact practical knowledge," are worth the orator's pursuit;[39] the different interpretation of this passage I have offered above has more points of connection to the way the author of *Regimen* thinks about his practical *tekhnē*.[40]

In fact, there is considerable uncertainty about which text from the Hippocratic Corpus, if any, to nominate as Socrates' referent, and this is symptomatic of the fact that all the Hippocratic writers, on both sides of the methodological debate to be found within the corpus, embrace the value both of system and of a realistic understanding of the limitations on applying precise knowledge to the circumstances of actual experience. Jaap Mansfeld was able to nominate *Airs, Waters, Places* instead.[41] The treatise *On Ancient Medicine*, rightly chosen by Hutchinson as a clear exponent of an empiricist methodology closer to Isocrates, in its turn contains many statements and tendencies closer to the kind of medicine Socrates admires. As Mark Schiefsky says:

> Though *Vict.* [=*Regimen*] and VM [=*On Ancient Medicine*] disagree sharply on the question of the *kind* of theory of human φύσις that should serve as the foundation of medicine ... they share the general assumption that medicine must be based on such a theory. *Vict.* also shares VM's focus on dietetics and conception of medicine as a systematic body of knowledge that takes into account all the relevant factors in human diet and regimen.[42]

In fact, Schiefsky comes to the conclusion that "only in *VM* do we find an *explicit* recommendation of something like the method Socrates describes as a method of investigating human φύσις," so that, "*If* Plato had in mind any of the texts that make up the present Hippocratic Corpus, surely it was VM," notwithstanding the evident differences between the two theories.[43]

This methodological ambivalence is everywhere in the Hippocratic Corpus. Joly has given reasons for skepticism about whether any neat, discoverable, or reconstructible Hippocratic analogue can lie behind Plato's "Hippocrates"; the search for "strict parallelism" could be misguided, since medicine in the

---

[39] Hutchinson 1988:35.

[40] Cf., more generally, Johnson 1959:29: "Just as the medical student for all his book learning is incompetent until years of clinical experience have taught him to recognize and deal with ailments, so the pupil is no rhetor until he can stand up to the fire and cunning of an opponent in public debate, and vanquish him by the arguments and style of delivery appropriate to that particular case."

[41] Mansfeld 1980.

[42] Schiefsky 2005:52.

[43] Schiefsky 2005:70f.

Phaedrus primarily serves the function of expressing what the orator's art does in connection with his hearers' souls.[44] Jouanna's characterization of the treatise *On the Nature of Man* is typical:[45]

> At first blush it seems that our treatise is a manifesto directed against the interference of philosophical theories in medicine, since our author announces clearly in his preamble his intention to treat human nature as a physician and not as a philosopher. In fact, his position reveals itself as fundamentally ambiguous: this is what we shall see in studying the complex connections between our treatise and the diverse philosophical and medical tendencies of its time.[45]

Indeed, I suggest that this methodological ambivalence is more generally appropriate to the practical arts (in particular, Isocratean rhetoric), and we have seen that we must take very seriously Plato's engagement with this kind of methodology in the *Phaedrus*.

Not Every Practical Art: The Counterexample of Harmonics

In fact, while in principle any practical art could and should have sought and developed a flexible methodology capable of marrying experience and doctrine, it seems that rhetoric and medicine were unusually advanced and sophisticated examples of this enterprise. An examination of harmonic theory shows that, even when we hear in our texts of an "empiricist/rationalist" polarity, this may not really betoken the existence of a school committed to facing the complex uncertainties of lived experience in the manner of some rhetorical and medical theories.

Among the various writers and movements in the practical arts,[46] the *harmonikoi* criticized by Aristoxenus, a Peripatetic harmonic theorist perhaps fifteen years younger than Aristotle, make a good test case. For their "empiricist" methods were found provocative in a field with a strong rationalist and mathematical tradition going back to Pythagoras. These *harmonikoi* seem to have offered "arguments [that] depend wholly on their views about the intervals that can reliably be identified by the ear."[47] "In this method of describing musical structures, then, it is possible to conceive, for example, the interval of a fifth as three and a half tones without reference to the ratio of 3:2 and in this way it is more compatible with the way that the human mind perceives music. Likewise ... a semitone could be perceived as an interval half the size of a tone."[48]

---

[44] Joly 1994:43f.
[45] Jouanna 2002:38.
[46] For a wider view of *tekhnai* in this period see Cuomo 2007.
[47] Barker 2007:95.
[48] Gibson 2005:18.

It is tempting to analogize the ear's data in this system to the imprecise experiential information upon which orators and physicians must base their actions. But there is no evidence that the errors and incompleteness of perception were problematized in this school, not to mention any evidence that such problems were then considered *practical* (as opposed to merely descriptive) problems. We can only speculate. Barker couches such a speculation in conditional form. Just as *On Ancient Medicine* rejects "empty postulates" about the "nature of man" and challenges physicians to "work on the basis of empirical observation of experience," "I suggest that the *harmonikoi* of this early period, *if* they had considered the matter, would have taken a similar view about their own art."[49] Unfortunately, the counterfactuality of this intriguing "if" must be underscored; by Barker's own analysis, the *harmonikoi* do not seem to have moved in this direction, but instead to have retained the theoretical framework of the systematic handbook.[50] This inability to develop principles of performance sophisticated enough to take into account their awareness of the "flux of phenomena" put the *harmonikoi* in the awkward position of singing and playing "intervals which are outlawed by their own theoretical position."[51]

If this characterization is correct, we have to do with a *failure* to develop a theory that makes room for experience's discrepancies from rationalistic canons. The most we can say is that perhaps this view of the *harmonikoi* as incompetent and inconsistent handbook-drafters (adherents to *tetagmenē tekhnē* in the Isocratean sense) is to some degree an incomplete and unfair caricature, based as it is on hostile witnesses.[52] There could have been an innovative critique here of music's epistemological foundation, in the spirit of Protagoras' man-measure doctrine.[53] But just as it is difficult to reconcile Protagorean epis-

---

[49] Barker 2007:104n58, emphasis added.
[50] Barker 2007:66, where the *harmonikoi* are described as "looking for invariance and determinacy amid the flux of phenomena" in the manner of rhetoricians who "tried to reduce the art of persuasive speech to a set of cut-and-dried rules." Cf. Barker 2007:104 ("no larger intellectual pretensions").
[51] Barker 2007:95.
[52] Blindingly hostile is the discussion in Plato *Republic* VII 530d–531d, in which harmonicists who substitute sense for reason (in the form of mathematical principle) are painted as complete fools who confuse the objects of perception with the objects of knowledge (the tones and semitones mentioned by Gibson [2005:18] correspond to the διάστημα ᾧ μετρητέον of 531a7). A more sympathetic reading could try to imagine the *harmonikoi* as developing something like Isocrates' theory of the orator's knowledge of *ideai* etc., but falling short of an account of how different principles from these are involved in the activation of *doxai* in performance at the *kairos*.
[53] Perhaps there was a stronger sophistic–harmonic convergence earlier with Protagoras' "sophist" (Isocrates *Antidosis* 235) associate Damon, with his interdisciplinary focus on *ēthos*: Barker 1984:168f., Brancacci 2008. Lord (1978:42) sees an echo of 37 B 6 Diels-Kranz in Aristides Quintilianus *De musica* 1.4 τέχνη πρέποντος and defends the view that the rhetorical-sounding "τὸ πρέπον appears to have been a fundamental category of Damonian theory." This at least

temology with the Protagorean theory of practice (the wise man's pursuit of virtue, as developed in Plato's *Theaetetus*), we are at a loss for evidence to say that the *harmonikoi* were led by their ear-criterion to engage in the problems of empirically based practice.[54] Medicine and rhetoric—to some degree because of the better extant sources, and equally importantly because of the serious-ness with which Plato and Aristotle were driven to engage with their ideas—are revealed in comparison as more than an effective working-out of problems by technical practitioners, but rather a theoretical tradition of broad importance for all rival Greek theories of practice.

---

shows that the topic of matching effects with souls, as we encounter it in the *Phaedrus* and in Aristotle's *Rhetoric*, could reflect a wider sophistic-rhetorical practice that informs Plato, Isocrates, and Alcidamas as a common source and stimulus. For a possible connection between Aristoxenian (and possibly Damonian) *sunkriseis* and the rhetorical technique of comparison found in Isocrates, see Gibson 2005:110.

[54] For an account of how rhetoric reflected on music as an analogous "sister discipline" in the Roman period, see Malhomme 2009.

3

Aristotle in the Afternoon
Rhetoric, Exoterica, and the Compromised Philosopher

The surviving Aristotelian corpus, which seems largely to preserve the teachings and discussions conducted by Aristotle within his school, contains multitudes enough for Aristotle's followers and interpreters. It establishes Aristotle, on the one hand, as the original example of the philosopher who has bequeathed us (*inter alia*) a system, and any of whose works will only be properly understood through a study of the didactic technicalities that the works share and whose exposition must be traced throughout the corpus. On the other hand, partly because of the very strength and flexibility of everything that can be called Aristotelian method, the Aristotelian corpus devotes a full measure of attention to matters of human social life—politics, poetry, persuasion, and the practical and performative demands of ethical perfection. While Aristotle's treatises on these subjects ask their questions and do their work under the obvious influence of the philosopher's more theoretical analysis of being, some scholars have nevertheless been tempted to approach a field such as Aristotelian rhetoric with the prejudice that, in Aristotle's own terms, it is third philosophy at best.[1] Working under the straightforward assumptions that Aristotle was motivated in his practical philosophy to be right, to reach an audience, and to have an effect, I have already given several reasons suggesting that these topics, for Aristotle, had affinities with the concerns of Isocrates and reflect serious engagement with the rival school's teachings and presentation of itself to the world. In Aristotle's *Protrepticus*, we had the advantage of a comparison text that was, at the same

---

[1] For example, Depew (2004) takes the status of Aristotelian ethics, politics, and rhetoric as "third philosophy" to mean that Aristotle and Isocrates' fundamental theories of knowledge and philosophy are so incompatible as to render insignificant the apparent analogies between their ideas, excluding Isocrates' concerns from Aristotle's conception of philosophy. Garver (2004) places a helpful emphasis on the two authors' shared interest in the practical and particular, but with a strong focus on the limitations of the merely practical in the rest of Aristotle's theory. Such comparative studies as Haskins 2004 have not looked beyond Aristotle's *Rhetoric* for the matter of the comparison. Poster (1997:243) concludes that rhetoric's role was "an unfortunate necessity" for Aristotle.

time, serious in its allegiance to high philosophical theory, ambitious to reach a popular audience subject to Isocrates' influence, and available to us in a (more-or-less) coherent literary form, so that we can analyze its rhetoric and ideas in their own terms.

Many other aspects of Aristotle's career and writings are mostly invisible to us as texts. Often we lack even the merest textual fragments and must work from prejudiced and confused testimonia. Still, whatever the historical and critical cautions imposed on us by these problems, we must digest this evidence, for it clearly records traces of a public and published Aristotle engaged with the topics and personalities of the Isocratean school. Our estimation of what is properly Aristotelian about an approach to rhetoric and politics is complicated by our knowledge of these exoteric writings and of the more public and rhetorical mode of instruction Aristotle may have practiced, for a period, alongside the stricter studies and teaching that produced the extant corpus. Several methodological difficulties attend any study of this strand in Aristotle's career: the evidence is extremely scant, usually late, and often derived from polemical and scholastic milieus whose tendencies are themselves difficult to reconstruct reliably. With so little positive information, it is tempting to base an interpretation of the exoteric Aristotle on what is more fully known—the surviving Aristotelian works, or, what is scarcely more satisfactory, the doctrines that Aristotle would have discussed in the Academy, as these can be reconstructed from the dialogues Plato is supposed to have composed at any given point.[2] If the investigation's purpose is to illuminate the significance of Aristotle's extant works from a new angle, or to place them in a new context, then this runs the risk of circular reasoning. If any reconstructions can be made that are relatively free of such circularity, it will still not be easy to know how boldly to use them to seek new insights into an Aristotelian corpus that, admittedly, has done an admirable job of holding together coherently quite apart from any historical context. Finally, when we begin to take the measure of Aristotle's lost works, we find ourselves, as with all studies into fragmentary doxographical testimonies, in the presence of many scholarly judgments whose authority, given the seldom-examined complexity of much of the evidence, has often fossilized into dogma; to move forward we have to glean much from these insights while making a fresh approach that does not simply rehash the terms of a debate without the requisite momentum.

It is sometimes assumed, based simply on Aristotle's Academic affiliation, that the young Aristotle, familiar already as he may have been with Plato's *Phaedrus*, as a committed Academic took as strident and partial a position against

---

[2]   I am primarily concerned with developments in Aristotle's career that unfolded, perhaps, in the middle 350s.

rhetoric as does Socrates in the *Gorgias*. Even if Aristotle's very early work, *Gryllus*, claimed that rhetoric is not a *tekhnē*, and may have explored this angle on rhetoric with some vehemence,[3] there is no reason to believe Aristotle's views were not flexible and rapidly evolving, given what we have seen of his own engagement with the subject and the complexity of the position of Plato's *Phaedrus*, upon which he could build. Even if our account of Aristotle does justice to the eventual expansion of his philosophy into areas whose political grounding and political consequences have departed far from Platonism (especially the kind of Platonism usually constructed to play a role in such histories), we must still beware the assumption that this growth does not have its seeds in Aristotle's (quite prolonged) "youth." I wish to discover whether we can arrive at equally coherent and tenable conclusions from the hypothesis that Aristotle became involved early in (relatively) public controversy, not purely as the defender of Platonic idealism, but precisely because he was willing to engage in something like the more political-rhetorical mode of education practiced by the Academy's rivals. We will see that it is just this for which Philodemus blamed, and Cicero praised, Aristotle. I will be content if I can review the evidence and open up the question again, not with totally fresh eyes, but neither taking the old postulates for granted, and not without any recourse to circular arguments, but at least probing whether a less commonly used set of assumptions may expand our view.

Cicero on Aristotle's Rhetoric Lectures

Several rhetorical writers of the Roman period make mention of a course of rhetorical lectures given by Aristotle. Cicero, as a Roman orator and a philosophical eclectic, is naturally interested in the intertwined histories of Greek philosophy and rhetoric. He turns to Aristotle more than once for an example justifying the principles of his own career. In a particularly prominent passage that culminates the short introduction to the *Tusculan Disputations*, Cicero—having claimed that all his work and success as an orator flowed from the "springs of philosophy" (1.6), to which he now returns—uses Aristotle as his chief analogy (1.7):

> Sed ut Aristoteles, vir summo ingenio, scientia, copia, cum motus esset Isocratis rhetoris gloria, dicere docere etiam coepit adulescentes et prudentiam cum eloquentia iungere, sic nobis placet nec pristinum dicendi studium deponere et in hac maiore et uberiore arte versari. hanc enim perfectam philosophiam semper iudicavi, quae de maximis quaestionibus copiose posset ornateque dicere ...

---

[3] Cf. Chroust 1965, Viano 1967. For the position of this work, see below, chap. 5.

But just as Aristotle, a man of supreme genius, knowledge and fertility of speech, under the stimulus of the fame of the rhetorician Isocrates, began like him to teach the young to speak and combine wisdom with eloquence, similarly it is my design not to lay aside my early devotion to the art of expression, but to employ it in this grander and more fruitful art: for it has ever been my conviction that philosophy in its finished form enjoys the power of treating the greatest problems with adequate fullness and in an attractive style.

(trans. King 1945)

Here Aristotle exemplifies the conjoined powers of philosophy and rhetoric *because* he was drawn to emulate the successful education that Isocrates called "philosophical," an education that was explicitly rhetorical and political. Like Isocrates himself, he offered that kind of instruction ("to teach the young to speak"). Cicero's account would have been based not only on the ancient secondary sources for Aristotle's career, but also on his familiarity with the exoteric writings, several of which may have been produced for the same audience before which this anecdote is situated. Indeed, "Aristotle" to Cicero meant, first and foremost, the exoteric Aristotle who wrote the elegant dialogues upon which Cicero modeled his own philosophical works, for Aristotle's esoteric works seem only to have been rediscovered in Cicero's lifetime, and the ancestor of our Aristotelian corpus was probably not produced until after his death.[4]

In a related passage of the dialogue *De oratore*, Cicero's character Crassus insists upon the broad range of the orator's proper knowledge; he is again concerned to demonstrate that exemplary statesmen have acquired their learning from philosophers, and that philosophy in turn is necessarily concerned (and ideally quite concerned) with the art of persuasive speaking. The former fact is shown through Classical Greek examples such as Pericles' attainment of mastery over Athenian politics and war on the basis of his education from Anaxagoras, *vir summus in maximarum rerum scientia* (3.138). This leads again to the story of Aristotle's entering the ring with Isocrates, which Crassus takes as defining Aristotle as the very type of the teacher who can best train the man of action (3.141):

Itaque ipse Aristoteles cum florere Isocratem nobilitate discipulorum videret, quod suas disputationes a causis forensibus et civilibus ad inanem sermonis elegantiam transtulisset, mutavit repente totam formam prope disciplinae suae versumque quendam Philoctetae paulo

---

[4] For some of the contradictions and nuances in this story, see Ford 2011:168f. and the literature cited at 214nn26f.

secus dixit: ille enim turpe sibi ait esse tacere, cum barbaros, hic autem, cum Isocratem pateretur dicere; itaque ornavit et inlustravit doctrinam illam omnem rerumque cognitionem cum orationis exercitatione coniunxit. Neque vero hoc fugit sapientissimum regem Philippum, qui hunc Alexandro filio doctorem accierit, a quo eodem ille et agendi acciperet praecepta et eloquendi.

Accordingly when Aristotle observed that Isocrates succeeded in obtaining a distinguished set of pupils by means of abandoning legal and political subjects and devoting his discourses to empty elegance of style, he himself suddenly altered almost the whole of his own system of training, and quoted a line from *Philoctetes* with a slight modification: the hero in the tragedy said that it was a disgrace for him to keep silent and suffer barbarians to speak, but Aristotle put it "suffer Isocrates to speak"; and consequently he put the whole of his system of philosophy in a polished and brilliant form, and linked the scientific study of facts with practice in style. Nor indeed did this escape the notice of that extremely sagacious monarch Philip, who summoned Aristotle to be the tutor of his son Alexander, and to impart to him the principles both of conduct and of oratory.

(trans. Rackham 1942)

From here, Crassus goes on to declare that, when faced with those who succeed in combining the two well-matched accomplishments, we may well grant the philosopher the name of *orator*, and the orator the name of *philosophus*; while wisdom is more fundamentally important, eloquence is undoubtedly its fairest crown (3.142f.).

Cicero's telling accords with modern judgments in casting Isocrates as the type of unphilosophical eloquence. Yet the facts as narrated again grant Isocrates a notably powerful influence over the educational arena. Aristotle evidently aspires to the success enjoyed by Isocrates in an arena marked off and dominated by Isocrates, and he is willing to deform the existing shape of his educational mission to compete for the students who will only choose an education that is rhetorical. Since Aristotle begins the story as an authentic philosopher, it is hard to accept that a transformation such as Cicero describes can be fully consistent with the philosophical principles that Aristotle had previously held. Historically, given the absence of evidence that Aristotle's independent philosophical career had yet begun in earnest, it is legitimate to wonder whether Aristotle even had much of a system to change, and whether we may not implicate the influence of Isocrates' school in Aristotle's very first steps into the career of offering philosophical instruction.

Isocrates died in 338, and Aristotle did not return to Athens until 335, so that the story takes place during Aristotle's period in the Academy (before Plato's death in 348/7), and almost certainly in the early 350s (the consensus of e.g. Solmsen 1929, Düring 1957, Chroust 1964). Another version (Quintilian 3.1.14) places Aristotle's rhetoric lectures in the afternoon (*postmeridianis scholis Aristoteles praecipere artem oratorem coepit*). This by itself is compatible with the Ciceronian testimony, but it may cause or evince confusion, since Aulus Gellius, without any mention of Isocrates, has the "exoteric lectures and speaking exercise" (*exotericas auditiones exercitiumque dicendi*, 20.5.5, more fully described in 20.5.2 as *quae ad rhetoricas meditationes facultatemque argutiarum civiliumque rerum notitiam conducebant*) taking place in the afternoon in the same place and during the same period as the morning "acroatic" instruction, i.e. the activities of the Lyceum after Isocrates' death. The "disgraceful to keep silent" quotation is combined with the idea of simultaneous instruction in two arts of persuasion—rhetoric and dialectic—by the fifth-century AD commentator (and scholarch of the Academy) Syrianus, who writes that Aristotle "would continually cry out to his companions, stirring them to exercise in speaking, 'It is a disgrace to keep silent and suffer Isocrates to speak'" (*Scholia in Hermogenem* IV.297 Walz = II.59.21 Rabe).[5]

David Blank has helpfully brought together the principal evidence for Aristotle's "course on rhetoric" in a recent publication[6] but focuses on the question of whether we should commit to the "lectures" as a likely item among the lost Aristotelian texts. I do not find it surprising that there is no evidence that these lectures had a permanent existence as *texts*; the testimonia in question are in fact more interesting, consistent, and congruent when taken as evidence for oral teaching and polemic: for school *activity* rather than authorial and school *production*. Our sources report a historical fact (the public rhetorical instruction provoked by rivalry with Isocrates) and interpret it in the light of the Aristotle known to them directly, especially his many exoteric writings. Thus our sources' handling of the historical report does reveal something about the literary Aristotle, because the literary Aristotle was the main context in which they could make sense of anecdotes about the scholastic Aristotle (though Philodemus should also be considered, to a greater extent, the inheritor of a purely scholastic set of attitudes, some of which can tenuously and partially be traced back to the fourth century). For example, Cicero (in *De oratore*) determines the credibility and interest of the historical report through his devoted

---

5   See also the version in Diogenes Laertius 5.3, where Ξενοκράτην is usually emended to Ἰσο-κράτην.

6   Blank 2007. Compare the earlier edition (of PHerc 832 col. 41.12–PHerc 1015 col. LIV.17 = Sudhaus 1896:57–59) and discussion of Angeli 1997.

knowledge of the exoteric writings, which had inspired him to take Aristotle as the preeminent model for himself as teacher-of-ornate-speech-*cum*-wisdom. I do not believe the anecdote would have resonated amid so much solid knowledge of the literary Aristotle, if Cicero had not found compatible and similarly targeted material in the exoteric corpus.

Likewise, in the *Disputations*, it is not the "lectures" that are important to Cicero—he does not mention them in this context—but the general portrait of Aristotle as conjoining, in his teaching (*disciplina*), theoretical study (*rerum cognitio*) with rhetorical practice (*orationis exercitatio*). This is compatible with Philodemus' testimony that Aristotle "used to train [*egumnazen*] (his students) in the afternoon."[7] Since there is no sign he is thinking about the "lectures" anecdote in this programmatic passage claiming the Aristotelian mantle, we may well believe that the whole of Cicero's information about Aristotle tends to confirm this practical-rhetorical strand. Blank rightly emphasizes that the conjoining itself is of exemplary importance to Cicero, but it is difficult to allow on that basis that Cicero's language of *exercise* implies nothing of "rhetoric on its own" but only Aristotle's incidental example, to his students, of doing philosophy "in an eloquent manner."[8] Could Cicero really have believed that Aristotle's charming expression of philosophical matter was his competitive response to Isocrates' success—not a turn to practical matter, but an improvement in his style? This seems unlikely. Cicero explicitly names two subjects of Aristotle's new instruction to Isocrates' audience of young men: speaking (*dicere*) and combining wisdom and eloquence (*prudentiam cum eloquentia iungere*). The second subject does not eclipse and contain the first. In *Orator* 46, Cicero plainly believes that Aristotle trained such young men (*adulescentes ... exercuit*) in an argumentative performance in the manner of orators and not that of philosophers (*non ad philosophorum morem tenuiter disserendi, sed ad copiam rhetorum*). This consistent Ciceronian belief says something about his Aristotle quite apart from any particular course of rhetoric lectures: that he was a force to be reckoned with in practical training in practical philosophy.

Philodemus on Aristotle's Rhetoric Lectures

Accordingly, if we follow the facts as Cicero sees them, it is not surprising to find Cicero's contemporary Philodemus (in Book VIII of his *Rhetorica*) citing the same event to upbraid Aristotle for his treachery to philosophy.[9] Philodemus—a

---

[7]   PHerc 832, col. 36: see below.
[8]   Blank 2007:19.
[9]   The relevant passages of Philodemus' *Rhetorica* may be consulted in Düring 1957:299–311 and Blank 2007. See Kleve and Longo Auricchio 1992 for an introduction to Philodemus' *Rhetorica*, and Gigante 1999 for an account of relations between the Peripatos and Epicurus and his followers.

deeply committed Epicurean philosopher whose technical and polemical writings would not have survived without the eruption of Mount Vesuvius in AD 79, which carbonized and buried a library full of Epicurean texts—holds a challengingly different point of view on the same episode, giving us the chance to look for recoverable truths between the two partial perspectives. If we are skeptical about how well Aristotle was yet known or established as a philosopher at the time of his alleged confrontation with Isocrates, then we may decide that Philodemus anachronistically charges Aristotle with betraying philosophical principles he had not yet developed. In any case, Philodemus knows the story of Aristotle's competitive charge into the field of rhetoric and is disgusted that Aristotle has despised true philosophy while still professing his compromised mixture under the name "philosophy." This is the most interesting point in Philodemus' tirade, because it allows us to rethink the valences and sympathies of Aristotle's *philosophia*:

> περὶ Ἀριστοτέλους ἀναγγέλλουσιν, ὅτι τῆς δείλης ἐγύμναζεν ἐπι-
> φωνήσας "αἰσχρὸν σιωπᾶν, Ἰσοκράτην δ' ἐᾶν λέγειν." ἐμφαίνει δὲ τὴν
> κρίσιν ἱκανῶς κἀκ τοῦ συγγεγραφέναι τέχνας ῥητορικὰς κἀκ τοῦ μέρος
> τῆς φιλοσοφίας τὴν πολιτικὴν νομίζειν, εἰ καὶ ψελλίζει διαφέρειν
> αὐτὴν φάσκων τῆς ῥητορικῆς ... τῶν περὶ τὰς πόλεις συμβαινόντων
> οὐθέν ἐστι φίλον· δεύτερον δὲ διὰ τὸ φιλοσοφίαν πολλὴν ἐπίδοσιν
> λαβεῖν τυχοῦσαν χρηστῆς πολιτείας· τρίτον δ' ἀγανακτήσαντας ἐπὶ τοῖς
> πλείστοις τῶν νῦν τὰ πολιτικὰ πραττόντων, ὡς εὐτελεῖς ὄντες οἱ μὲν
> ἄρχουσιν, οἱ δ' ἄρχειν ἀξιοῦσιν.

> [Finally let us examine what] they report about Aristotle, that he used to train (his students) in the afternoon, commenting "it is shameful to remain silent while allowing Isocrates to speak." He makes his judgement quite clear both by having written rhetorical handbooks and by considering politics to be part of philosophy, even if he does lisp when he says that politics is different from rhetoric ... [*ca. 70 words*] [He used to give three reasons why his students should go into politics. First, ...] nothing is dear [*to one who pays no attention to*] what happens concerning cities; second, because of the fact that philosophy makes great progress when it happens to find a good constitution; third, because they are angry with most of those who are now in politics, since they either rule or think they should rule, though they are worthless.

> PHerc 832 cols. 36–37 + PHerc 1015 col. XLVIIIb
> (ed. Blank 2007:34f. = Sudhaus 1896:50 = Düring 1957 T
> 31 a, b) (trans. Blank 2007:44)

This passage seems relatable to the context of Aristotle's teaching and dialogues before Plato's death.[10] Philodemus goes on immediately to emphasize the rewards available to someone like Aristotle if he is willing to subvert his high philosophical principles and regress to the level of teaching a junior and preparatory (but popular) subject like rhetoric.[11] Rhetoric is dismissed as something appropriate for the education parents have provided to their children (ἐμ παισὶν διὰ τὴν τῶν γονέων ἐπιμέλειαν, XLIX.17–19); if an Aristotle surrounds himself with adults who value it as a serious undertaking in preference to truly satisfying philosophical pursuits, he will inflict on himself the toilsome kind of service that involves tolerating the ignoble souls that fall short of philosophical tastes (ἐπίπονον … τὸ λειτούργημα καὶ τὸ τοιούτων ἀνέχεσθαι ψυχῶν, ὅσαι πρὸς ῥητορικὴν ἐσπουδάκασιν, 38.8–13). As Düring has remarked, "If this text had been found isolated from its context, we might have conjectured that it was an echo of an attack by Aristotle on Isocrates." That we do not, in fact, have this kind of attack by Aristotle on Isocrates could reflect Aristotle's care in appropriating Isocratean protreptic to his own use: his transformation of his educationally successful predecessor's limited attempt to fuse wisdom, knowledge, and *praxis* into a rival protreptic that better satisfied his own philosophical principles.

Philodemus' framing—in terms of preliminary and youthful versus better and mature pursuits—is suggestive of the fourth-century schools' protreptic overtures to intellectually inclined youth. The word restored at PHerc 1015 col. LIII.1, προτροπ[ὰ]ς, indicates that Aristotle's response to Isocrates induced him to debase the "exhortations" of protreptic.[12] We have seen previously that a school may use the preliminary stage of training to incorporate its rivals' fields of specialization into a more complete vision of educational self-realization (Isocrates' attitude towards eristics and geometry, or the Platonic school's eventual acceptance of Isocratean parenetics as ethical propaedeutic). It is in part by reading these maneuvers uncharitably that Philodemus found the raw material for his chastening tirade about the corruption and betrayal of philosophy. Protreptic's fundamental claim that the philosophical life is also

---

[10] In particular, the call to political engagement is likely from one of the dialogues, perhaps the *Statesman* (Düring 1957:303, cf. Bignone 1936:II.97ff.). To see the rest as allied to this and likely to be of the same vintage is a matter of interpretation.

[11] PHerc 1015 col. XLIX + PHerc 832 col. 38. At XLIX.5f., Düring 1957:303: "keeps up a kind of school in rhetoric" is perhaps better for ἔχοι δὲ ποσὴν τριβὴν ἐν τοῖς ῥητορικοῖς than Blank 2007:44: "has some familiarity with rhetoric," given the constant association of the *trib-* stem with school activity.

[12] The reference to protreptic survives even if the dialogue *Protrepticus* is not specifically meant. See Angeli 1997:11–15, suggesting a reference to the Aristotelian *Gryllus* "and to the exhortation to the youth, mediated by it, not to dedicate themselves to rhetoric *qua* non-art."

the more practically successful life (with more or less obfuscation of how well this may agree with worldly standards) only adds to the exploitable confusion. What is more surprising is to notice that Philodemus feels the need to stake out protreptic territory of his own by claiming that true philosophy (in comparison to Aristotle's debased compromise) not only leads its practitioner toward the Epicurean aim of stability and tranquility (ἡσυχίας εὐσταθοῦς, PHerc 1015, col. L.3f.), but also wins in the struggle for reputation and ("natural") material abundance (the rhetoric teacher's "toilsome service" is οὔτε περιουσίας φυσικῆς οὔτε δόξης ποριστικώτερον, L.10–12).

The differences between these rival versions of what is to be undertaken and why may be serious and consequential, yet, even in Philodemus' polemics, we can see how partial and complicated any distinction is bound to be between *philosophoi* who share so many elements from the common philosophical tradition, whose prestige they arrogate to themselves. As a further example of this, we may note the low rank Philodemus seems to assign geometry; he lumps it in with the proverbially junior and instrumental skills of literacy (*grammatika*), music, and military tactics.[13] This surface echo of Isocrates' idea that geometers have distracted themselves from true wisdom, goodness, and care for their souls suggests the complexity of the array of positions from which Philodemus constructed his polemic. As we will see, Philodemus may well have created (with however much deliberate distortion or sarcasm) a portrait of Isocrates as slowly and eventually progressing towards philosophy, in contrast to Aristotle's degeneration from philosopher to popularity seeker.

Philodemus cites the authority of Epicurus himself to say that Aristotle (offering a false hope of real philosophy) was a more pernicious force than the unabashedly and practically political teachers who "oiled up" (*aleiphontōn*) their students for the arena of public life.[14] According to Philodemus' view, political and forensic oratory did not depend on an expertise and had no place among the philosopher's pursuits, whereas "sophistical" epidictic was at least a *tekhnē*, built "on understanding which is available to rational persons in common" and thus useful to the philosopher.[15] Aristotle, then, in this polemic has gone farther

---

[13] PHerc 1015 col. LI.9–11, τὰ γεωμετρικὰ διδάξειν καὶ γραμματικὰ καὶ μουσικὰ καὶ τακτικά. Blank (2007:45n83) rightly finds that "This passage is still puzzling, and I have little confidence in its reconstruction." At any rate, in XLIX.15f., γράμματα was included alongside παλαιστρική as an analogy for the suitability of rhetoric to children, so that, while acknowledging that Philodemus may here be listing pursuits somewhat more worthwhile than rhetoric (and not forgetting the sophisticated moral purpose for *mousika* that Philodemus argues elsewhere), the parallel supports my claim that these studies are all being considered here as distractions from wisdom.

[14] PHerc 1015, col. LIV.10–17.

[15] See Blank 2009:229f.

than Isocrates in leaving even philosophical rhetoric behind. Cicero could look at Isocrates and Aristotle both and appreciate "philosophy" free to contribute to practical politics; Philodemus looked at Isocrates and saw "sophistic" able to rise above practical politics and reach the philosophical realm. Together these two partial perspectives imply an Isocrates who ably established his claim to both political and philosophico-ethical authority.

Did Isocrates' boundary-blurring use of *philosophia* for his school's education influence Aristotle's move to compete in some sense with this mode of instruction?[16] If we accept Philodemus' evidence, how does Aristotle's reorientation towards such a *philosophia* stand in relation to his mature philosophy and *tribē*? Some of the ideas in this passage can be paralleled in Aristotle's extant works on ethics and politics, among his writings on "the philosophy that concerns human matters" (ἡ περὶ τὰ ἀνθρώπινα φιλοσοφία).[17] The real question is not whether Aristotle practiced human-focused practical philosophy during both periods—he certainly did—but how much the earlier practice, if we knew more about it, might expand and challenge our view of the limits that define how practical the aims and context of such "philosophical" teaching were for Aristotle. As Philodemus' tirade develops, he is pleased enough to include, anachronistically, the Lyceum's later activities, such as its collections of *polis* constitutions, as further evidence of Aristotle's disloyalty to philosophy in its Epicurean bounds:

> Of course he inspired great admiration for the (rhetorical) power but contempt for his proper business, and because of this he was caught red-handed collecting the laws together with his pupil (Theophrastus) as well as the large number of constitutions and the decrees concerning places and those regarding particular occasions and everything which belonged to this sort of [study]. [ca. 20 words] choosing to be seen both to know and to teach philosophy, rhetoric, politics,

---

[16] The usual restricted (rhetorical) interpretation of Isocratean *philosophia* may present an obstacle to this interpretation. But this group of testimonia suggests that Aristotle felt the need to challenge Isocrates intellectually as well as rhetorically. Mulvany (1926:167) argues this specifically with attention to the context in *De oratore*, concluding, "If Isocrates was merely a teacher of eloquence ... then Aristotle could not contend with him except in rhetoric ... In §139 we read that Timotheus was trained by Isocrates in the same accomplishments as Dio by Plato, Epaminondas by Lysis, Agesilaus by Xenophon, Archytas by Philolaus, and all Magna Graecia by Pythagoras; for, §140, there once was a single comprehensive system of instruction, which satisfied the needs both of the scholar and of the statesman ... So the sense required in §141 ... is that ... Isocrates imparted both learning and eloquence, whereas Aristotle imparted learning only." (Mulvany supports this interpretation by setting aside the clause *quod ... transtulisset*, which all editors acknowledge involves some corruption.)

[17] *Nicomachean Ethics* X 1181b15, cited by Düring (1957:303).

agriculture, perfumery, metallurgy, stopping just short of the activities of people who are ashamed of what they do and say that they pursue under compulsion.

PHerc 1015 col. LIII + PHerc 832 col. 42
(trans. Blank 2007:45f.)

But here too comparison with Isocrates is illuminating. In this description of the "political" pole of corruption to which Aristotle has been drawn, a modern reader may well see a point of connection to the Isocratean school. Isocrates praises the study of history,[18] and his school produced such notable historians as Theopompus and Ephorus, the first universal historian.[19] Yet it seems that, far from this being Philodemus' point, he is actually ignoring the applicability of these interests to Isocrates, damning Aristotle by contrasting the utterly unphilosophical status of the political oratory to which Aristotle has descended with the relative worth of sophistic (epidictic) oratory. Once more Philodemus seems to give us a valuable perspective on Isocrates in spite of his own doctrinal principles. For he accepts Metrodorus' critique of political rhetoric, precisely because political advice depends on experience *and research*, whereas "sophistical" rhetoric constructs *ethical* advice on a rational basis compatible with philosophy.[20] With his counterintuitive appraisal of how wisdom and politics interacted in Isocrates' and Aristotle's "rhetoric," Philodemus helps us see just how much potential overlap could be discovered in the ambits of their two careers in this area. The most conservative interpretation of Philodemus' account is that it corroborates Cicero quite independently from the Ciceronian desire to rhetoricize all philosophy.

---

[18] See e.g. Isocrates *To Nicocles* 35.

[19] The work of these historians, which survives only in fragments, shows a range of interests that defies the label "rhetorical history" used by many scholars based on presuppositions about the Isocratean *paideia*. Arguments against the ancient sources' testimony that Theopompus and Ephorus were Isocrates' students are generally limited by taking for granted these same presuppositions about what it would mean to be an "Isocratean." See the discussion in the following chapter.

[20] See Blank 2009:229f. The seeds of Isocrates' dual political/sophistical significance in the public arena as envisaged by Philodemus may be seen *in nuce* at *Antidosis* 84f., where Isocrates distinguishes himself from esoteric philosophers who have to exert themselves to attract students through protreptic (*protrepein*). Isocrates, in contrast, promotes a praxis of universally accessible virtue and intelligence (*tēn aretēn kai tēn phronēsin ... tēn hupo pantōn homologoumenēn*, cf. Alexiou 2007), with both ethical and (*pace* Philodemus) political dimensions: "I endeavor to persuade the whole city to undertake the kind of actions from which they will both enjoy happiness themselves [*eudaimonēsousin*] and will rid the rest of the Greeks from their present evils." Even the former is collective for Isocrates, read apart from Philodemus' distorting lens.

I have already suggested that Philodemus focuses our attention on the possible positive significations of Isocratean philosophy.[21] Just as Cicero was unable to cleanse his account of the implication of Aristotle's offense against (one kind of) philosophy, Philodemus is either polemically driven to claim, or is unable to suppress the idea, that Isocrates' school practice is legitimately valued as philosophy:

Σιωπῶ γὰρ ὅτι τῶν παρ' αὐτῷ τὰ ῥητορικὰ μαθόντων ὁλόκληρος οὐδεὶς ἐν οὐδετέρᾳ κατέστη . . καὶ . . . . . . νετικα παρά τισι ἐδίδασκεν, Ἰσοκράτους καιτο . τοῖς χρόνοις προκόψαντος· ὥστε κἄν, εἰ πρότερον ἐδίδασκεν τέχνην, ἐπὶ τὴν ἡσυχιωτέραν καὶ δαιμονιωτέραν, ὥσπερ εἶπε, φιλοσοφίαν ἀποχωρεῖν.

I shall not mention the fact that of those who learnt rhetoric with him [=Aristotle] no one became a perfect practitioner in either kind of rhetoric.[22] And he taught [ca. 3 words][23] to some people, whereas Isocrates, as time went on, advanced (to the opposite standpoint), so that even if he taught the art before, he could retire to the "more peaceful" and "more divine" (art of) philosophy, as he called it.

> PHerc 832 col. 43 + PHerc 1015 col. LV = Sudhaus
> 1896:59f. = Düring 1957 T 31 g = Blank 2007:40f.[24] (trans.
> Blank 2007:46 and Düring 1957:307 for Ἰσοκράτους ...
> προκόψαντος)

Who retired from rhetoric to philosophy? It is not perfectly clear that it is not Isocrates. Düring has probably overstated the case to say that "from the point of grammar, it would be most natural to assume that Isocrates is the subject of εἶπε," but he voiced this conviction despite himself feeling forced to go against his grammatical instinct and refer the retirement and description of *philosophia* to Aristotle, based on the assumption that Isocratean *philosophia* could not be described in these terms.[25] Blank, in his discussion, because of the "garbled" state of the papyrus after Ἰσοκράτους, does not even mention the possibility or significance of Isocrates' involvement in this asser-

---

[21] Cf. Di Matteo 1997, who sees Philodemus' allusions to Isocrates as integral to the polemic of the *Rhetorica*.

[22] I.e. Isocratean "school" rhetoric (δοκοῦσαν ὁμοίαν Ἰσοκράτει ῥητορικήν, 43.1f.) or the "political" rhetoric Aristotle distinguished from this (τὴν πολιτικὴν ἣν ἑτέραν ἐκείνης ἐνόμιζεν, 43.4–6).

[23] Blank makes the attractive suggestion τὰ παραινετικά based on the papyrus' νετικα.

[24] I have followed Blank's text, also accepting Sudhaus's restoration of προκόψαντος (something of the kind is wanted).

[25] Düring 1957:308.

tion,[26] despite his observation that the quoted description of *philosophia* is as unknown in our texts of Aristotle as it is in Isocrates.[27] In any case, a reference to Isocrates would accord with some of the loftier intellectual pretensions of Isocratean protreptic and glorification of *logos* and his own *philosophia*. Philodemus' philosophical prejudice seems to compete with an ingrained ambivalence towards these pretensions. This derives in part from the complex Epicurean attitude towards rhetoric developed in the *Rhetorica*: epidictic orators and teachers are *sophistai*, alone of all teachers and practitioners of eloquence *tekhnitai* in possession of an art[28]; Aristotle is deluded to believe that political rhetoric (*rhētoreuein*) can come about through the epidictic scholasticism (*sophisteuein*) that has drawn him into contest with Isocrates.[29] Aristotle's students presumably failed to achieve either result, according to Philodemus, because their teacher did not have the sense to focus on one or the other. Isocrates, in contrast, is more amenable to progressing from a lower form of philosophy to a higher one, somehow better aware of the relation between artful and artless practice, whereas Aristotle is going in the opposite direction, trying to make higher philosophical principles suddenly and crudely practical. Hubbell took the ascent to "more divine *philosophia*" as Isocrates' and saw a surprisingly extreme polemical tactic on Philodemus' part:

> Perhaps the most remarkable part is his exaltation of Isocrates; "while Aristotle descended from philosophy to rhetoric, Isocrates rose from rhetoric to philosophy." This passage must rest on a misinterpretation of Isocrates' use of φιλοσοφία, a misinterpretation which must be deliberate on the part of Philodemus, and not due to any love of Isocrates, but to a desire to take a fling at Aristotle.[30]

---

26 Blank 2007:30. Compare the translation of Di Matteo (1997:124): "col tempo il progresso di Isocrate è innegabile, sì che, anche se prima insegnava la retorica, si ritrasse, come egli stesso disse, nel grembio della filosofia, più tranquilla e demonica della retorica."

27 Blank 2007:30n71.

28 Blank 2009:229f., cf. Hubbell 1920:255–257; Di Matteo 1997:128–130, quoting the important passage, PHerc 1580, fr. 4 = Sudhaus 1896:122: Καὶ λέγουσι τὸν Ἰσοκράτην καὶ τὸν Γοργίαν καὶ τὸν Λυσίαν ὁμολογεῖν οὐκ ἔχειν ἐπιστήμην. Ἀπιθάνως δὲ λέγεται καὶ ἀδυνάτως, ἐπειδὴ τεχνῖται τε ἐπηγγέλλοντο εἶναι καὶ διδάξειν ἄλλους ..., in which "Philodemus would be lashing out against all who declared—in his opinion ἀπιθάνως and ἀδυνάτως—that Isocrates, Gorgias, and Lysias had admitted not possessing knowledge" (with a good account following, 130ff., of the anti-rhetoric side of Philodemus' argument); Ferrario 2007:217.

29 PHerc 1015 col. LI.12–19, following immediately on τὰ γεωμετρικὰ διδάξειν καὶ γραμματικὰ καὶ μουσικὰ καὶ τακτικά, quoted above. See Blank 2009:231 for additional passages in which Philodemus denies that "sophistic" training has any effective, real-world political result.

30 Hubbell 1920:320.

Yet a purely polemical explanation of this statement does not seem adequate[31]; if Aristotle is to be contemned as untrue to philosophy, and Isocrates had never professed fidelity in the first place, then Aristotle's gravitation in Isocrates' direction would prove how far he has fallen, which would have served the polemic just as well.

So this passage provokes us to consider Isocrates' participation in something perceived as truly philosophical, whosoever estimation is reflected. Whatever our interpretation of this vexed passage, Philodemus weighed both Aristotle and Isocrates against Epicurean values and found Aristotle's showy display of polymathy dangerous and mercenary in comparison to the ideal rhetorical education's cultivation of ability, tranquility of the soul (τῆς κατὰ ψυχὴν γαλήνης χάριν), and bodily health:

> And in this respect he was actually much more shameful than the orators, who try to train (their students) in the afternoons for (speaking) on [*these sorts of topics*] not just for the sake of their tranquility of mind, but also for the sake of the good temperament of their body which conduces to health...

> PHerc 832 col. 42 + PHerc 1015 col. LIV
> (trans. Blank 2007:46)

Philodemus would have been primarily familiar with Aristotle through the exoteric works, and his perspective may thus help us recover what the profile of Aristotle's career could be made to resemble when viewed in the absence of the esoteric corpus, while challenging us with an Isocrates whose style of rhetoric could play a role in the philosophical life precisely because of its impractically ethical mode.

The Academy's Attitude toward Rhetoric

Is the idea that Aristotle wanted, at this stage of his career, to meet Isocrates on a common field of pedagogical contest (whether this would constitute a "descent" or not) at odds with the picture we are usually given of Aristotle in his late twenties as a devoted partisan of the Academy? Here again the terms of the received wisdom—what does it mean to be a partisan of the Academy?—can interfere with a clear assessment. It is certainly not clear that this must mean the determined enemy of Isocratean rhetoric. Every reader of the *Phaedrus* knows how seriously it engages with the necessary and proper use of

---

[31] No doubt Philodemus' construction of Isocrates in the role of sophist is very partial, but we lack the evidence that it is driven by duplicity, and we should consider the possibility that ambivalence or confusion about Isocrates' actual status is also at play.

rhetoric in philosophy, and it is this work that provides the natural backdrop for Aristotle's engagement with Isocrates.[32] It is worth looking in more detail at the only passage in all of Plato's works in which he names Isocrates: the praise of Isocrates at the end of the *Phaedrus*, whose sincerity I briefly suggested in the previous chapter. It is all the more relevant to the question we have been considering by its speaking of "some divine impulse" and "some *philosophia*" in this connection. In some ways it is a strange echo of the Philodeman appreciation of Isocratean "sophistic."

ΣΩ. Τίνα τοῦτον;

ΦΑΙ. Ἰσοκράτη τὸν καλόν· ᾧ τί ἀπαγγελεῖς, ὦ Σώκρατες; τίνα αὐτὸν φήσομεν εἶναι;

ΣΩ. Νέος ἔτι, ὦ Φαῖδρε, Ἰσοκράτης· ὃ μέντοι μαντεύομαι κατ' αὐτοῦ, λέγειν ἐθέλω.

ΦΑΙ. Τὸ ποῖον δή;

ΣΩ. Δοκεῖ μοι ἀμείνων ἢ κατὰ τοὺς περὶ Λυσίαν εἶναι λόγους τὰ τῆς φύσεως, ἔτι τε ἤθει γεννικωτέρῳ κεκρᾶσθαι· ὥστε οὐδὲν ἂν γένοιτο θαυμαστὸν προϊούσης τῆς ἡλικίας εἰ περὶ αὐτούς τε τοὺς λόγους, οἷς νῦν ἐπιχειρεῖ, πλέον ἢ παίδων διενέγκοι τῶν πώποτε ἁψαμένων λόγων, ἔτι τε εἰ αὐτῷ μὴ ἀποχρήσαι ταῦτα, ἐπὶ μείζω δέ τις αὐτὸν ἄγοι ὁρμὴ θειοτέρα· φύσει γάρ, ὦ φίλε, ἔνεστί τις φιλοσοφία τῇ τοῦ ἀνδρὸς διανοίᾳ. ταῦτα δὴ οὖν ἐγὼ μὲν παρὰ τῶνδε τῶν θεῶν ὡς ἐμοῖς παιδικοῖς Ἰσοκράτει ἐξαγγέλλω, σὺ δ' ἐκεῖνα ὡς σοῖς Λυσίᾳ.

Soc. Whom do you mean?

Phdr. The beautiful Isocrates. What are you going to tell him, Socrates? What shall we say he is?

Soc. Isocrates is still young, Phaedrus. But I want to tell you what I foresee for him.

Phdr. What is that?

Soc. It seems to me that by his nature he can outdo anything that Lysias has accomplished in his speeches; and he also has a nobler character. So I wouldn't be at all surprised if, as he gets older and continues writing speeches of the sort he is composing now, he makes everyone who has ever attempted to compose a speech seem like a child in comparison. Even more so if such work no longer satisfies him and a higher, divine

---

[32] I will not attempt to review arguments for the dating of *Phaedrus*, but it is reasonable to suppose that its ideas, at least, were current in the Academy at this period.

impulse leads him to more important things. For nature, my friend, has placed the love of wisdom in his mind. That is the message I will carry as if to my beloved, Isocrates, from the gods of this place; and you have your own message, as if to yours, Lysias.

278e7–279b3 (trans. after Nehamas and Woodruff 1995)

Naturally, many readers have been tempted, or even compelled, to read the passage as an ironic deflation of Isocrates' pretensions, with a view to (what we are all supposed to know already) how little of this philosophical potential Isocrates realized. But this is to set aside everything that is most remarkable and distinctive about the dialogue as a whole (that it takes rhetoric seriously[33]) in order to make it conform to a view of the Plato–Isocrates relationship that has been constructed from much more tenuous and allusive stuff than this passage. Moreover, such a reading turns a deaf ear to Plato's literary habits, for the best parallel to the tone of this encomium is the praise of the philosophical youth Theaetetus. Besides the echo of the word *gennikos* in both passages (noted in the previous chapter), they are also linked by the prophetic context: Socrates in *Theaetetus* also has reason to admire Theaetetus' *phusis* and prophetically— μαντικῶς, cf. μαντεύομαι here—anticipates the high repute he will earn (142c4–d3).

Aristotle's Exoteric Writings

With a wider conception of Aristotle's interests, and even of his willingness to practice philosophy in a more public context in Athens and in the rhetorical-political mode of philosophy's alleged rivals, we may be more fully receptive to the dazzlingly encyclopedic range of interests displayed in the surviving catalogues of Aristotle's writings.[34] These testify to Aristotle's full immersion in his age's consuming "nonphilosophical" questions and suggest a considerable variety of style and method. Moreover, their wide appeal may be felt through Cicero's passionate praise of their style: "Aristotle, pouring forth a golden stream of eloquence" (*flumen orationis aureum fundens Aristoteles, Academica* 2.119), "an unbelievable charm and richness in his style" (*dicendi quoque incredibili quadam cum copia tum etiam suavitate, Topics* 1.3). Even more important for my argument

---

[33] This is a fairly widespread interpretation of *Phaedrus*, though there are those readers for whom not only this concluding passage, but every apparent overture towards rhetoric in the dialogue, can be interpreted away. Guthrie (1975:413) says that *Phaedrus* "by pretending to take [rhetoric] seriously only discovers that 'true' rhetoric is philosophy." I hope I have shown in the preceding chapter how "only" is particularly awkward to reconcile with the rich complexity of the dialogue.

[34] For a full discussion of these lists, see Moraux 1951.

is that Cicero associates the style of the exoteric Aristotle with that of Isocrates (and the members of his school—a reminder of the scholastic structures through which Aristotle and Isocrates encountered each other), regarding them both as models for his own brand of writing: "Now *my* book [about his consulship, in Greek] has used up Isocrates' entire perfume cabinet with all the little scent boxes of his pupils, and some of Aristotle's rouge as well."[35] Cicero again mentions Aristotle and Isocrates together as stylistic models in connection with his composition of a *Letter of Advice* to Caesar.[36] All of Isocrates' addresses to rulers have strong didactic elements that can be seen, in comparison to Platonic examples, as indicating philosophical ambitions.[37] Aristotle seems to have composed letters to Macedonian kings and officials, and the Isocratean texts are worth studying before speculating on the approaches and purposes Aristotle's epistles may have adopted.

One lost work often discussed in studies of Aristotle's early rhetorical writings and compilations is the *Collection of the Art of Theodectes* (Τέχνης τῆς Θεοδέκτου συναγωγή), or *Theodectea* (Θεοδέκτεια). Whether Aristotle's "Theodectean" rhetoric was an original work or a digest of Theodectes' *ars rhetorica*,[38] there has been a broad consensus that Theodectes' prior example furnished an important point of departure for Aristotle's eventual *Rhetoric*. In the archaeology of Aristotelian rhetoric, it is sometimes noted that our ancient sources give Theodectes a scholastic affiliation with Plato,[39] Aristotle, and Isocrates, but this fascinating convergence of philosophical schoolings is not really explored. Because Theodectes lives on in most histories of philosophy for the sole purpose of contributing something to the *Rhetoric*, the full range of his scholastic and literary career remains in the dark. I wish, therefore, to provide here a more complete sketch of our fragmentary knowledge of this remarkable intellectual, as an example of the quasi-philosophical and rhetorically oriented career that could have been served by sitting in the audience of Aristotle's public rhetoric lectures.

---

[35] *Letters to Atticus* II 1, no. 21, trans. Shackleton-Bailey 1999.
[36] Ibid. XII 40, no. 241.
[37] That this is so of Isocrates' *Philip* and *Evagoras* will be argued in chap. 5.
[38] See Moraux 1951:98–101. The ambiguous reference by "Aristotle" to ταῖς ὑπ' ἐμοῦ τέχναις Θεοδέκτη γραφείσαις (*Rhetoric to Alexander* 1421a38) has evidently influenced the traditions.
[39] But the statement of Berti (1962:180)—that "Theodectes would have himself occupied the chair of rhetoric in the Academy" after Aristotle's departure from Athens—is, more than Berti seems to acknowledge, a speculative embellishment on the reference by Diels (1866:13) to the Academic Theodectes as "Lehrer der Beredsamkeit in Athen."

The Careers of Theodectes of Phaselis and Isocrates of Apollonia

> It falsifies the historical development to distinguish sharply between philosophical schools, such as the Academy and the Peripatos, and the schools of the sophists and the minor Socratics. To call one "philosophical schools" and the other "mere rhetorical schools" as if there were no essential similarity between them is to foster a rather extreme form of the Platonic viewpoint.
>
> John Patrick Lynch, *Aristotle's School*[40]

Theodectes of Phaselis[41] seems to have spent most of his life in Athenian intellectual circles, and he is remarkable to us especially for the versatility with which he moved from one to another. Today, as in his own maturity, he is best known as a successful tragic poet[42]; he probably won his first victory at the Great Dionysia when Plato and Isocrates were in their fifties.[43] But the difficulty of pigeonholing him becomes obvious when we look into the evidence for his scholastic career, which overlaps and intermingles with his life as a poet.

Several sources identify Theodectes as a student of Isocrates: the *Suda* (s.v., θ 138), Photius,[44] the pseudo-Plutarchian *Life of Isocrates* (837c), and Hermippus' *On the Students of Isocrates* (the sole pertinent surviving fragment of which[45] concerns him as a tragedian).[46] Besides these testimonia, Theodectes' attested literary versatility, from prose to verse, from oratory to rhetorical theory, fits the broader picture of the directions in which Isocrates' pupils scattered (or at least ended up classified into disciplines that are usually segregated by modern scholarship). Michael Flower, in his study of Theopompus, hits on Theodectes' name first of all when searching for fourth-century parallels to the astonishing variety of Theopompus' writings—all the more interesting since Flower is skeptical of the traditions placing Theopompus in Isocrates' school, and he does not mention the tradition that says the same of Theodectes.[47] In any case, though, the Phaselite was not associated with the supposed "rhetorical history" of

---

[40] Lynch 1972:63f.

[41] See Matelli 2007 with bibliography.

[42] See Martano 2007 with bibliography.

[43] IG II² 2325b.

[44] *Library* 176.120b31, 260.487a1.

[45] Athenaeus 10.451ef = fr. 77 Wehrli = FGrHistCont 1026 F 48, ed. Bollansée (1999).

[46] Other traditions name Theodectes together with Theopompus, Ephorus, and Cephisodorus, who are discussed below (e.g. Dionysius of Halicarnassus *To Ammaeus* 2).

[47] Flower 1994:40f. Note that the parenthetical dates Flower assigns to Theodectes are too late to agree with the epigraphic evidence of his dramatic victories.

his day that has been used to cast doubt on the tradition of Theopompus and Ephorus as Isocrateans.

Finally, Theodectes is said to have participated in the funeral competitions for the Carian ruler Mausolus (winning with his tragedy *Mausolus* but bested by Theopompus in oratory), in which the other known contestants—the contemporaries Naucrates of Erythrae, Isocrates of Apollonia, and Theopompus—were all traditionally said to have studied with Isocrates.[48] The import of the varied sources for this has often been minimized, because in some of them the familiar Athenian Isocrates has displaced the obscure Isocrates of Apollonia. Jacoby's apparent bestowal of his authority to this view—that Theodectes and Theopompus were the Athenian Isocrates' contemporary rivals and thus couldn't have been his students—was not as confident and consistent as it could have been. Jacoby did claim that Photius' intriguing report ("[Theopompus] himself says that he was in his prime together with [*sunakmasai*] Isocrates the Athenian, Theodectes of Phaselis, and Naucrates of Erythrae, and that these together with himself occupied the first place among Greeks in the *paideia* of *logoi*"[49]) renders impossible the student–teacher relationship between Theopompus and Isocrates "unless one wishes to see in συνακμάσαι a deliberate cover-up."[50] But the plain meaning of *sunakmasai* raises an obvious chronological difficulty: Theopompus, though his year of birth is uncertain,[51] would have outlived the ninety-eight-year-old Isocrates by approximately twenty years. We must, therefore, believe that Theopompus actually spoke of Isocrates of Apollonia, especially since this correction yields the selfsame list of competitors in the Mausolus *agōn* as is found elsewhere.[52] Oddly enough, Jacoby later in the same comment accepts the solution to the latter problem: "The information concerning competition between Isocrates and Theopompus in the Mausolus-agon (T6) has to be ruled out: if the list of competitors together with the variants is not merely conjecture (Blass Ber.² II 75), then Theopompus' competitor was not the Athenian (T6b) but the Apolloniate (T6a)." The same argument should be applied to the fragment in Photius, but Jacoby's judgment continues to be cited with approval.[53]

---

[48] In chap. 5, I will show that the Mausolus competition was part of a larger pattern of novel prose funerary commemoration that originated in the Isocratean school.

[49] FGrHist 115 F 25 = Photius *Library* 176.120b31–35.

[50] FGrHist II D, p. 352, lines 11–34, *ad* 115 T 1.

[51] See Flower 1994:14–17.

[52] FGrHist 115 T 6a (*Suda*, s.v. Θεοδέκτης, θ 138, cf. T 6b, where Aulus Gellius 10.18.6 shares Photius' difficulty with the obscurity of the lesser Isocrates, remarking *sunt etiam qui Isocratem ipsum cum his certauisse memoriae mandauerint*).

[53] E.g. Flower 1994:60n63, seizing on the apparent availability of "the most difficulty for those who believe in the connection [between Theopompus and Isocrates] ... in the words of Theopompus himself."

The *Suda* entry on the lesser Isocrates[54] indicates many parallels with Theodectes and contains enough detailed information to give us a plausible impression. This Isocrates' place in Athenian intellectual circles reminds us of Theodectes'. He is said to be the son of an unknown *philosophos* (Amyclas) and to have soaked up some Academic instruction on his way to becoming Isocrates' "successor." For this last point, we have apparent corroboration from none other than Speusippus (Plato's nephew and successor as head of the Academy) in his *Letter to Philip* (11), where a "Pontic student" of Isocrates is named (at a time when the master was ancient but still living) as his successor. This Pontic student—and the "successor" (*diadokhos*) designation, coincident with the *Suda*, makes it hard not to suppose that it is Isocrates from Pontic Apollonia—was evidently as deeply mired in scholastic polemics as anyone at the time, for Speusippus, in calling him the most hateful of all sophists, abuses him more harshly than he does even Isocrates or Theopompus. The *Suda*'s attestation of an "Amphictyonic" speech means that Isocrates of Apollonia had something to say about a topic intensively exploited for its propaganda value, versus Isocrates, in the *Letter to Philip*. As for the work *On Not Performing a Taphos for Philip*, it hardly matters whether it was hostile or flattering, so directly does it place the younger Isocrates beside Speusippus in the business of investing intellectual capital in Philip's public image.

Theodectes becomes all the more interesting as a participant in this scene if there is any truth to his Academic associations. The *Suda* identifies him as a student not only of Isocrates, but also of Plato and Aristotle.[55] Though some would doubt that Aristotle had the older Theodectes under his tutelage, it is indisputable that Aristotle took a close interest in Theodectes' work. Theodectes' point of connection to philosophy in general is the same as the point of connection between Aristotle and Isocrates: the art of rhetoric. Aristotle's extant works show that he was not only intimately acquainted with Theodectes' tragic oeuvre,[56] but also a reader of Theodectes' political-theoretical *Nomos*[57] and his

---

[54] "Isocrates (2): Son of Amyclas the philosopher, of Apollonia in Pontus (or Heraclea, according to Callistratus); the orator. Pupil and successor of the great Isocrates; he also studied with the philosopher Plato. This Isocrates took part in a rhetorical contest with Theodectes, the orator and tragic poet, and Theopompus of Chios, and also with Erythraeus of Naucratis, to give the funeral speech for Mausolus, the king of Halicarnassus. His speeches are five: *Amphictyonic Speech*; *Protreptic* [Προτρεπτικός, an intriguing connection to our discussion of Aristotelian and Isocratean protreptic in chap. 1]; *On Not Making a Tomb for Philip*; *On Being Resettled*; *On His Own Political Career*" (*Suda* ι 653, trans. Natoli, *Suda On Line*, http://www.stoa.org/sol/).
[55] This tradition is accepted by, among others, Ostwald and Lynch (1994:602).
[56] Aristotle *Nicomachean Ethics* 1150b9; *Poetics* 1455a9, 1455b29; *Rhetoric* 1397b3, 1399b29, 1400a28, 1401a36.
[57] *Rhetoric* 1398b6, 1399b1.

Apology of Socrates.[58] While these are valuable confirmations of overlapping lives and interests (the *Apology of Socrates* leaves us to make the perhaps false choice between whether it was written by Theodectes *qua* confirmed Isocratean, or was a product of sympathy or closer association with an explicitly "Socratic" school), it is in the fragmentary and indirect record of Aristotle's rhetorical work that he is most closely connected to Theodectes. Quintilian even indicates that there was some ancient doubt about the attribution of the Aristotelian *Rhetoric* to Aristotle or to Theodectes,[59] which implies a close connection indeed. But the more general picture that emerges from the lost works of Aristotle *deambulantis ad auram post meridiem* is of a fellow rhetorical theorist taken seriously as such and known personally to Aristotle. Not only did Aristotle write a work entitled *Theodectea*, but the book-length Τέχνης τῆς Θεοδέκτου συναγωγή is the only attested work focused on an individual to complement the two books of the Aristotelian Τεχνῶν συναγωγή.[60] Cicero classed Theodectes, an author of a *tekhnē*, with Aristotle and Theophrastus,[61] and Dionysius of Halicarnassus also joined Theodectes and Aristotle in their setting the model for this kind of *philosophia*.[62] Plutarch tells the story of how Alexander in Phaselis honored Theodectes' statue "because of the association he had with the man through Aristotle and philosophy" (τῇ γενομένῃ δι' Ἀριστοτέλην καὶ φιλοσοφίαν ὁμιλίᾳ πρὸς τὸν ἄνδρα),[63] which has generally been considered to support at least the philosophical association of Theodectes and Aristotle. Finally, a particularly fascinating mention is made by the contemporary comic poet Antiphanes:

> οὐχ ὁρᾷς ὀρχούμενον
> ταῖς χερσὶ τὸν βάκηλον; οὐδ' αἰσχύνεται
> ὁ τὸν Ἡράκλειτον πᾶσιν ἐξηγούμενος,
> ὁ τὴν Θεοδέκτου μόνος ἀνευρηκὼς τέχνην,
> ὁ τὰ κεφάλαια συγγράφων Εὐριπίδῃ.

---

[58]   *Rhetoric* 1399a9: cited here as *Socrates* but clearly a reply to the charges against Socrates; for the fuller title, cf. Aristotle fr. 465 R³.

[59]   *Training in Oratory* 2.15.10. Cf. the proem attached to the *Rhetoric to Alexander* (1421b1, proem §§16f.), περιτεύξῃ δὲ δυσὶ τούτοις βιβλίοις, ὧν τὸ μέν ἐστιν ἐμὸν ἐν τοῖς ὑπ' ἐμοῦ τέχναις Θεοδέκτῃ γραφείσαις, τὸ δὲ ἕτερον Κόρακος. (Here "Aristotle" gives examples of the particularly useful and well-written antecedent treatises he will incorporate into his present work: "You will find two such books, one of which is my own, viz., the Oratorical Art which I wrote for Theodectes, while the other is the treatise of Corax," trans. after Revised Oxford Translation.)

[60]   Diogenes Laertius 5.24.

[61]   *Orator* 194.

[62]   ταῦτα δὲ Θεοδέκτης μὲν καὶ Ἀριστοτέλης καὶ οἱ κατ' ἐκείνους φιλοσοφήσαντες τοὺς χρόνους ἄχρι τριῶν προήγαγον, ὀνόματα καὶ ῥήματα καὶ συνδέσμους πρῶτα μέρη τῆς λέξεως ποιοῦντες (*De compositione verborum* 2). Rose gives this, together with another branch of the same tradition, as Aristotle fr. 127 R³.

[63]   *Life of Alexander* 17.9.

> Don't you see the
> pansy dancing with his hands? He's not ashamed—
> the man who explains Heracleitus to everyone,
> and is the only person able to make sense of Theodectas' art
> and the author of summaries of Euripides.

fr. 111 Kassel-Austin = Athenaeus 4.134bc
(trans. Olson 2006)

That Theodectes' *tekhnē* could be represented on the stage in his own lifetime as something that a womanish idiot would profess in the same vein as he might busy himself with pedantically expounding Heraclitus and writing prefaces to Euripides' plays is powerful (but hitherto unremarked) evidence for his stature as a theorist in Athenian intellectual circles.[64] Indeed, the intellectual concerns of Isocrates' school left their mark elsewhere in iambus and on the comic stage. In particular, the methodological fixation on the respective roles played by nature, practice, and knowledge was enough of a commonplace to be treated humorously twice in the fourth century: by Simylus in relation to the art of the playwright, and by Dionysius' *Thesmophoros* in relation to the art of cookery.[65] In the latter fragment, "cookbook" learning is literally disparaged: cookery cannot be written down in black-and-white precepts, the *kairos* cannot be defined by rule, and the cook whose attention goes to all the precepts misses the opportune moment and labors in vain.

Crossover between the Schools

As we review more evidence of this kind, a general framework emerges of inter- and intrascholastic relations. It is the cumulative weight of such evidence that creates the context in which we can understand Isocrates of Apollonia's involvement with Plato,[66] and the evidence suggesting Theodectes' association with the Aristotle of the afternoon rhetoric lectures. But there is one important direct, Academic source furnishing us with a comparandum for, and a confirmation of, the idea that a student could migrate from Isocrates' school to Plato's: the Platonic *Epistle* XIII. This letter contains a recommendation of a certain Helicon to Dionysius (360b7–e3):

---

[64] Cf. the title of σοφιστής given him by Pollux *Onomasticon* 6.108.

[65] Shorey 1909:185–187, 198. Simylus fr. 727 Lloyd-Jones and Parsons 1983 (who point out that the iambic poet who made these nondramatic verses is not the same as the comic poet, the two having been distinguished by Meineke) = Stobaeus 4.18α.4; Dionysius fr. 2 Kassel-Austin = Athenaeus 9.404e (on which further Giannini 1961). See also Strattis *Atalante* fr. 3 Kassel-Austin with the interpretation of Azoulay (2010:38f.).

[66] On Isocrates of Apollonia see further Fricel-Dana 2001–2003.

... πέμπω σοι ... καὶ ἄνδρα, ὥσπερ ἐδόκει ἡμῖν τότε, ᾧ γε σὺ καὶ Ἀρχύτης, εἴπερ ἥκει παρά σε Ἀρχύτης, χρῆσθαι δύναισθ᾽ ἄν. ἔστι δὲ ὄνομα μὲν Ἑλίκων, τὸ δὲ γένος ἐκ Κυζίκου, μαθητὴς δὲ Εὐδόξου καὶ περὶ πάντα τὰ ἐκείνου πάνυ χαριέντως ἔχων· ἔτι δὲ καὶ τῶν Ἰσοκράτους μαθητῶν τῳ συγγέγονεν καὶ Πολυξένῳ τῶν Βρύσωνός τινι ἑταίρων. ὃ δὲ σπάνιον ἐπὶ τούτοις, οὔτε ἄχαρίς ἐστιν ἐντυχεῖν οὔτε κακοήθει ἔοικεν, ἀλλὰ μᾶλλον ἐλαφρὸς καὶ εὐήθης δόξειεν ἂν εἶναι. δεδιὼς δὲ λέγω ταῦτα, ὅτι ὑπὲρ ἀνθρώπου δόξαν ἀποφαίνομαι, οὐ φαύλου ζῴου ἀλλ᾽ εὐμεταβόλου, πλὴν πάνυ ὀλίγων τινῶν καὶ εἰς ὀλίγα· ἐπεὶ καὶ περὶ τούτου φοβούμενος καὶ ἀπιστῶν ἐσκόπουν αὐτός τε ἐντυγχάνων καὶ ἐπυνθανόμην τῶν πολιτῶν αὐτοῦ, καὶ οὐδεὶς οὐδὲν φλαῦρον ἔλεγεν τὸν ἄνδρα. σκόπει δὲ καὶ αὐτὸς καὶ εὐλαβοῦ. μάλιστα μὲν οὖν, ἂν καὶ ὁπωστιοῦν σχολάζῃς, μάνθανε παρ᾽ αὐτοῦ καὶ τἆλλα φιλοσόφει· εἰ δὲ μή, ἐκδίδαξαί τινα, ἵνα κατὰ σχολὴν μανθάνων βελτίων γίγνῃ καὶ εὐδοξῇς, ὅπως τὸ δι᾽ ἐμὲ ὠφελεῖσθαί σοι μὴ ἀνιῇ.

... I am sending you ... also a man whom we thought, you remember, that both you and Archytas, if Archytas comes to you, could use to advantage. His name is Helicon, his family is of Cyzicus, and he is a disciple of Eudoxus and well versed in all that eminent man's doctrines. Moreover he has been associated with one of the pupils of Isocrates and with Polyxenus, one of the followers of Bryson. But, what is rarer with such men, he is pleasant to meet, seemingly not difficult, but easy and mild mannered. I put it thus cautiously, for it is a man I am giving my opinion of; and though man has his good qualities, he is, with rare exceptions and in the greater part of his actions, quite changeable. I had my fears and doubts even about this man, so I not only conversed with him myself but also made inquiry among his fellow citizens, and nobody had anything to say against him. But look him over yourself and be on your guard. Above all, if you can in any way find leisure for it, take lessons from him as part of your studies in philosophy. If not, have him instruct someone else so that when you do have leisure you can learn and thereby add to your character and your good name. In this way I shall continue to be of help to you.

(trans. Morrow 1997)

I have quoted this passage at such length both because it is so rarely brought into discussions of Isocrates as head of a "philosophical" school, and because the author's curious ambivalence seems wryly to comment on how a monarch can be expected to receive a philosopher, with the sympathies of "Plato" seeming to be on the tyrant's side while critiquing the all-too-human weaknesses of a junior "philosopher" (!)—or is he really just hedging his bets? The similarities to the letter telling Perdiccas about Euphraeus (*Epistle* V)[67] are clear: a man is recommended to the monarch for the utility of his *logoi*, which here are even more definitely in the realm of serious philosophy. But this Academic source is able to recommend a man not only based on his association with Academic mathematics (Eudoxus of Cnidus[68]), but also—these are arguments in the man's favor, not accidental details of his circuitous life—based on his connection to extra-Academic mathematics (in a line traceable back to an association with Socrates, through Bryson[69]) and, most strikingly, to Isocrates (at the remove of two handshakes). If anything, the reference in this curriculum vitae to study with "a certain one of Isocrates' students" accords Isocrates more respect than if Isocrates himself were named as the teacher, as we might easily imagine that the master's variant passion for philosophy would be better tolerated in Academic circles than the pedagogical activities of his students who used his name (as the one here does: he is anonymous, his significance and value defined by the name of his teacher). What is the best explanation for the author's reservations about Helicon? Is this man's human weakness of changeability manifested in his flitting from one scholastic environment to another? Is it that an apologetic tone must be taken with Dionysius for sending the "kind of man" who is a school creature in the first place, these days? If so, is it reassurance that, despite or perhaps because of his tortuous career, Helicon is free of the usual polemical toadiness of philosophical men at court? What, in this context, do his links to the rival Isocratean school suggest about how objectionable a philosopher he can be expected to be, in comparison to others who might come with the Academic imprimatur? The text does not answer these questions, leaving us only with the net fact that this Academic source has some positive motivation for bringing up the Isocratean connection.

It is interesting to observe that some of the notable orators most widely attested to have studied with Isocrates—Lycurgus and Hyperides—are also explicitly said to have been "hearers" of Plato.[70] Getting beyond mere nuggets of biographical testimonia, it is perhaps most rewarding to focus on the case of the lesser-known orator Philiscus of Miletus, Isocrates' pupil (credited with producing a handbook of Isocratean rhetoric and a collection of his master's say-

---

[67] To be discussed in chap. 5.

[68] Eudoxus' presence at the court of Mausolus—where so many Isocrateans competed on the occasion of the king's death—is connected to his rivalry with Plato by Diogenes Laertius 8.87.

[69] On Bryson see Giannantoni 1990:I.475–483, IV.107–113. The report of the *Suda* (s.v. Σωκράτης), connecting this Bryson (of Heraclea) with Euclides and the Megarian school, as suggestive as it would be for our purposes, may reflect conflation with a later philosopher.

[70] Engels 1998:363 with n6.

ings[71]) and the author of a *Life of Lycurgus* in which he seems to have reflected upon the interscholastic milieu in which both Lycurgus and he were educated. Philiscus' adherence to Isocrates' school is stated in an abundant variety of sources (probably including Dionysius of Halicarnassus and Cicero). Less clear is whether he may also have received instruction at the Academy, though his epigram for Lysias has been found to show that he "was familiar with Platonic eschatology."[72] It is Philiscus' work on Lycurgus' life that more remarkably shows the Isocratean's esteem for Plato. Olympiodorus preserves this fragment of it: [73]

καὶ πάλιν ὁ Φιλίσκος τὸν βίον γράφων τοῦ Λυκούργου φησὶν ὅτι μέγας γέγονε Λυκοῦργος καὶ πολλὰ κατώρθωσεν, ἃ οὐκ ἔστι δυνατὸν κατορθῶσαι τὸν μὴ ἀκροασάμενον τῶν λόγων Πλάτωνος.

... and again Philiscus, writing on the life of Lycurgus, says that Lycurgus became a great man and accomplished many things that are impossible to accomplish for a person who never attended Plato's lectures.

(trans. after Engels 1998:361)

Engels rightly finds significance in the fact that "he, a prominent pupil of Isokrates, nevertheless stressed Plato's influence on Lykurgos, another well-known pupil of Isocrates ... Philiskos regarded Plato's philosophical teaching as the basis for the astonishing political achievements of Lykurgos in his later years."[74] To this we may add a reminder that the project of prose biography itself was still quite new in Philiscus' day; in chapter 5 below I will consider the formative influence of Isocrates and his school in establishing it, all of which makes the simple existence of a prose work on an individual's life a likely sign of Isocrateanism.

Let us turn to Clearchus, the tyrant of Heraclea Pontica, who crossed from the scholastic to the political world, in addition to his crossover between Plato and Isocrates' schools. Memnon, the first-century AD historian of Heraclea,[75] said he was "not untrained in philosophical education, but was one of Plato's students, and studied with Isocrates the orator for four years" (222b10–13). Isocrates confirms his tuition of Clearchus in his letter to the tyrant's son and successor Timotheus (*Epistle* 7), which is both a didactic overture to a powerful ruler (and thus to be read alongside such a ruler-address as his

---

[71]   Engels 1998:367f.
[72]   "Plutarch" *Lives of the Ten Orators* 836c, Engels 1998:364.
[73]   Olympiodorus, *Commentary on Plato's Gorgias* 515c Westerink 41.10 p. 215.23–37 = FGrHistCont 1013 F 1.
[74]   Engels 1998:370.
[75]   According to the report of Photius *Library* 224.222b9ff. = FGrHist 434 F 1.

Philip[76]) and a related *apologia*, distinguishing the fine qualities and conduct of Clearchus the pupil from the notorious savagery of Clearchus the tyrant. Timotheus is praised for using his power with more intelligence (*phronimōteron*, 1) than his father,[77] and for choosing virtue and the fine reputation that accompanies it over wealth. Isocrates predicts that if he continues on this path, he will not lack for encomia of his intelligence (*phronēsis*) and of this admirable choice (*proairesis*).[78] He adopts a somewhat ambivalent attitude to the father's violent rise to power. On the one hand, this was the necessary and only way to gain the rulership of Heraclea and so to put Timotheus in the position of using his dynastic power nobly and humanely (*kalōs kai philanthrōpōs*, 6), as Isocrates advises him to do in some detail. On the other hand, Isocrates is at pains to insist that Clearchus too possessed such mild and humane qualities while he was still a student (*eleutheriōtaton ... kai praotaton kai philanthrōpotaton*, 12), undergoing a shocking change with his acquisition of power, which led to an estrangement between teacher and student (13). Memnon's account of Clearchus sees the contradiction in his character as persisting, for it contrasts his ruthless dispatch of his enemies with his innovative program of intellectual patronage ("However, he built a library before the others to whom tyranny has given her name," 222b25–27).[79] His fellow Isocratean Theopompus, however, is only known to have recounted Clearchus' poisoning of rivals (FGrHist 115 F 181), not his better qualities.

The phenomenon of scholastic "crossover" in the Hellenistic period has attracted some attention from Christian Habicht, and it is worth asking if the same spirit Habicht finds in this period (including in early Hellenistic Athens) can be usefully carried back into our part of the fourth century, as a hypothesis challenging the easy assumption that divisive polemics were definitive of scholastic interactions. Diogenes Laertius, so eager to report on polemics when he can, has plenty of evidence for exchanges that qualify the "permanent rivalry" of the schools. Examples of school adherents freely attending rival lectures include:

> Zenon used to go to the lectures of the Platonists Xenokrates and Polemon, to those of the Cynic Krates and those of the Sceptic Stilpon.[80]

---

[76] See chap. 5. "Plutarch" *Life of Isocrates* 837c reports that Isocrates accepted commissions and fees from Timotheus. For a productively political approach to Isocrates' Timotheus, see Ober 1998:268–273.

[77] Memnon repeats and confirms this.

[78] οὐκ ἀπορήσεις τῶν ἐγκωμιασομένων τήν τε φρόνησιν τὴν σὴν καὶ τὴν προαίρεσιν ταύτην (1).

[79] Memnon goes on to make a contrast between Clearchus and his brother Satyrus (Timotheus' guardian), who was crueler still and who had no truck whatsoever with learning (*mathēmata* and *philosophia*).

[80] Diogenes Laertius 7.2, SVF 1 T 11.

In the second century, Kleitomachos followed the teaching of the masters of the Academy, the *Peripatos*, and the *Stoa* before he himself became headmaster of the Academy (DL 4.67). A hundred years earlier, his predecessor Arcesilaus even encouraged his students to attend the classes of others (DL 4.42). Such may have been the exception, but there is nowhere any indication that the freedom of choice was limited.[81]

This evidence is strengthened by cases in which a student left one school for another: Heraclides Ponticus' switch from the Academy to the Peripatos (Diogenes Laertius 5.86), his student Dionysius' departure for the Stoa (Diogenes Laertius 7.166), another case where the Academic Arcesilaus himself introduced a Chian student to the Peripatetic Hieronymus, to whom the student transferred his adherence (Diogenes Laertius 4.42), and this same Arcesilaus' migration from Theophrastus' Peripatos to Polemo's Academy (Diogenes Laertius 4.22, 28).[82] In short, there is an overall picture that "personal relations were generally friendly and collegial, even between philosophers engaged in sharp polemical exchange."[83] Similar conditions may also have prevailed, for many of the same reasons, in our earlier period.

Other Entanglements between Aristotle and Isocrates

The relationship between Aristotle and Isocrates can be fleshed out further. The following is a brief account intended to put the material discussed above into perspective. Aristotle's early work *Gryllus* was probably published before the Isocrates-inspired rhetoric lectures and within a couple of years of the death of Xenophon's son Gryllus at the Battle of Mantinea (362).[84] The most definite and useful context for it is found in Diogenes Laertius' life of Xenophon (2.55):

φησὶ δ' Ἀριστοτέλης ὅτι ἐγκώμια καὶ ἐπιτάφιον Γρύλλου μυρίοι ὅσοι συνέγραψαν, τὸ μέρος καὶ τῷ πατρὶ χαριζόμενοι. ἀλλὰ καὶ Ἕρμιππος ἐν τῷ Περὶ Θεοφράστου καὶ Ἰσοκράτην Γρύλλου φησὶ ἐγκώμιον γεγρα-φέναι.

Aristotle mentions that there were innumerable authors of epitaphs and eulogies upon Gryllus, who wrote, in part at least, to gratify his

---

[81] Habicht 1988:5.
[82] Habicht 1988:5.
[83] Habicht 1988:6.
[84] The *Gryllus* will be discussed again in the context of competitive scholastic innovations in funerary commemoration in chap. 5.

father. Hermippus too, in his *Life of Theophrastus*, affirms that even Isocrates wrote an encomium on Gryllus.

(trans. Hicks 1925)

It is possible to conclude, from "ingratiating" and the mention of Isocrates' encomium, that Aristotle criticized Isocrates among others for finding in Gryllus' death the occasion for a self-serving rhetorical display; moreover this could fit into Plato's critique of rhetoric in the *Gorgias*.[85] On the other hand, the qualification ("in part at least") is then odd, and the idea of Xenophon, a Socratic, as the addressee of these compositions perhaps makes it only more necessary to consider whether this could have been a case of more scholastic polemics among parties with different claims to "philosophy." It is just as easy to imagine Aristotle's work as a "higher" praise of Gryllus rather than as a polemic against all rhetoric.

In any case, whether provoked by the *Gryllus* (as scholars generally maintain[86]) or by the rhetoric-lecture activities Aristotle undertook in the following years, Isocrates' "most genuine pupil,"[87] Cephisodorus of Athens, published a book *Against Aristotle*. A fragment of a second-century AD treatise by Numenius, who was apparently well informed about Cephisodorus and his work,[88] has been much discussed:

ὃς δὴ ὁ Κηφισόδωρος, ἐπειδὴ ὑπ' Ἀριστοτέλους βαλλόμενον ἑαυτῷ τὸν διδάσκαλον Ἰσοκράτην ἑώρα, αὐτοῦ μὲν Ἀριστοτέλους ἦν ἀμαθὴς καὶ ἄπειρος, ὑπὸ δὲ τοῦ καθορᾶν ἔνδοξα τὰ Πλάτωνος ὑπάρχοντα οἰηθεὶς κατὰ Πλάτωνα τὸν Ἀριστοτέλην φιλοσοφεῖν, ἐπολέμει μὲν Ἀριστοτέλει, ἔβαλλε δὲ Πλάτωνα καὶ κατηγόρει ἀρξάμενος ἀπὸ τῶν ἰδεῶν, τελευτῶν εἰς τἆλλα, ἃ οὐδ' αὐτὸς ᾔδει, ἀλλὰ τὰ νομιζόμενα ἀμφ' αὐτῶν ᾗ λέγεται ὑπονοῶν. Πλὴν οὕτως μὲν ὁ Κηφισόδωρος, ᾧ ἐπολέμει μὴ μαχόμενος, ἐμάχετο ᾧ μὴ πολεμεῖν ἐβούλετο.

Cephisodorus, when he saw his master Isocrates being attacked by Aristotle, was ignorant of and unversed in Aristotle himself; but seeing the repute which Plato's views enjoyed, he thought that Aristotle was following Plato. So he waged war on Aristotle, but was really attacking Plato. His criticism began with the Ideas and finished with the other doctrines—things which he himself did not know; he was only guessing

---

[85] This is the view of Berti (1962) and Chroust (1965). For a work by Speusippus entitled *Gryllus*, see Theys 1998:219n11.

[86] See esp. Berti 1962:185, for the dating of Cephisodorus' attack.

[87] Dionysius of Halicarnassus *Isocrates* 18.

[88] Düring 1957:390.

at the meaning of the opinions held about them. This Cephisodorus was not attacking the person he was at war with, but was attacking the person he did not wish to make war upon.

Eusebius, *Praeparatio evangelica* 14.6.9–10, 732bc =
Düring 1957 T 63 c = Numenius fr. 25 des Places
(trans. after Revised Oxford Translation)

Cephisodorus has mistaken Aristotle for a Platonist—what is the explanation? For scholars like Jaeger, this can be pressed into the service of a larger account of the early, Platonist Aristotle.[89] For our purposes, what is most significant is that this polemical work did engage with philosophical doctrines, so that just as we may see Plato's school (in the person of Aristotle) as encountering rhetoricians on their field of contest, so may we see Isocrates' school (in Cephisodorus) as countering Aristotle on the ground of more abstract philosophical discourse. The evidence as a whole for Cephisodorus and his book does not allow us to dismiss the composition as a shallow tirade. It was lengthy, in four books (Athenaeus 2.60de), and Dionysius of Halicarnassus (*Isocrates* 18) regarded it as a reliable source to rebut insinuations Aristotle had made against Isocrates.

I differ with the view of Düring[90] that another passage of Dionysius of Halicarnassus, *Letter to Pompey* 1, is "our most trustworthy witness," or even that this text "says that Cephisodorus had written his book not in order to start a quarrel but to seek the truth." Düring takes this interpretation to the point of claiming that entirely friendly relations prevailed between Aristotle and Isocrates. The passage in question reads:

Πολλοὶ γὰρ εὑρεθήσονται πρὸ ἐμοῦ τοῦτο πεποιηκότες [sc. criticize Plato], οἱ μὲν κατὰ τὸν ἐκείνου γενόμενοι χρόνον, οἱ δὲ λίαν ὕστερον ἐπακμάσαντες. καὶ γὰρ τὰ δόγματα διέβαλον αὐτοῦ τινες καὶ τοὺς λόγους ἐμέμψαντο πρῶτον μὲν ὁ γνησιώτατος αὐτοῦ μαθητὴς Ἀριστοτέλης, ἔπειτα οἱ περὶ Κηφισόδωρόν τε καὶ Θεόπομπον καὶ Ζωίλον καὶ Ἱπποδάμαντα καὶ Δημήτριον καὶ ἄλλοι συχνοί, οὐ διὰ φθόνον ἢ διὰ φιλαπεχθημοσύνην κωμωιδοῦντες ἀλλὰ τὴν ἀλήθειαν ἐξετάζοντες.[91]

For many will be found who have criticized Plato before me, some in the time of Plato, and others who flourished a good deal later. Some of them attacked his doctrines and found fault with his writings, first his most genuine pupil Aristotle, and then Cephisodorus, Theopompus,

---

[89] Jaeger 1948:37.
[90] Düring 1957:389.
[91] Cited according to Düring 1957:379 (T 63a).

Zoïlus, Hippodamas, Demetrius—both they and their associates—and many others, not out of envy or quarrelsomeness, but in an effort to discern the truth.

It is indeed noteworthy that Dionysius credits Cephisodorus and his colleagues with serious intellectual purposes and states that they took up *dogmata* and *logoi* as the subject matter of their works. What does not seem sound to me, however, is to draw a neat line distinguishing a "favorable" notice such as this one from the churlish scribbling of hacks. Note how easily the regard for the critics as serious writers sits in Dionysius beside such terms as *diebalon*, whose slanted and slanderous connotations cannot be argued away. With regard to accusations of tendentious and empty howling (which itself is characterized by Dionysius with the word *kōmōidountes*, evoking Owen's category[92] of "good" verbal warfare among philosophers), we must not allow ourselves to forget that such dismissal is itself the commonest currency of intellectual contest. What proof do we really possess that allegedly vituperative treatises were in fact wholly different from those purported to make serious critiques? All that is clear is that individual sources regard them in those different lights; and when the sources seem to be sending a mixed message, it is hardly the most economical solution to decide that a simple truth is hiding behind a complex range of reactions. In any case, the passage before us cannot bear Düring's burden, since it doesn't seem to refer to the same book Dionysius called an *apologia* in the *Letter to Pompey*. If Dionysius is indeed the "most trustworthy," we should look to the place where he speaks clearly and specifically about the book, and the relationship behind it (between Aristotle and Isocrates),[93] that interests us.

In evidence like this, the names and scholastic lineages associated with Cephisodorus are very suggestive of the intellectual milieu of genre-crossing intellectuals I have been evoking. Zoïlus is a particularly good example. For one thing, the attribution of serious motivations to him by Dionysius can be

---

[92]   See the introduction to the following chapter.

[93]   Indeed, in this passage, Aristotle and Cephisodorus are placed on the same side. Note that Düring (1957:389) is led—in part by his interpretation—to find "baffling," and a "mistake," the testimony of Aristocles of Messene (in Eusebius *Praeparatio evangelica* 15.13–15 = F 2, §7, in the edition of Chiesara [2001]). Chiesara (2001:72n6) does note that the more vulgar charges leveled by Cephisodorus according to Aristocles are not those we encounter in our other sources for Cephisodorus. In this she sees the likelihood of Aristocles' dependence on Hermippus' book *On the Disciples of Isocrates*. This is an alternative solution to the difficulty seen by Düring in what he considered the anachronistic charge against Aristotle of being *tenthēs*. In any case, Chiesara does not join Düring in questioning the unanimity of our evidence for Cephisodorus' critical attitude towards Aristotle. And I must add once more that serious critiques may sometimes mingle with scurrilous slanders.

put alongside the more complete picture we possess of him[94] as a notoriously savage critic of Homer, Plato, and Isocrates. On the other hand, in two genres— Homeric criticism and rhetorical theory—he fits in closely with Aristotle and was evidently an interlocutor whose writings demanded such a response as the Aristotelian *Aporēmata Homērika*. A critic of both Plato and Isocrates, Zoïlus has additional importance as a "nonaligned" figure who is nonetheless utterly exemplary of the world of intellectual contest that we are studying. There is some evidence that Zoïlus may have counted as a force to be reckoned with in conjunction with a group of students, especially in the area of rhetorical theory—one of his pupils being Anaximenes of Lampsacus (ἐν ἁπάσαις ταῖς ἰδέαις τῶν λόγων τετράγωνόν τινα, "an all-round performer in every branch of literature").[95]

Theopompus' presence here is interesting; we will consider his connections and controversies with contemporary writers below. A word should also be said about the collocation of Zoïlus and Theopompus in its own right. While the former is considered a cynic and the latter a historian, the overlap in generic range between these two is striking. Besides their common interest in philosophical invective, oratory and history were outlets for both men. Zoïlus, whom the *Suda* calls "*rhētōr* and *philosophos*" (s.v., ζ 130), also wrote a history terminating with Philip II.

A few notices in Athenaeus help us form a more specific impression of Cephisodorus' work. The first of these reports (2.60de):

ὅτι Κηφισόδωρος ὁ Ἰσοκράτους μαθητὴς ἐν τοῖς κατὰ Ἀριστοτέλους (τέσσαρα δ᾽ ἐστὶ ταῦτα βιβλία) ἐπιτιμᾷ τῷ φιλοσόφῳ ὡς οὐ ποιήσαντι λόγου ἄξιον τὸ παροιμίας ἀθροῖσαι, Ἀντιφάνους ὅλον ποιήσαντος δρᾶμα τὸ ἐπιγραφόμενον Παροιμίαι· ἐξ οὗ καὶ παρατίθεται τάδε·

Isocrates' student Cephisodorus in his *Against Aristotle* (fr. 3 Radermacher = Arist. fr. 464)—there are four books—faults the philosopher for not treating collecting proverbs as a worthwhile activity, even though Antiphanes wrote an entire play entitled *Proverbs*. The following lines (fr. 186) are cited from it.

(trans. Olson 2006)

While the dearth of examples of whole works of this type and period does stand in the way of our appreciation of a notice like this, we learn more here than elsewhere about the actual character of the work—the fact of its publication at

---

[94] FGrHist 71.
[95] Dionysius of Halicarnassus *Isaeus* 19 (trans. Usher 1974).

a certain length, and a little about the nature of the disputations it contained. The loss of Aristotle's early works renders this latter part obscure. Adolf Stahr, in one of the fullest discussions of this whole matter yet written, aggressively argued against the interpretation followed here. The understanding of Stahr, who develops Athenaeus' testimony into an elaborate reconstruction of the date of the incident and the published nature of Aristotle's criticisms of Isocrates that provoked it, was that Cephisodorus rather criticized Aristotle for having authored "a work of no account, the collection entitled *Paroimiai*."[96] Even if we accept this, the actual nature of the dispute remains in doubt, beyond the likelihood of its connection to Aristotle's early rhetorical writings.[97]

Athenaeus 3.122a–c has Cephisodorus in book 3 of his *Pros Aristotelēn* demonstrating through quotations that vulgar expressions (φαῦλα, πονηρῶς εἰρημένα) can be found in the best canonical authors. Stahr draws out from this the inference that "Cephisodorus uses examples from the best-known and most famous poets to turn *bonus interdum dormitat Homerus* into a generally valid basis for pardoning stylistic mistakes in turning phrases and aphorisms; and this fragment allows me to conclude that in this locus Isocrates is being stood up for against similar accusations made against him by Aristotle."[98] It would indeed seem that these defensive arguments imply that Aristotle had gone enough on the offense to make stylistic criticisms of Isocrates.[99] Athenaeus 8.354bc, in which "not even Cephisodorus" ventured into the basest kind of accusations against Aristotle preferred by Epicurus, is another piece of mixed evidence in which Cephisodorus' motives and methods are neither black nor pure.

---

[96] Stahr 1830–1832:I.68–71, II.42–46, II.285–288. Blass (1892:452) gives the same interpretation. The title *Paroimiai* is given in the catalogue of Aristotle's works at Diogenes Laertius 5.26. It is interesting to observe in Stahr's discussion how he too wrestled with the seeming ambiguity in our sources about whether Cephisodorus' book was scurrilous or estimable. He accepts that Isocrates' pupil defended his teacher in part by attacking Aristotle's moral character, but he is impressed by the high regard in which Cephisodorus seems to have been held (Dionysius of Halicarnassus *Isocrates* 18 as cited above, Athenaeus 3.122ab, Themistius *Sophistēs* 285c3; the citation of Aristotle's *Rhetoric*, however, depends on the confusion between Cephisodorus and Cephisodotus [a confusion also present in the manuscripts of Athenaeus], although it is parallel to Düring's valid speculation on the basis of that work's quotations of Isocrates).

[97] Blass (1892:452) is allowing himself considerable license to speculate when he suggests that "ein beschränkter, wenig liberaler Sinn und eine unverständige Verachtung des Volks und seiner Weisheit" is to be seen in Cephisodorus' criticisms of a work on proverbs.

[98] Stahr 1830–1832:I.70f. Reinhardt (1873:43) suggests that Aristotle had *Panathenaicus* 117 in view.

[99] Thus Blass (1892:451f.) characterizes Cephisodorus' work as a "Schutzschrift für Isokrates gegen Aristoteles' Angriffe, welche Schrift Dionysios ausserordentlich bewundert. Jene Angriffe werden, da sie veröffentlicht sein mussten, in dem Dialoge 'Gryllos oder über die Rhetorik' enthalten gewesen sein ... und entsprechend scheinen auch die Angriffe gegen den Ankläger, die sich nothwendig mit einfanden, gemässigt gewesen zu sein; wenigstens hören wir nichts von ehrenrührigen Beschuldigungen."

One of the most important points on which we have consistent evidence is that Cephisodorus in this matter is behaving in his capacity as a follower of Isocrates. The sources are less helpful in situating the incident in an Academic context. In any case, this may count as early creditable evidence of a more overt rivalry between the Academy and Isocrates' school than we can infer from Plato and Isocrates' works—a rivalry that by the 340s would be unmistakable, as we will see.[100]

Cephisodorus' emergence from Isocrates' school to fight the philosophers with philosophical weapons is paralleled in Isocrates' student Theopompus, famous as a historiographer, but also the author of a work *Against the Diatribē of Plato* that attacks the theory of forms cogently enough to be quoted later in Simplicius' commentary on Aristotle's *Categories*.[101] I will discuss this strand of Theopompus' career in the following chapter. We may well wonder whether Theopompus' mode of engagement was not as respectable and serious as Cephisodorus' is generally granted to be (however real and fierce the assault on the reputation of a rival intellectual and school).

The tradition of "Platonism" in turn was eventually to take a friendly interest in Isocratean parenesis. The Neoplatonic commentators on Aristotle gave an important propaedeutic role to the Isocratean *To Demonicus, To Nicocles*, and *Nicocles* as "ethical studies."[102] These were just one element in a wide syncretism, but the manuscripts show that the Neoplatonists edited these works as part of their students' canon, and considered their author Isocrates an authority on *ēthē* among other ethical writers (*ēthika grapsantes*). Isocrates was harmonized with philosophical authorities, as when Olympiodorus turns to the *Busiris* to shed light on Socrates.[103] The last scholarch of the Academy, Damascius, praises his teacher Severianus for infusing these Isocratean readings with their full measure of philosophical significance: "He took me through the most important and political of Isocrates' speeches, not in the technical manner of a sophist, but with the wisdom of a philosopher."[104] Already in the fourth century BC Xenocrates, the Academy's scholarch, was writing parenetic works.[105] The two

---

[100] On Cephisodorus, see further the bibliography in Düring 1957:389.

[101] CAG VIII, p. 216; see FGrHist 115 T 48, F 259, and F 359. Simplicius does not seem to quote popular versions of philosophical ideas.

[102] Hoffmann 2006:605.

[103] See Menchelli 2007.

[104] οὐ τὸν τεχνικόν τε καὶ σοφιστικόν, ἀλλὰ τὸν ἔμφρονα καὶ φιλόσοφον τρόπον, Damascius, *Life of Isidore* fr. 282 Zintzen = *The Philosophical History* 108 Athanassiadi (trans. Athanassiadi 1999). Compare the identification of Proclus' teacher Syrianus as Ἰσοκρατίων in *Suda*, s.v. Συριανός (σ 1662).

[105] See Diogenes Laertius 4.11 (Xenocrates' extant works are συγγράμματα καὶ ἔπη καὶ παραινέσεις) and 4.14 (three titles of the form *pros* + name).

schools' mutual (and not always hostile) interest in each other's topics seems to have a long history.

Still, caution is called for in evaluating evidence of philosophical polemics. In my readings of *Nicomachean Ethics*, *Protrepticus*, and *Phaedrus*, I have laid an emphasis on the possibilities of reflective engagement with "Isocratean" ideas across the boundary of scholastic rivalry. I would not claim that this completely refutes the results of the scholarly game of detecting hostile allusions, especially between Isocrates and Plato.[106] It is my hope, however, that readers will return to those possible allusions with less certainty about their significance. In some cases, skepticism is needed to avoid the circular reinforcement of existing prejudicial constructs of these authors. For example, it is often repeated with near-certainty that Isocrates' attacks on "eristics" in the proem of his *Helen* and elsewhere are aimed at Plato and his circle, rather than at the type of eristic whom Plato's dialogues also engage in polemic.[107] Recently Sandra Zajonz has given persuasive and satisfying reasons for doubting this facile conclusion.[108] Yet it was precisely the less careful commonplace that Chroust, who applied it to *Antidosis* 258ff., uses to maintain the connection between the *Antidosis* and Aristotle's *Protrepticus*.[109] Now, I have accepted on other grounds that Isocrates *is*, in fact, an important voice in the *Protrepticus*, but we may legitimately worry whether the edifice of common wisdom about Isocrates and Plato deserves our confidence. I have defended my doubts about whether Plato's works can be read as simply inimical to Isocrates, but Chroust accepts this and makes it the necessary first link in the chain that leads him to see Aristotle's early rhetoric lectures as having "taught this 'new dialectics' or scientific form of argumentation and presentation."[110] If we are less certain about the tone and even reference of the intellectual position-taking we discover in our texts, then we will be less likely to base our understanding of the historical testimonia on questionable assumptions. Our direct examination of these testimonia shows them to be often cryptic and uncertain, and we should leave ourselves open to being surprised by the conditions of scholastic politics that they imply.

The likely motivations and concerns of Aristotle appear in a different light if we are more fully and open-mindedly acquainted with the surprisingly varied range of evidence for the interests and interactions of different

---

[106] Eucken 1983 is a starting point for exploring such evidence; important earlier work includes Teichmüller 1881–1884, Blass 1892:28–41, and Ries 1959.

[107] For a more nuanced view, see Cooper 1986:87.

[108] Zajonz 2002: esp. 86.

[109] Chroust 1964.

[110] I also question the use Berti (1962) and Chroust (1964) make of the testimony that Gorgias was Isocrates' teacher; we have an extensive Isocratean corpus on which we may base our understanding of Isocrates, instead of substituting the convenient "sophist Gorgias."

but interconnected scholastic circles during the period when Plato (d. 348/7), Isocrates (d. 338), and Aristotle (d. 322) were all active. The historical sources understand Aristotle as fully engaged in a mode of education usually associated with rhetorical "rivals" to philosophy. It has usually been taken for granted that Aristotle championed a very Platonizing "cultural ideal" in these encounters, but this assumption may not be helpful. What seems beyond doubt is that Aristotle felt the rhetorical arena, and the Isocratean school, to be impossible to ignore and highly relevant to his own self-definition. Rather than joining Philodemus in denouncing Aristotle for this flexibility and curiosity about working in *ta anthrōpina*, we can better take these entanglements as a suggestive background against which to understand the range of approaches and ideas of the Aristotelian works we do possess (including the features with Isocratean affinities that we have explored in chapter 1).

Part II

School Creatures

Literary Competition, Philosophy, and Politics

4

Philosophical Politics, Tooth and Nail

An Introduction to Philosophical Polemics

> What to the ostentatious smuggling verbalists are the thoughts of thinkers but Loose-Fish?
>
> Herman Melville, *Moby-Dick*

When we study the generation of Plato and Isocrates' students, and their often polemical intercourse, across lines of genre and scholastic affiliation, we are presented with an unfamiliar picture of a space for debate and competition. Within this space are writers who have been variously remembered as philosophers, historians, orators, sophists, and poets. This raises multiple questions. What place did "philosophy" take for itself in the intellectual and political life of the later fourth century? Was the state of intellectual life at this period in some sense a legacy of the careers of the older generation, of Plato, Xenophon, and Isocrates? Will a close look at the activities of the students reflect light back upon the political and social import of the teachers' lives?

Thus in this part of my study I continue my inquiry into the practical meaning and political organization of specifically intellectual activity, still aiming to take its measure not in terms of affiliation with political factions, but through an appreciation of how, in the internal rivalries among intellectuals, we may sometimes be able to observe more clearly the manner in which their specialized field of activity fits into the larger fabric of the life of the Athenian, and later Hellenic, community. My aim is to shed some light on the "school politics" of a poorly understood but vital transitional period in literary and intellectual history—the years between Plato's death and the familiar figures of Hellenistic literature.[1] In this period, the intellectual giants of the last years of the independent Athenian polis, particularly Plato and Isocrates, saw their legacy handled and developed by the products of their schools.

By "school politics" I mean two sometimes quite irreconcilable things: first, in the sense of our own professional politics or office politics—rivalries, alliances, empire-building, and backstabbing that seem to be more about status in the intellectual arena than anything of consequence in what we would call the "real world"; second, how the scholastic institutions did, in fact, find a place for themselves in the Greek world's inescapable political pressures, political events, and political fabric of life.

The impact of purely political power on the field of philosophy presents itself much more unmistakably in the students' generation. Yet due caution must be applied to any attempt to answer the more familiar question of how philosophical or intellectual movements may have translated their own internal activities, configuration, and contests into a force capable of altering political history. This question has excited great interest and controversy, especially given the copious indications in the ancient literature that Plato's Academy trained a cohort of students to further a common political agenda, or at least to apply themselves to reforming government by the criteria of philosophy. Studies by P. A. Brunt and Kai Trampedach have reacted to persistent sympathy for this simplified story in modern scholarship by addressing the issue strictly in these terms and producing refutations of any direct and successful application of the Academy's organized activities to politics. Brunt took up "the thesis that it was a primary aim of Plato to produce political experts" and concluded that "the evidence on the political activities of Plato's pupils is too weak to sustain in itself the thesis that it was one of his chief aims to prepare them for statecraft," and finally that "whatever importance the school has in the history of political *theory*, its influence on the history of states was nil."[2] Trampedach is similarly blunt about the political inconsequentiality of such noteworthy Academic–ruler relationships as those between Euphraeus and Perdiccas III, the "Platonics" and Hermias,[3] and Aristotle and Alexander: "These connections between philosophers and rulers, as has been seen, did not have political consequences."[4]

---

[1]   As recent work (see Acosta-Hughes and Stephens 2011; White 2007; White 1994) is showing, the Hellenistic authors considered Plato very topical, but in their own peculiar way. I aim to complement such studies by suggesting how "Plato," to early Hellenistic authors, could signify not merely a literary classic and famous defier of the poets but also a figure of authority and controversy in the school polemics of the intervening generations (which transmitted a strikingly different emphasis in intellectual circles).

[2]   Brunt 1993:283, 330, 332.

[3]   These two relationships will be taken up below.

[4]   Trampedach 1994:282. Sonnabend (1996) similarly adopts the limiting framework of "interstate politics," though he acknowledges the inadequacy of partisan categories to account for the

It must be emphasized that neither of these studies took as their subject the form of life, politically conditioned and itself internally subject to a "political" organization, that brought the earliest students of the Academy together with their philosophical colleagues and quasi-philosophical quasi-colleagues in confrontations that were sometimes shaped for the consumption of rulers and other political notables. Even Trampedach's book, despite having a decidedly prosopographical bent in its first half, neglects these complex interactions within the philosophical field in order to focus on the evidence for the philosophers' purely political activities and relationships across the politician-philosopher divide. A consideration of the *intrinsically* political nature of ancient intellectual careers has not fit into the design of these modern political studies, just as philosophically trained scholars, in turn, have quite logically and consistently turned their attention away from the "distraction" of partisan squabbles in their investigations into the development and influence of philosophical doctrines in the schools of this period.

Movements and projects of a philosophical kind can often be shown to breathe the political spirit of their time, but attempts at direct intervention in the political order are less frequent. Even allowing for the relatively low degree of professional differentiation that still obtained in the Classical *polis*, Plato's own formulation (whether in the seventh letter or in the *Republic*) of the divide between the phenomenon of political life and the way of philosophy strongly suggests that the criteria by which philosophy articulates a "higher politics" may not be those of its suitability to practical implementation.[5] While I would lay stress on Plato's serious attention to imagining a marriage between the stringent demands of philosophy and the real parameters of a functioning political community,[6] which suggests the possibility that, for Plato, the philosopher's life can be a model civic life, nonetheless these concerns are distinctly more universal than the necessary parameters of effective political action. Moreover, it should be enough for us to establish that, on the basis of what we can learn from Plato's published works, it is not obvious how philosophy can or should affect politics. This is why Brunt and Trampedach's tests for a direct effect

---

"intellectual competitive struggle played out in the Athenian public sphere" seen in Speusippus' *Letter to Philip* (92).

[5] We may make the provocative reflection that as such differentiation and specialization increased with the rise of philosophical schools, explicit contacts with politics and politicians increased as well. But any signs that intellectuals were the influencing and not influenced participant in these transactions are, if anything, scarcer than before.

[6] This Platonic concern for "practical politics" may be seen in regard to legal norms (*Crito*) and religious norms (*Euthyphro*) that are apparently subject to philosophical clarification and validation, and in Plato's serious engagement, in common with Isocrates, with rhetoric as a mode of effective citizenship whose powerful workings in politics can (or cannot) be reconciled with the guiding principles of philosophy (*Phaedrus*, cf. *Gorgias*).

produced negative results. And so, the connections between the philosophizing of Plato's school and the shape and course of political life have to be sought through the layers that Plato deliberately interposed between them. This does not require regarding the activities of a philosopher as entirely autonomous or irrelevant, but we must be prepared to think in terms of the subtler translations of work that has specific value for philosophers (or, more generally, seems specifically provocative to other intellectuals) into the kind of capital that has currency in the political administration of states or in the contest among political entities for supremacy.

A better approach, and one that displays independent affinities to the present study, is that of Vincent Azoulay, whose Bourdieusian analysis is meant to "understand the way in which intellectual life in Athens organizes itself into a field of confrontations and rivalries, from which, *in fine*, individuals emerge by a series of strategies of distinction."[7] This reading finds a "rupture" and deep division within the intellectual field in Athens, between a civically embedded pole (exemplified by the logographers and dramatic poets) and an assertively independent pole reflecting an "autonomization" due to Isocrates' foundation of the first Athenian school in the late 390s, which would constitute the birth of a distinct intellectual field.[8] The study of Isocrates, therefore, affords us "a privileged means of access for decoding the play of the symbolic struggles that structure the field."[9] Azoulay's perspective thus leads him to deploy the term "politique au second degré" for some of the same motives for which I speak of "philosophical politics," but second-degree politics is still a form of politics *tout court*, maintaining the same ends but pursuing them by specialized means, so that the philosophers' activities are still fundamentally political in the ordinary sense (in Azoulay's image, the umbilical cord joining politics and philosophy is stretched but not broken).[10] Although retaining the corrective points of Brunt and Trampedach, I am not prepared to allow power politics so decisive a role in determining the shape of the intellectual field and its internal politics.

Leaving open the questions of how effectively autonomous the field of philosophical and intellectual competition may have been,[11] and of what degree of

---

[7] Azoulay 2007:174.

[8] Azoulay 2007:180, 182, 185–187. Philosophy as a refuge or exile from civic politics is expressed in Isocrates *Panathenaicus* 11, with a corresponding reorientation towards the more general *Hellēnika kai basilika kai politika pragmata* (193), and Azoulay emphasizes this disengaged stance (*apragmosunē*, 192).

[9] Azoulay 2007:186f.

[10] Azoulay 2007:184, citing Schuhl 1946–1947 in support of the view that "the goal of the Platonic school is evidently to train politicians."

[11] I have already tried to suggest a high degree of specifically and autonomously intellectual life in our period, with noticeable freedom to form projects according to theoretical motivations,

correlation existed between its configuration and the political power dynamics more-or-less external to it, we must first attempt to describe the scene by assembling the participants who act upon it, their public and published interactions with each other, and the private relationships frequently alleged to cloud their integrity as agents of their texts and teachings. A structural account of such a personal network, together with some basic assessments of its characteristics as a field and as a group, may serve as the foundation for an account of the political dimension of their philosophical activity and do more to develop and complicate this account than another attempt to prove or disprove the existence of a philosophical cabal in the halls of power.

In what follows, I will take as the initial nodes on the network those whom tradition has identified as "students" of Plato or Isocrates. We have already considered several of these individuals. We want to understand better to whom they were talking, and about what. The network can then be expanded to include those whose intellectual or political converse connects to these figures. The principle of this method is to delimit a space within which persons worked recorded social effects on each other. It may also throw some light back on the institutional, social, and political context of Plato and Isocrates, who originated some of the most influential scholastic structures and modeled the philosophical career, and who by courting monarchs initiated an endeavor that continued among the younger group.

This later-fourth-century group of philosophers and others affords us a special opportunity to study these contextual intersections because of several notable changes that can be observed in progress among them. First, there is the sheer growth of the intellectual profession, manifested in a proliferation of schools, in the solidification of rhetoric and philosophy as organized disciplines with articulated doctrines, and in the emergence of a professionally literate class communicating across disciplinary lines. A second notable phenomenon, which may seem at odds with the first, is the apparently increased influence of courts and rulers on many intellectuals. Affiliations of this kind will be seen to come about through a mix of forces, including newly urgent practical necessities; ideal or theoretical proclivities are still important but are losing the determinative influence they had on Plato and Isocrates' address to monarchs in the

---

and intellectual debate often conducted in relatively disinterested and impersonal terms. Our study of the generation of Plato and Isocrates' students sees these qualities under stress and sometimes at risk of breaking down. This may seem somewhat surprising against the common perception of the strong Athenian roots of Plato and Isocrates' schools in comparison to a higher degree of scholastic specialization and autonomy in succeeding generations. A better understanding of this particular history is one of the goals of this chapter specifically, and of the larger study that confronts the teachers' interactions with those of their students.

days before Philip. In the extreme instances we will observe a free-for-all of competition by any means necessary.[12]

Important aspects of this emergent generation and its quarrelsome obsessions have attracted some attention from students of fourth-century philosophy and history. G. E. L. Owen notably protested against the usually inadequate appreciation of the partial and polemical nature of our evidence for this moment in the history of philosophy in his "Philosophical Invective." Owen deserves great credit for casting a ray of light on what is, indeed, still "a rich century of calumny whose measure the historians of philosophy are only starting to take."[13] And his skepticism about castles made of such evidentiary sand can be nothing but salutary, if it prevents the misuse of hostile witnesses in reconstructing the *philosophical ideas and doctrines* developed and held by thinkers of the past. The *communis opinio* on such philosophically pressing questions as the tendencies and sympathies of Aristotle's earliest philosophical writings has too often depended on such frail constructions, their own history—of coming to be out of ancient fragments in the modern scholarship of previous centuries—forgotten.[14] However, once we declare ourselves interested not only in doctrines, but also in controversies and position-taking among ancient intellectuals, the same evidence becomes invaluable, despite its problems.

It is important to recognize Owen's focus: the ease with which historians may be misled when they are ignorant of the tradition's wide stream of attack and manipulation. Accordingly, his results are primarily negative, as he demolishes the claim of unfounded and recycled accusations to serve as bases for making factually acceptable history. He concludes by expressing satisfaction if he has "put us on our guard *against* some evidence that wears an innocent face."[15] So the tales of the talebearers are misleading if misappropriated. But if we do survey them with a skeptical eye, can we enlighten ourselves about anything beyond the dangers faced by the historian of philosophy and by the thin-skinned philosopher of antiquity? The vast supply of dubious evidence is itself positive evidence of something. Academics, Isocrateans, and Aristotle

---

[12] It would be revealing to consider the path on which Plato's and Isocrates' students were set in relation to a modern ideal of a disinterested and specialized intellectual profession. It seems that at this period there are both important convergences and important divergences in progress between ancient and modern ideals.

[13] Owen 1983:3. I will have several occasions to cite this article, which is one of very few to have gathered together in one place many of the names that concern me in this chapter. Work on this topic began with the valuable collection of material in Luzac 1809:101–318.

[14] Indeed, Owen's paper on philosophical invective (1983) seems most likely to have grown out of his important earlier work (Owen 1965) questioning the evidence that had been considered to bear on this question, and its interpretation, for he handles our material so as to produce further arguments against the influential account of Jaeger (1948).

[15] Owen 1983:25, emphasis added.

are all seen to pour their energy into rivalries and attacks that are variously personal, political, and professional.

Besides his detailed criticisms of specific pieces of evidence, which will be relevant to my own survey of personalities and entanglements, one of Owen's contributions is his good sense in adapting what is familiar about stock slanders in the context of the works of the orators to the conditions specific to philosophers. In circles where literacy and education are paramount, plagiarism corresponds almost exactly to the charge of common theft that is regularly brought in ordinary disputes between "laymen," while the teacher–pupil relationship is as ripe to be exploited for proxy smears among intellectuals as is the parent-child relationship in the contests fought in the Athenian lawcourts.[16] Owen uses this modest critical toolkit to make some elegant and persuasive refutations.

Owen also invites us to examine the evidence that some fourth-century pamphleteers went far beyond the weak invective of the Middle Comic stage and took up a coordinated program of propagandistic eulogy and vituperation, as in Athenaeus' report (5.220a) that Socrates' followers outdo the comedians in their destructive slander of all opponents.[17] At the same time, he draws a line between rhetorical "calumny and adulation by way of an epideictic exercise" and the more seriously drawn battle lines of the philosophers. From this point of view, Polycrates was a subphilosophical rhetorician, understood aright by Isocrates in the reply of his technical and playful *Busiris* (responding to both Polycrates' earlier encomium of Busiris and his *Accusation of Socrates*), whereas Xenophon displays naïve misjudgment when he responds in serious earnest to the same allegedly playful *Accusation of Socrates*.[18]

This account valuably focuses at the same time on the conjunction of programmatic seriousness and comic-rhetorical touches in the polemics of these overlapping circles of writers, and on the exchange of encomia along tracks running near and parallel to the economy of invective. However, I believe that a better solution to this puzzle is to be found through the hypothesis that all of these writings and confrontations were part of a single serious-and-playful literary culture (at the very least, that some unity of topic and audience held together contemporary prosateurs' treatment of the question of Socrates' guilt). We do not need to seek refuge in the view that a Polycrates and a Xenophon miscommunicate with each other if we are willing to admit that a serious attack can wear a smiling face, and that purely technical display (rhetorical or philosophical) can itself be an effective weapon and assertion of superiority.

[16] Owen 1983:17, 14–16.
[17] Owen 1983:18–21.
[18] On Polycrates, see Livingstone 2001:28–40.

Can we believe that Polycrates' intention had to be misjudged by Xenophon or unusually distorted in its general reception in order for the *jeu* to elicit from Xenophon a response in a supposedly different register? I do not doubt Owen's literary instincts that the manner of confrontation in these sources is often surprisingly distant from political and forensic oratory, and closer to comedy. But this discrepancy should be placed in the context of the generally novel literary and political mores of philosophers and of the various obscure figures on the margins of recognized philosophy. This evolving group may have developed its own specific weapons, whose literary subtlety and deviousness should not cause us to forget that serious struggles (as over the status of Socrates and his legacy) were being fought. It may be helpful to consider the example of Plato himself, whose display of affinities to comedy at moments where he is engaged in serious philosophy and intellectual positioning is generally appreciated. Thus it may not be very useful to treat malice and jest as opposing poles, if so-called comic moments are in reality instances of specialized and subtle form of intellectual contest. The possibility that this mode of argument is a specialized creation within the broadly philosophical genre deserves further study. Moreover, one of Owen's most penetrating observations, if fleshed out, may lend strong support to my account of generic and professional specialization. I refer to the trend in the fourth century wherein invective against philosophers "becomes weak and repetitive and generalized in the comedians in proportion as it becomes ruthless and uninhibited in the pamphlets of the sophists and philosophers themselves." Owen can point to the well-read Athenaeus, who is in concurrence that such philosophers as the early Socratics are more slanderous than the comedians themselves.[19] I suggest that, as attacks and controversies are increasingly concentrated within the broadly philosophical profession, we must be more receptive to the special generic forms of intercourse that accompany the demonstrable formation of a more specialized space of discourse. A further result of these considerations is that Owen's working distinction between the "philosophers" and the "pamphleteers" may not be tenable.

Whose voices were heard in the arena we wish to describe? Let us begin with Plato's students, Isocrates' students (and we must include Isocrates himself because of his remarkable longevity), their antagonists, allies, and patrons. This group is remarkable for its size and its lack of resemblance to the cast of characters that feature in the history of philosophy or any other recognized discipline.

The nucleus of this group—meaning not necessarily the most influential actors, but the ones whose recorded actions and publications give us the clearest picture of controversy and competition, while also allowing us to draw

---

[19]   Owen 1983:19. Athenaeus 5.220a.

lines of personal connection that cross and multiply more prolifically than with others—includes Plato's students Speusippus and Aristotle, and Isocrates' students Cephisodorus and Theopompus. Still closely linked to this center are such figures as the Academic Euphraeus, Aristotle's associate Hermias of Atarneus, and Eubulides of the Megarian school.[20] As we branch farther out, we will consider some of the minor orators and sophists with connections to Theopompus, and Isocrates' other famous historian-student, Ephorus. The majority of these persons led careers that were subjected to the direct influence of Philip and the Macedonian court, a factor that will be impossible for us to ignore.

Theopompus

The historians Theopompus of Chios and Ephorus of Cyme are said not only to have been Isocrates' students,[21] but to have received decisive guidance from him in their literary careers. This would have applied to both the subject matter of their histories,[22] and the marshaling of their intellectual energies according to their differing natures—the oft-repeated *discunt, alter, uti dixit Isocrates in Ephoro et Theopompo, frenis eget, alter calcaribus.*[23] This ancient tradition, together with a distinctly modern exclusive conception of these alleged students as writers of history, has created a literary bias, so that scholarly discussion is dominated by the question of whether there was a "school of rhetorical history" represented by Ephorus and Theopompus.[24]

My purpose in this section is not to examine again the evidence of "rhetorical history" in the pages of Ephorus and Theopompus, and then to ask again whether the literary influence that was apparent to so many ancient readers[25] implies personal contact and rhetorical training. Rather, in the context of the evidence we have already reviewed for the interpersonal and interscholastic

---

[20] On Eubulides, see Aristocles F 2 Chiesara 2001 = T 58f Düring 1957, Ford 2011:63–65.

[21] See the sources gathered at FGrHist 115 T 5 and 70 T 3. Interesting among the former is the *Suda's* reference (s.v. Δημοσθένης, δ 454 = T 5b) to "Theopompus the Chian philosopher," which makes Jacoby remark, "auch φιλόσοφος merkwürdig" (*ad loc.*). For a wider overview of the ancient traditions concerning Isocrates' students, see Engels 2003.

[22] Cicero *De oratore* 2.57, Photius *Library* 176.121a27–34. The latter passage (and it alone from the first three quarters of Photius' account of Theopompus) is not in FGrHist, even though it continues the same indirect speech included as T 5a (φασί, 121a23).

[23] Cicero *Letters to Atticus* VI 1.12, cf. Quintilian *Training for Oratory* 2.8.10 and *Suda*, s.v. Ἔφορος, ε 3953.

[24] Those who have rejected the teacher–pupil relationship include Schwartz (1907) and Flower (1994); those who accept it include Kalischek (1913), Barber (1993 [1935]), Shrimpton (1991), and Bollansée (1998:149).

[25] N.B. that modern scholars who argue against putting the historians in Isocrates' school without exception claim that manifest stylistic similarities are at the root of the biographical tradition.

relations of other alleged Isocrateans, I wish to focus on whether the historians show an awareness of, and a need to be involved in, a rivalry with those in schools of philosophy (especially the Academy). The modern construct "rhetorical history" focuses our attention on Ephorus and Theopompus' methods and styles as historians rather than on what evidence exists that the two "historians" may have been much more typically "Isocratean" in aspects of their writing and lives that have little or nothing to do with historiography—especially Theopompus' involvement in scholastic polemics. It is notable that the idea of rhetorical education attributed to Isocrates' school in studies of Theopompus and Ephorus is extremely conventional, with little emphasis on the claim Isocrates lays to a political *philosophia* or on his students' close ties with acknowledged sophists and philosophers. The appropriateness of substituting a test of "philosophical" awareness for a rhetorical litmus test can be illustrated as follows. Martin Ostwald and John Lynch, in their excellent survey of "The Growth of Schools" for the *Cambridge Ancient History*, declare that "it is difficult to detect Isocrates behind the rambling discussions of Sicily, of a utopian myth ascribed to Silenus, of Zoroastrianism, of Athenian demagogues" that we find in Theopompus' *Philippica*.[26] This has the sound of reason—but what if we substituted Plato for "Isocrates"? Few would then deny that, indeed, perhaps the topics of discussion at the Academy left their mark, still visible, in the fragments of the *Philippica*.[27] These topics could fit into the ambitions of an Isocratean, not *qua* historian, but as a denizen of the interconnected, polymath scholastic world.[28] We have already taken some notice of one of the strongest indications of this interconnection—Speusippus' concern with Theopompus'

---

[26] Ostwald and Lynch 1994:601.

[27] One specific example of topical convergence between Academic dialogue and Theopompan *muthos* (see Strabo 1.2.35 = FGrHist 115 F 381 for Theopompus' candid embrace of the way *muthoi* are deployed in his history) is the extraordinary *muthos* of the Μεροπὶς γῆ told by Silenus to Midas in book 8 of the *Philippica* (FF 74–75, cf. Brown 1955, Ferguson 1975:122f., Aalders 1978, Romm 1996:134f.). Theopompus deploys the myth as a very general meditation on the unlikely happy fulfillment of human life, and it is in this same guise, with altogether different details, that Aristotle presented the Silenus–Midas encounter in his *Eudemus* (fr. 44 R³, cf. Jaeger 1948:48f.). We may compare the significance of this to the common use of *topos* and *paradeigmata* in Isocrates' *Philip*, Speusippus' *Letter to Philip*, and Aristotle's *Rhetoric*.

[28] The unusual range of subject matter handled by Theopompus in his *Philippica* and minor works has led some scholars who were unimpressed with the explanatory power of the Isocrates tradition to draw the portrait of a Cynic historian under the guidance of Antisthenes (upon whom, alone of all the Socratics, the notoriously and unsparingly bitter Theopompus bestowed his rare praise, FGrHist 115 F 295 = Diogenes Laertius 6.14): see e.g. Hirzel 1892, Murray 1946, and Flower 1994:94–97. That such a construction has been found tempting in the absence of any reliable ancient testimony perhaps speaks to the perceived inadequacy of placing Theopompus' literary career in so seemingly unremarkable an intellectual context as the fourth-century rhetorical manner.

anti-Plato slanders in the course of the *Letter to Philip*'s extended assault on Isocrates.[29] But before discussing the historian's attitude towards the Academics we will review his links to the Isocrateans.

Theopompus' relations with Theodectes and Theocritus—neither primarily a historiographer, and the former not at all—are a good example of a connection to the Isocratean circle that occurs outside the circle of "rhetorical history." It will be recalled that Theodectes—variously called tragedian, orator, and sophist—was, together with Theopompus, one of the several Isocrateans who competed at Mausolus' funeral. We may add to this that Theopompus himself wrote about Isocrates and Theodectes together, stating that they both were logographers and teachers for pay.[30] Significantly, in both of these testimonia there is a hint of rivalry between Theopompus and his putative schoolmates, something that is paralleled in the traditions about Theocritus and also in Theopompus' relations with his political patron Alexander. At their worst, these tensions never approach the vehemence of the historian's passionate hatred of anything Platonic, but they are an interesting subphenomenon in their own right. The link between Theopompus and Theodectes is mainly circumstantial— to be accepted and analyzed only on the basis of the evidence for Theopompus' better-attested relations with others in the same circle—and it is as such that I present it here.

The case of Theocritus of Chios is more complex and more interesting. Our main interest in Theocritus in the following chapter will be as an attacker of Hermias, and this is something he has in common with Theopompus, as we will see shortly in our discussion of the abuses of Hermias addressed to Philip by the historian. Their togetherness on this point, however, did not keep Theopompus from abusing his fellow Chian[31] in his *Advice to Alexander*, quoted by Athenaeus. The target is Theocritus' rise to a luxurious standard of living—now he drinks from gold and silver instead of from chipped ceramic.[32] It is interesting to compare the attacks on Harpalus also included in his *Letter to Alexander* or *On the Chian Letters* (FF 253–254), as they demonstrate that in Theopompus' claims on

---

[29] Speusippus' *Letter to Philip* will be discussed in detail in the following chapter.

[30] FGrHist 115 F 25 = Photius *Library* 176.120b35–37: ἀλλὰ Ἰσοκράτην μὲν δι᾽ ἀπορίαν βίου καὶ Θεοδέκτην μισθοῦ λόγους γράφειν καὶ σοφιστεύειν, ἐκπαιδεύοντας τοὺς νέους κἀκεῖθεν καρπουμένους τὰς ὠφελείας.

[31] For the possible import of Theopompus' fellow Chians as his rivals, cf. *Suda*, s.v. Ἔφορος, ε 3953 = T 8: φυγὰς δὲ γενόμενος ὁ Θεόπομπος ἱκέτης ἐγένετο τῆς Ἐφεσίας Ἀρτέμιδος· ἐπέστειλέ τε πολλὰ κατὰ Χίων Ἀλεξάνδρῳ.

[32] Θεόπομπος δ᾽ ὁ Χῖος ἐν ταῖς Πρὸς Ἀλέξανδρον συμβουλαῖς περὶ Θεοκρίτου τοῦ πολίτου τὸν λόγον ποιούμενός φησιν· "ἐξ ἀργυρωμάτων δὲ καὶ χρυσῶν πίνει καὶ τοῖς σκεύεσιν χρῆται τοῖς ἐπὶ τῆς τραπέζης ἑτέροις τοιούτοις, ὁ πρότερον οὐχ ὅπως ἐξ ἀργυρωμάτων [οὐκ] ἔχων πίνειν ἀλλ᾽ οὐδὲ χαλκῶν, ἀλλ᾽ ἐκ κεραμέων καὶ τούτων ἐνίοτε κολοβῶν" (F 252).

Alexander's attention, slights to an orator, historian, and polemicist not unlike himself held the same currency as lurid accounts of the powerful Macedonian insider and treasurer's decadence. For this, we may think of the concoction of political propaganda and scholastic polemics in Speusippus' *Letter to Philip*, but in Theopompus' case the relations with powerful political figures are more definite and significant than in Speusippus' case.

The mere fact that such men as Theodectes and Theocritus are on Theopompus' mind constitutes a stronger connection to Isocrateanism than the misguided quest to discover Isocrates' "views" in Theopompus' history. Besides the inherent difficulties in establishing which of the Athenian schoolmaster's perspectives on the world we would use for such a comparison, there is the larger problem that Theopompus' greatest proximity to the Isocratean circle occurs when he is pursuing the polemical strategies that place him on the far side of a generational divide from Isocrates. The danger of false comparisons is especially acute when it comes to "political views," that traditional criterion of factional affiliation. For example, there is little about the Isocratean variant of Panhellenism, which had been addressed in part to Athenians before Chaeronea, that would not inevitably be lost in the Theopompan translation.[33] Indeed, the same divide that separated Isocrates' *Philip* from the Speusippean response to it, in which Theopompus was attacked, also separates Isocrates' "politics" from the "political" activities of his younger associates. The term "political" is used with caution here, since it has to be stretched to cover something like relations with monarchs in general. If Theopompus' Macedonian politics have decisively departed from the strategies of Isocrates' *Philip*, they are so much more distant from earlier Isocratean flirtations with kings. Contrast, for example, the idealized son of Sparta's ruling Eurypontid king fictively made to speak in *Archidamus* (ca. 366 BC) with the *akrasia*-afflicted Archidamus whom we encounter in Theopompus' *Philippica* (FF 232–233, 312). Or consider how all the advice dispensed to the young monarch in Isocrates' *To Nicocles*—concerning how to stay free from pleasure's spell—is vividly shown as scorned and forgotten by the monarch at the center of the *Philippica*.[34]

The engagement with monarchs by Plato, Xenophon, and Isocrates' generation, even when it tempts us to regard it as "really" political, kept much of its idealistic, or at least symbuleutic, character. This was simply not viable in the rough-and-tumble new philosophical politics. This change in the weather had more to do with the progress of history than with one's scholastic affiliation. What was (at worst) a détente between Plato and Isocrates themselves was

---

[33]   Nevertheless, this kind of Isocratean influence has been argued to exist, providing in turn a basis for disputing such allegations (e.g. Flower 1994:44f. and esp. 83–90).

[34]   Cf. Flower 1994:90.

supplanted by a virulent struggle that aroused no less passion in Speusippus than in Theopompus.

Still, the literary comparisons between Isocrates and Theopompus do hold some interest in respect to the particular case of the polemical letters. For example, Jacoby, who was not ready to allow that Theopompus had actually attended Isocrates' school, still felt that the Isocratean epistles provided the most relevant antecedent to the form of Theopompus' missives to Philip and Alexander,[35] in which are found his attacks on both Theocritus and Hermias.

Theopompus' attacks on Hermias and on Plato himself are by far the strongest evidence available for how invested he was in the status game played in philosophical circles (which, in turn, is the strongest evidence for the truth of his association with Isocrates). Didymus quotes, on the side of those who speak against Hermias, the *Letter to Philip* of Theopompus:

ὁ δ' α[ὐτὸς ἐν τῆι Πρ]ὸς Φί[λιππον ἐπ]ιστολῆι καὶ ἣν π[αρεσκεύαστο (sc. Ἑρμείας) π]αρ[ὰ τοῖς] Ἕλλησι δόξαν ἱστορε[ῖ . . . .]ρ[. . . . .]λως δὲ χαρίεις καὶ φιλ[όμουσ]ος γεγ[ον]ώς· καὶ [βάρβ]αρος μὲν ὢν μετὰ τῶν Π[λατ]ωνείων [φ]ιλο[σο]φεῖ, δοῦλος δὲ γενόμενος ἀδηφάγοις ζεύγεσιν ἐν ταῖς πανηγύρεσιν ἀγωνίζεται, σκοπέλους δὲ [καὶ] μικρ[ὰ χωρί]α κεκτημένος ἔτυχε μὲν τῆς [τ(ῶν)] εὐέκ[τ(ων) δόξ(ης), τ(ὴν)] δὲ πόλιν τὴν Ἠλ<ε>ίων ἐπ[αγγέλλ]ειν [πρὸς αὐτὸν τὴν] ἐκεχειρία[ν] ἔ[π]εισ[εν . . . .]·

The s[ame author in his l]etter [t]o Phi[lip] also writes about the reputation [he (Hermias) had cultivated with t]he Greeks. [Though he was a eunuch, he behaved like] a man of innate cul[tivati]on and grace. [Barb] arian though he is, he philosophizes with the P[lat]onists; and though he has become a slave in the bonds of gluttony, he competes at the sacred festivals. He has acquired some headlands [and] tiny [regions] and has won the esteem of [the] bodily fit. So he persuaded (?) the city of Elis to an[nounce the] cessation of hostilities [with him] ... [presumably with a view to competing in the Olympic games].

> *Commentary on Demosthenes* col. 5.21ff. = F 250
> (trans. Shrimpton 1991:270f.)

This present-tense denunciation would seem to be motivated by a desire on Theopompus' part to counter the standing of Hermias and his circle at court—a desire that is directly and obviously comparable with the aim of the

---

[35] "The letters should be put beside Isocrates' circular letters. The comparison, to the extent that it is possible, is of great interest for Theopompus' manner" (FGrHist II D, p. 390, ad 115 FF 250–254).

Academic Speusippus' words against Theopompus in his *Letter to Philip*. Given that Theopompus is elsewhere quoted as attacking not only Hermias,[36] but also Plato (see below), the tyrant's Academic philosophizing must be more than just another civilized pursuit of which he is unworthy. Indeed, the best way to read this line is in precisely the manner I will suggest below for Theocritus' poetic assault on Aristotle's departure from the Academy. Though Theopompus' βάρβαρος μὲν ὤν is concessive, it still insinuates that the Academy's standards must not actually be as incompatible with such a creature as Hermias is alleged to be. Bertelli recognized this:

> The disparaging intention expressed through the antithesis is, in my view, also evident in βάρβαρος μὲν ὢν μετὰ τῶν Πλατωνείων φιλοσοφεῖ. Only that in this case the polemic's objective is double: it is not limited to Hermias alone but also involves the milieu of the Academy, as if Theopompus wished to say that Plato's school admitted even barbarians to its teaching.[37]

Elsewhere in Theopompus' surviving words, his opposition to the *Platōneioi* is not indicated so indirectly. Platonic thinking is not only a laughable indulgence for a barbarian, it is wrong and worth writing against. Athenaeus quotes from a book by Theopompus entitled *Against the Diatribē of Plato*,[38] where we may understand *diatribē* to mean "discourse" or even "dialogue style" (a sense in which it is used in the quoted text), "school" (quite likely), or "philosophical activity" in general:

> καὶ γὰρ Θεόπομπος ὁ Χῖος ἐν τῷ Κατὰ τῆς Πλάτωνος διατριβῆς "τοὺς πολλούς" φησί "τῶν διαλόγων αὐτοῦ ἀχρείους καὶ ψευδεῖς ἄν τις εὕροι, ἀλλοτρίους δὲ τοὺς πλείους, ὄντας ἐκ τῶν Ἀριστίππου διατριβῶν,

---

[36] See F 291, Didymus' quotation from Theopompus' *Pros Philippon*, which (as Shrimpton says) sounds more like an obituary: "Hermias set out on this path a eunuch and a Bithynian by race (or: disfigured in appearance) [short gap] thirdly [gap], with Eubulus he took Assos and its tower and Atarneus and its environs. Of all people this man accomplished the most violent and wicked things against all, both its citizens and others, doing away with some by poisoning and others by the noose. When the Chians and Mytilenaeans put him in charge of some land over which they were disputing, he played many drunken tricks with unpaid military expeditions and grievously insulted most of the Ionians. A money-grubber and money-changer, he did not hold his peace when the Chians fell into misfortune [large gap] to restore their established constitutions. However, he did not altogether escape nor get off with his impious and disgusting manners, but he was arrested and sent to the King where he was extensively tortured and ended his life in crucifixion" (trans. Shrimpton 1991:125f., following the text of Pearson and Stephens 1983:13ff.).

[37] Bertelli 1997:96.

[38] For this work, under a slightly different title, see also Theopompus, FGrHist 115 T 48 (list of titles from Rhodes, ca. 100 BC): Καταδρομὴ τῆ[ς Πλάτωνος] διατριβῆ[ς].

ἐνίους δὲ κἀκ τῶν Ἀντισθένους, πολλοὺς δὲ κἀκ τῶν Βρύσωνος τοῦ Ἡρακλεώτου."

For Theopompus of Chios too, in his *Against the Diatribē of Plato*, says, "One would find that the majority of his dialogues are useless and false, and the greater number of them the work of someone else, being from Aristippus' works [*diatribai*], and others from those of Antisthenes, and many from those of Bryson of Heraclea."[39]

F 259 = Athenaeus 11.118c–d

Here the attack is mainly personal, using the stock charge of plagiarism (the intellectual equivalent to common thievery, as above). Even *akhreious kai pseudeis* need not be taken as a negative assessment of what Plato has achieved philosophically in his writings. This is possible, but the sense could also be that Plato has put out books that are "useless and counterfeit" because un-original.

If this fragment, then, is useful for establishing the existence of the book and showing the kind of libelous smear that we would expect to have balanced Speusippus' *Letter to Philip*, other Theopompan material from this book or something in a similar vein shows that occasion did prompt the "historian" to take up philosophical language to claim his position in the scholastic field: "And Theopompus, too, declared for these reasons that the sweet body exists, but not sweetness" (καὶ Θεόπομπος δὲ τὸ μὲν γλυκὺ σῶμα διὰ ταῦτα ἀπεφήνατο συνεστηκέναι, τὴν δὲ γλυκύτητα οὐκέτι, F 359). Here Theopompus judges an opponent's position not as plagiarized drivel, but as not convincingly argued with proper supports (*dia tauta apephēnato*). This is the sort of philosophical testimonium that, if it named Speusippus or Antisthenes instead of Theopompus, would have to be taken seriously as indicating a position on the ontology of abstracts. Moreover, the quotation occurs in Simplicius' commentary on Aristotle's *Categories*,[40] and it seems unlikely that Simplicius would have noticed and preserved the citation if it had come from a gossipy polemic devoid of intellectual interest. In truth, the context we should most likely imagine is, if not an abusive tirade, then perhaps neither a critique with strictly intellectual motivations (one starts to wonder just how common such a thing could have been in Theopompus' time). Rather, the fragments taken together preserve something of the wild mix that was the new philosophical politics.

Something of this hybrid character is more perceptible in another text in which Theopompus names Plato, quoted in Epictetus:

---

[39] For Bryson, compare the discussion of Plato *Epistle* XIII in the previous chapter.
[40] Simplicius *Commentary on Aristotle's Categories*, CAG VIII p. 216.

τὸ δ' ἐξαπατῶν τοὺς πολλοὺς τοῦτ' ἔστιν, ὅπερ καὶ Θεόπομπον τὸν
ῥήτορα, ὅπου καὶ Πλάτωνι ἐγκαλεῖ ἐπὶ τῷ βούλεσθαι ἕκαστα ὁρίζεσθαι.
τί γὰρ λέγει; "οὐδεὶς ἡμῶν πρὸ σοῦ ἔλεγεν ἀγαθὸν ἢ δίκαιον; ἢ
μὴ παρακολουθοῦντες τί ἐστι τούτων ἕκαστον ἀσήμως καὶ κενῶς
<ἐ>φθεγγόμεθα τὰς φωνάς;"

What deceives the many is just what deceives Theopompus the orator in the passage where he charges Plato with wanting to define each
thing. What does he say? "Did none of us say anything good or just
before you? Or, unless we pay [paid] minute attention to what each of
these things is, do [did] we utter sounds emptily and without meaning?"

F 275 = *Dissertationes ab Arriano digestae* 2.17.5
(trans. Shrimpton 1991:254)

The reference to Theopompus as a *rhētōr*, and the fact that he is lumped in with
hoi polloi, may show some skepticism about Theopompus' credentials for making
this criticism. But the protestation regarding the danger that the forest will be
lost for quibbling over the trees, although somewhat commonsensical, is not
invalid and can certainly be paralleled in the interlocutors of Socrates in Plato's
dialogues (e.g. *Protagoras*). More to the point, what Theopompus says here is
certainly not the smear of a polemicist in a hurry to say whatever will most hurt
Plato's image in the eyes of those outside the specialized scholastic universe.
Rather, if it has any bite at all, it is only for the audience of those who know what
Plato says in his books and care whether it is right or wrong (out of a love for
knowledge or from jealous rivalry—and the two motives need not be segregated
from each other).

  Of course, from everything that we know about Theopompus, we expect
anything he had to say about Plato to have had a political edge, however often
his statements may have employed the manner of philosophical argumentation instead of philosophical polemics. We will see in the following chapter that
Theopompus was also the source for the testimonium that Plato was honored at
his death (or rebuked, following an alternative translation) by Philip.[41] Whatever
the sense of this text, it should be unsurprising that Theopompus commented
not only on the philosopher's ideas, but on his relations with the Macedonian
court. It should also be unsurprising that Plato's standing among the Socratics
mattered to Theopompus, and not only his standing with politicians (though it is
always possible that the former was taken up in a polemic that bore on the latter,
given the complexity of scholastic rivalry vis-à-vis the field of political power).

---

[41] Diogenes Laertius 3.40 = F 294.

This is reconfirmed by the terms in which Diogenes Laertius cites Theopompus' praise of Antisthenes.[42] As noted above, the personal-sounding touch of the philosopher's "leading anyone along with harmonious companionship"[43] has inspired ideas of a Cynic Theopompus. The decisive counterargument to this is the prosopography of Theopompus' references to the world of philosophers, so rich in Isocrateans and Academics, to the virtual exclusion of all others.

When it came to the political game, Theopompus' high-stakes polemics and high-risk literary style seem to have left him dangerously on both sides of the all-important pole of the political world, the Macedonian court. This corroborates our sense from other sources of the position of a participant in scholastic polemics. The prospect of disfavor was very real because the battles were vigorously contested on both sides, as we can see by juxtaposing Theopompus' addresses to Philip and Alexander, on the one hand, and Speusippus' *Letter to Philip* and the fact of Aristotle's great success at Macedon, on the other hand. Thus Theopompus' mixed bag of relations with both Philip and Alexander makes sense if we consider it apart from the assumptions of conventional factional politics.

The most obvious aspect of this political "inconsistency" was already to Polybius a cause for complaint.[44] This is the obvious dissonance between the statement in the proem of the *Philippica* that Theopompus was impelled to write his history "because Europe has never at all produced such a man as Philip son of Amyntas" (F 27) and the subsequent depiction of the same man in the lowest possible terms.[45] We may add that Philip's promise is clearly celebrated in a surviving fragment of Theopompus' *Encomium of Philip*.[46] Likewise, we may suspect that it was not an irresistible urge towards impolitic honesty that made

---

[42] τοῦτον (sc. Ἀντισθένη) μόνον ἐκ πάντων Σωκρατικῶν Θεόπομπος ἐπαινεῖ καί φησι δεινόν τε εἶναι καὶ δι' ὁμιλίας ἐμμελοῦς ὑπαγαγέσθαι πάνθ' ὁντινοῦν (Diogenes Laertius 6.14 = F 295).

[43] Or perhaps "with his elegant conversation," as Shrimpton 1991:257.

[44] Polybius 8.8–11 = T 19, cf. Hammond and Griffith 1979:275n1.

[45] In the characterization of Shrimpton (1991:206): "Immediately after that [=F27], in his proem and throughout the entire history, he depicts him as a most uncontrolled woman-chaser, to the point of destroying his own household, as far as he could, through his impulsive predilection for that sort of thing; and, moreover, as a most unjust man and thorough mischief-maker in the manipulation of friends and allies; as the enslaver of a great number of cities, deceiving them with treachery and force; and as an impassioned alcoholic, so as frequently to be seen by his friends obviously drunk even in the day-time."

[46] ὡς Θεόπομπος ἐν τῷ Φιλίππου ἐγκωμίῳ, ὅτι εἰ βουληθείη Φίλιππος τοῖς αὐτοῖς ἐπιτηδεύμασιν ἐμμεῖναι, καὶ τῆς Εὐρώπης πάσης βασιλεύσει (Theon *Progymnasmata* 8 = F 256). Here I am considering Theopompus' literary handling of the person Philip; for his broader political orientation, it is enough to see how Plutarch must constantly defend his sympathetic portrait in his *Life of Demosthenes* against Theopompus' analysis.

Theopompus write harshly about Mausolus, at whose funeral he had delivered the prize-winning oration.[47]

The situation with Alexander, from whom Theopompus evidently enjoyed some strong support, is equally ambivalent in the end. The *Suda* entry on Ephorus, after mentioning Theopompus' exile and many letters to Alexander against the Chians, goes on to mention both encomia and invective (*psogos*) directed at Alexander.[48] The existence of the encomia is attested elsewhere,[49] but this is the only source for a work dedicated to the rebuke of Alexander (no longer extant in the time of the compiler). The pattern Theopompus followed with Philip and Mausolus suggests that there may be some truth behind this testimonium. In any case, the true situation may have been less simple than that "Theopompus was a political supporter and, one might even say, an agent of Alexander."[50]

Ephorus

Theopompus' exuberant polemics illustrate one of the many layers of truth in the *ben trovato* tradition that Isocrates thought he needed the reins while Ephorus required the goad. Indeed, for all Ephorus' fame, our traditions do not tell of his virulent attacks on his fellow writers. Perhaps this should restrain our tendency to believe that late writers invented scandalous stories willy-nilly about all the authors they read. One instance of the thematic and verbal connections between Ephorus and Isocrates is, however, worth reviewing briefly here.

Strabo transmits a passage from Ephorus' treatment of Zaleucus' legislation for Archaic Locri.[51] This passage figured in the earlier dispute about Isocrates' influence, with Niese proposing, and Jacoby denying, that Ephorus' inclusion of *Areopagitika nomima* as sources for Zaleucus' legislation in addition to the classical *Krētika* and *Lakonika* clearly links this passage to Isocrates' *Areopagiticus*. In the fragment of Ephorus, the Thurians misguidedly make the wise lawgiver's simple and flexible code the object of an effort to achieve exactitude (*akriboun*). This recalls the passage in Isocrates' *Areopagiticus* (39–43) in which the venerable Areopagus, in its care for good order (*eutaxia*), despises the ignorance of

---

47 φησὶ δὲ αὐτὸν (sc. Μαύσωλον) Θεόπομπος μηδενὸς ἀπέχεσθαι πράγματος χρημάτων ἕνεκα (*Suda*, s.v. Μαύσωλος, μ 299 = F 299).

48 καὶ μέντοι καὶ αὐτὸν Ἀλέξανδρον ἐγκωμιάσας πολλά. λέγεται δὲ καὶ ψόγον αὐτοῦ γεγραφέναι, ὃς οὐ φέρεται (*Suda*, ε 3953 = T 8).

49 ἔχομεν ... καὶ Θεοπόμπου τὸ Φιλίππου ἐγκώμιον καὶ Ἀλεξάνδρου (Theon *Progymnasmata* 2 = F 255/257).

50 Flower 1994:23; at 23–25 material from the same context in the *Suda* is used to support this depiction without mention of the *psogos*.

51 Strabo 6.1.8 = FGrHist 70 F 139.

those who imagine that men turn out most perfect where the laws have the greatest *akribeia*.[52]

This passage from Isocrates' political program, whose discussion of legislation Ephorus seems to have had in mind, is full of language remarkably suggestive of Isocratean educational theory. Laws work by practices and character dispositions (*epitēdeumata* and *ēthē*), and lawfulness resides in the soul (*psukhē*). Most impressively, Isocrates fixates on the term *grammata* (used to describe the errors inherent in sophistic education, which applies the model of the *epistēmē* of *grammata* to the *epistēmē* of *logoi*, *Against the Sophists* 10), repeating it four times in reference to the educative mechanism that is *not* effective in establishing *eutaxia*.[53]

The value of these connections is increased by the fact that the question of the role of legislation in political theory and practice was one on which Isocrates had expressed contrarian (minimizing) views that in turn were rejected in Aristotelian theory.[54] The topic thus stands out as the subject of active debate in the scholastic circles we have been describing.

---

[52] Niese 1909, FGrHist II C, p. 77, lines 25–32, ad 70 FF 138–139. Besides Ephorus' invocation of *Areopagitika*, his εὐνομεῖσθαι ... τοὺς ἐμμένοντας τοῖς ἁπλῶς κειμένοις is strikingly parallel to Isocrates *Areopagiticus* 41, τοὺς δὲ καλῶς πεπαιδευμένους καὶ τοῖς ἁπλῶς κειμένοις ἐθελήσειν ἐμμένειν.

[53] οὐδὲν γὰρ ἂν κωλύειν ὁμοίοις ἅπαντας εἶναι τοὺς Ἕλληνας ἕνεκά γε τοῦ ῥᾴδιον εἶναι τὰ γράμματα λαβεῖν παρ' ἀλλήλων, 39; ἀλλὰ γὰρ οὐκ ἐκ τούτων [= τῶν γραμμάτων] τὴν ἐπίδοσιν εἶναι τῆς ἀρετῆς, ἀλλ' ἐκ τῶν καθ' ἑκάστην τὴν ἡμέραν ἐπιτηδευμάτων, 40; δεῖν δὲ τοὺς ὀρθῶς ποιλτευομένους οὐ τὰς στοὰς ἐμπιπλάναι γραμμάτων, ἀλλ' ἐν ταῖς ψυχαῖς ἔχειν τὸ δίκαιον, 41; καὶ τοὺς κακῶς τεθραμμένους καὶ τοὺς ἀκριβῶς τῶν νόμων ἀναγεγραμμένους τολμήσειν παραβαίνειν, ibid.

[54] Brunt 1993:286f.

Speusippus' *Letter to Philip*

Epistula Socratica 30 Hercher, ed. Bickermann and
Sykutris 1928

A COMPLETE TRANSLATION OF THIS TEXT is offered here, since frequent
reference will be made to it in the following chapter.

[1] Antipater, the bearer of this letter, is a Magnesian by birth, but he
has been writing his *Greek History* at Athens for some time, and he says
that he is being done wrong by someone in Magnesia. So hear this
matter out from him, and help him as zealously as you are able. There
are many reasons why you would do right to help him, and in particular because when the discourse sent to you by Isocrates was read out
among us in school [*en diatribēi*] he praised the subject it proposed [*tēn
hupothesin*] but laid to its charge its omission of the benefits [*euerge-
sias*] you and your family have brought about for Greece. I will attempt
to speak of a few of these.[1] [2] For Isocrates, in contrast, has neither
set forth the benefits you and your ancestors have brought about for
Greece, nor dispelled the false accusations made against you by some,
nor kept away from Plato in the discourses he has addressed to you.

And yet, in the first place, your friendship towards our city ought
not to have escaped his attention, but rather he ought to have made it
conspicuous to your descendants as well. For Heracles, since we had
a law in ancient times that no foreigner be initiated into the myster-
ies, wishing to be initiated, became Pylius' adopted son. [3] This being
so, Isocrates could have addressed his discourses as to a fellow citizen,
since your family's descent is from Heracles. In the next place, he ought

---

[1]   I.e. the benefits (feminine), not the criticisms (Natoli).

to have made known the benefits brought about for Greece by your ancestor Alexander and by your other ancestors. But in fact he has kept silent about them as if they were unspeakable misfortunes. For when Xerxes sent ambassadors to Greece asking for earth and water, Alexander killed the ambassadors; later when the barbarians advanced in arms, the Greeks faced them at Macedonian Heracleum; and when Alexander revealed to the Greeks the treachery of Aleuas and the Thessalians, the Greeks withdrew and were saved because of Alexander. [4] And yet these benefits ought to have been mentioned not only by Herodotus and Damastes, but also by him who declares in his *tekhnai* that his hearers must be well disposed towards you because of [your ancestor the benefactor of Greece].[2] It would have been fitting to have set forth also the benefit done at Plataea in the time of Mardonius and that great series of benefits done by your ancestors. For in this way the discourse written about you would have gained the goodwill of the Greeks rather than saying nothing good about your family's kingdom. And discoursing about ancient matters would be proper to Isocrates' old age, whereas discoursing rhythmically, as he himself says,[3] belongs to a speaker's purpose in its prime.

[5] Furthermore, it would have been possible for him to dispel the false accusations made largely by the Olynthians. For who would consider you so simpleminded as to begin a war against the Olynthians at a time when Illyrians and Thracians, and the Athenians and Spartans and other Greeks and barbarians besides, were making war on you? I

---

[2] In the corrupt τησασιν πρόγονον ητους, there is certainly some reference to Isocrates *Philip* 76f., which declares how unseemly and provocative it would be to accuse Philip of plotting against those whom his ancestor Heracles chose to benefit at risk to himself (ἁπάσης τῆς Ἑλλάδος εὐεργέτης ... ὁ πρόγονος αὐτοῦ προείλετο κινδυνεύειν ... τὴν μὲν εὔνοιαν, ἣν ἐκεῖνος κατέλιπεν τοῖς ἐξ αὐτοῦ γεγενημένοις). I would rather see εὐεργέτους in ητους than Sykutris's suggestion ἤθους (*in apparatu*). The use of *tekhnai* in reference to Isocrates' epidictic political oration is striking and exemplifies the intellectual terms of engagement I emphasize in my interpretation of Speusippus' letter. Compare the use in §10, in more straightforward reference to Isocrates' (traduced) standards of rhetorical propriety, and Too 1995:166f. and Natoli 2004:144.

[3] Speusippus seems to refer directly not only to Isocrates *Philip* 10, but also to *Philip* 27, in which Isocrates says he has not adorned his discourse with the *eurhuthmiai* and *poikiliai* he would have used when younger, blaming his old age (*hēlikia* as here) and claiming it is fitting in any case for Philip to devote his attention to just the facts (*praxeis*). This may also be taken to support Dobree's emendation εὐρύθμως for εὐρυθαλῶς/εὐθαλῶς (MSS). *Against the Sophists* 16f., with its assertion that the speaker's intelligent composition of the forms (*ideai*) of speech and subsequent rhythmic performance of the result (εὐρύθμως καὶ μουσικῶς εἰπεῖν) is the work of a brave and imaginatively conjecturing soul (ἀνδρικῆς καὶ δοξαστικῆς ἔργον), also deserves close comparison, especially given the possible echo of it in Plato *Gorgias* 463a6–8 (cf. Dodds *ad loc.*, Hutchinson 1988:29f.). Cf. Natoli 2004:122.

needn't go on at length about this in a letter to you; but the things that the common run of speakers do not find it in their way to say,[4] and which have been passed over in silence by everyone for a long time, but which it is to your advantage to learn, I think that I will tell forth and will claim the reward of these good tidings, a just return of the favor, to be given from you to Antipater. For concerning the country that came to be the Olynthians', the bearer of this letter is the first and only to have told trustworthy stories [*muthous*][5] showing that in ancient times it belonged not to the Chalcidians but to the sons of Heracles. [6] For he says that Neleus in Messene and Syleus around the region of Amphipolis were both in like manner killed by Heracles as being violent men, and that Messene was given to Neleus' son Nestor to keep in trust, and the country of Phyllis to Syleus' brother Dicaeus, and that many generations later Cresphontes recovered Messene, whereas the country of Amphipolis, although it belonged to the Heraclidae, was taken by the Athenians and Chalcidians. And he says that in just this way, as wrongdoers and lawbreakers, Hippocoon was killed while tyrant in Sparta, and Alcyoneus in Pallene, and that Sparta was entrusted to the keeping of Tyndareus, and Potidaea and the rest of Pallene to Sitho the son of Posidon, and that during the restorations of the Heraclidae the sons of Aristodemus recovered Laconia, and the Eretrians, the Corinthians, and the Achaeans returning from Troy took possession of Pallene, although it belonged to the Heraclidae. [7] And he makes known how likewise Heracles killed the tyrants Tmolus and Telegonus, the sons of Proteus, around the country of Torone, and, when he had killed Clides and his sons around Ambracia, how he assigned the country of Torone to the guardianship of Aristomachus the son of Sitho, a country which the Chalcidians colonized although it belongs to you and yours; and how

---

[4]   Sykutris's translation accepts a more usual meaning for *empodōn* ("But what can be told to anyone, and yet has been passed over ..."), followed by Pina Polo and Panzram (2001:360), but (1) the word order *estin ouk empodōn* (as opposed to *ouk estin empodōn*) would be extremely unusual for "there is no obstacle"; (2) it is quite a strain to take the following *te* adversatively; and (3) it would be strange to tout how Antipater will be the "first and only" from whom Philip can "learn" what is commonly available knowledge. Natoli (2004:124) agrees with the general thrust of this interpretation, citing Harder 1930:251 in agreement. Compare Euripides *Phoenician Woman* 706 (ἃ δ' ἐμποδὼν μάλιστα, ταῦθ' ἥκω φράσων).

[5]   Of the *muthoi* offered to Philip in this letter, Nilsson (1951:105) remarks, "These tales are certainly invented by Antipatros, for they are not mentioned elsewhere. This letter is unusually full of references to myths, some of them are bold inventions, one invented for the purpose of giving reasons for an enterprise which failed. This is an extreme and most flagrant instance of the use and abuse of mythology for political propaganda. The author knew it, for finishing his account of the myths he says that they may be useful for Philip's power."

he put the country of Ambracia in the hands of Ladices and Charattes, with the requirement to return to his own descendants what was given in trust. Furthermore, all Macedonians know Alexander's recent acquisitions of the land of the Edoni. [8] And these are not the excuses of Isocrates, or a mere noisy sounding of names, but discourses with the capacity to benefit your rule.

Since your seriousness about Amphictyonic affairs is clear, I also wanted to point out to you a *muthos* from Antipater, of the way in which the Amphictyons first joined together, and of how, when they were Amphictyons, the Phlegyans were destroyed by Apollo, the Dryopes by Heracles, and the Crisaeans by their fellow Amphictyons. For although these had all been Amphictyons they were deprived of their votes, and others took their votes and gained shares in the union. He asserts that you have imitated the example of some of these and taken the Phocians' two votes from the Amphictyons as the Pythian prize of your Delphic campaign. [9] In this, the man who professes to teach how to speak of what is old in a new way and of what is new in an old way[6] in fact has made no *muthos* [*memutheuke*] either of the ancient deeds, or of those newly ventured in contest by you, or of those that happened in the times between. And indeed he seems not to have heard of some of them, not to know about some, and to have forgotten about others.

[10] In addition, in exhorting you to just actions, the sophist approves and sets forth as an example the exile and restoration of Alcibiades,[7] while omitting the greater and fairer deeds done by your father. For Alcibiades was exiled for impiety and returned to his country after having done it the greatest harm, but Amyntas, when he had been defeated in factional strife over the kingdom, withdrew for a short time and afterwards ruled Macedonia again. Then, Alcibiades went back into exile and ended his life shamefully, whereas your father grew old as king. And he cites to you the monarchy of Dionysius,[8] as if it were befitting for you to imitate not the most serious men, but the most impious, and to become an imitator not of the most just men, but of the worst. And he says in his *tekhnai*[9] that it is fitting to apply examples that are within your family and familiar, but he takes no heed of his *tekhnē* and uses examples from outside that are most shameful and as opposite as can be conceived in relation to his account. [11] And

---

6   Isocrates *Panegyricus* 8.
7   Isocrates *Philip* 58–61.
8   *Philip* 65.
9   *Philip* 113.

yet, in writing such stuff, the most ridiculous thing of all is when he says that he "gracefully fended off" those of his students who found fault with it.[10] Those of his associates who had been defeated, able to say nothing to this despite being in the very prime of rhetorical power, approved so fully of his discourse that they have bestowed on it the first prize for speeches.[11] You may understand in brief compass Isocrates' historical work and learning [*paideia*]: for by their means he makes the Cyrenaeans, who are called Theraeans by everyone, into Spartan colonists,[12] and he has appointed his Pontic student as the successor of his wisdom,[13] than whom you, who have seen many sophists, have not seen one more loathsome.

[12] And I hear that Theopompus is with you, being exceedingly frigid, and that he is slandering Plato, and that as if Plato had not constructed the beginning of your rule during Perdiccas' reign and invariably borne it hardly if anything ungentle or unbrotherly arose between you. In order, then, that Theopompus may cease being uncouth and savage, bid Antipater read out to him his own *Greek History* in comparison [*paranagnōnai*], and Theopompus will recognize that by right he is erased by everyone, while it is unjustly that he receives your generous patronage.

[13] Likewise Isocrates [will recognize the justice of his own erasure], since when he was young he wrote shameful letters against you to the people, with Timotheus, and now that he is old he has omitted, as if from hatred or envy, the majority of the good things that belong to you and yours, and he has sent you a discourse that he was writing at first to Agesilaus, and then, fixing up some small points, hawked to Dionysius, the tyrant of Sicily, and in the third place, deleting some things and adding others, tried to pass off on Alexander of Thessaly, and finally now he has shot it off in his miserly way to you. [14] I wish that the papyrus had enough room to mention the excuses that have been sent to you by him in his discourse. For he says that the peace that had been concluded prevented him from writing a discourse on the subject of Amphipolis,[14] and that later he would offer you personally an

---

[10] *Philip* 22.

[11] *Philip* 23.

[12] *Philip* 5.

[13] See chap. 3 above on the identification of this successor as Isocrates of Apollonia, whose literary output as listed in the *Suda* (*Amphictyonic Speech*, *Protrepticus*, and the work on Philip's *taphos*) corroborates his topicality for Speusippus.

[14] Isocrates *Philip* 7.

explanation concerning Heracles' immortality,[15] and, conceding that he writes rather weakly concerning some things because of his age, he asks for forgiveness,[16] and that you not be astonished if the Pontic [Isocrates of Apollonia], by also reading it in some rather feeble way, makes the discourse "seem more paltry,"[17] and as for the Persian, he says that you yourself know how you will outdo him in generalship.[18] But I don't have enough papyrus to write the rest of his excuses: such a scarcity of papyrus has the King's conquest of Egypt created.

Be well, and, having taken care of Antipater in good speed, send him to us.

---

[15] *Philip* 33.

[16] *Philip* 149.

[17] *Philip* 26f. (cf. ibid. 1, 81), where Isocrates says that by sending the *Philip* as a *written* discourse, he risks the persuasive failure that is always possible without the living speaker's *ēthos* and other contributions, when "someone" reads it "unpersuasively" and "as if ticking off a list." Speusippus (building on his sarcastic point above about the ineptitude of the "flower of rhetoric" in Isocrates' school) willfully finds a reference in this to a particular poor reader, whom he identifies as Isocrates of Apollonia (the teacher's designated successor and thus chosen deputy).

[18] *Philip* 105.

5

Preaching and Patronage
The Intellectual and the King

DO THE ENCOUNTERS OF FOURTH-CENTURY INTELLECTUALS with the field of political power require us to change the terms of our analysis from "scholastic politics" to politics *simpliciter*? Plato, Aristotle, Isocrates, and numerous other Academics and Isocrateans had close dealings with powerful rulers in the Greek world. Yet our evidence for these episodes shows that it was inevitably as intellectuals that they addressed these rulers. Whether doing service, conferring benefit, or attacking rivals, they strove to establish their claims in terms of their philosophico-rhetorical achievements and status. This is true whether we look at the agonistic speeches for politically important individuals (in which the fourth-century's school-adherents took the first steps towards the eventual Greek genre of biography), or at particular philosophers' addresses to rulers (Aristotle to Hermias, Isocrates to Philip, Speusippus to Philip).

The First Obituary Eulogies for Individuals in Their Scholastic Context

> Moreouer, the swete Isocrates exhorteth the kynge Nicocles, whom he instructeth, to leaue behynde him statues and images, that shall represent rather the figure and similitude of his mynde, than the features of his body, signifienge therbye the remembraunce of his actes written in histories.
>
> Elyot *The Boke named the Governour* I.xi

The encomium that traces a life from birth to death claims an unquestioned and seminal place in the history of Greek biography, and Isocrates' foundational importance to the prose genre of such encomia has been recognized in the studies of Momigliano, Pernot, and Sonnabend.[1] However, because of an unjustly narrow and marginalizing understanding of Isocrates' school, its contribution to the development and exploration of the genre's possibilities has not been fully appreciated. In the fourth century, encomia of dead individuals were motivated not only by political considerations and literary ambitions, but equally by scholastic competition over the capital of intellectual authority. A brief survey of the obituary eulogies produced in the years between the death of Evagoras in 374/3 and the death of Philip in 336 will suggest that Isocrates did more than merely setting the stage with his *Evagoras* for Xenophon's *Agesilaus* a few years later. Rather, Isocrates and Isocrateans were responsible for continued and complex contributions to encomiastic commemoration and the other genres into which it was being transformed. Thus, while it is true that these crucial early steps in the history of Greek biography were taken by intellectuals focused on Athens, we must expand the range of those whose works we take into account: not only philosophers with Socratic connections, but also Isocrates and the fragmentary remains of Isocrates' students' works during these years.

Isocrates' *Evagoras*, from approximately 370, is the earliest serious speech that stands on its own as the eulogy of a recently deceased individual.[2] If we seek its closest antecedents in prose, we will find the historians' summing-up portrait sketches: Thucydides on Themistocles and, about contemporary with the *Evagoras*, Xenophon's eulogies of Cyrus and Clearchus in the *Anabasis*.[3] Isocrates himself had produced something in a similar vein much earlier, in the defense of Alcibiades delivered by Alcibiades the Younger in *On the Team of Horses* of ca. 397.[4]

Isocrates as he begins *Evagoras* is quite self-conscious, and self-promotional, of his innovation. Even as he puts his performance in the context of established funeral contests and traditional poetic praise, he insists that he "pursues / things unattempted yet in prose or rhyme":

---

[1] Momigliano 1971; Pernot 1993; Sonnabend 2002. Cf. Velardi 1991:227; Nightingale 1995:93–132; Alexiou 2007:10f.

[2] Wilamowitz-Möllendorff (1900:533f.) points to Aristotle *Rhetoric* I 9, 1368a16f. (where a certain Hippolochus is named as the first subject of *enkōmion*), in order to cast doubt on the agreement otherwise prevailing between the historical record and Isocrates' own claim. Aristotle's contradiction of his rival Isocrates on this point is consistent with my argument about the scholastic environment in which the genre developed; Stuart (1928:94–97) answers Wilamowitz and sees in Aristotle's reference "a covert but deliberate revision of Isocrates' assertion."

[3] For the focus of Herodotus' proto-biographical sketches on historical figures in the East, see Momigliano 1971:35, Murray 2001:40. In *Evagoras* 37f., Isocrates feels it important to establish Evagoras as more to be praised than Cyrus the Great; he does Evagoras this credit through the familiar soul/body (*psukhē/sōma*) opposition.

[4] Pernot 1993:21. See Too 1995: chap. 6, and the thorough study of Gribble (1999:98–148).

Nicocles, as I saw you honor your father's tomb not only by the abundance and beauty of the offerings, but also with dances, songs, and gymnastic contests, and in addition, with competitions involving horses and triremes, leaving no room for anyone to outdo you in these matters, I thought that, if the dead know anything about what occurs here, Evagoras gladly receives these tributes and rejoices in seeing your concern for him and your lavish expenditure, but he would be thankful above all else if someone could give a deserving account of his activities and of the dangers he undertook. ... Expenditures produce none of these things but are (merely) a sign of wealth. Those who participate in music and other contests—some demonstrating their powers, others their skills—gain more recognition for themselves. But a fine speech that recounts Evagoras' deeds would make his excellence ever-remembered among all men. ... As it is, who would not become discouraged when he sees that those who lived at the time of the Trojan War and earlier are celebrated in song and on the tragic stage but realizes that he will never be thought to deserve such praises, not even if he should surpass their virtues? ... particularly as we know that progress in the arts and in all other things is not due to those who adhere to the status quo but to those who make improvements and dare always to change things that are wrong. I know that what I am about to do is difficult—praising a man's excellence through a speech. The greatest proof of this is that those who concern themselves with philosophy venture to speak on many other subjects of every different kind, but none of them has ever attempted to write on this matter.[5]

Particularly notable is that he sees his task of "giving an encomium of a man's virtue through discourses" (ἀνδρὸς ἀρετὴν διὰ λόγων ἐγκωμιάζειν, 8) as extending the range of subjects attempted by writers concerned with *philosophia*.[6] The emphasis on contests is pervasive, but constructed to emphasize Isocrates' originality. Evagoras' funeral had *mousikē* and had *agōnes* (1), but musical contests (the natural combination of these two) are only barely mentioned

---

[5]   Isocrates *Evagoras* 1, 2, 4, 6–8, trans. after Mirhady and Too 2000.

[6]   Cf. Nicolai 2004:88–93. Note how well this fits the function of protreptic discourse as identified by Ford (2011:124), "forming in [its audience] a habit of taking pleasure in the proper praise of excellent actions." Ford rightly highlights the continuity between traditional poetic *ēthos-paideia* and its philosophical counterpart (Ford 2011:204n15). Ford's focus on Aristotle's *Hymn to Virtue* leads him to dwell extensively on claims about what is best (*presbiston, kalliston*), a familiar Isocratean topos (*Nicocles* 43, cf. *To Nicocles* 20, *Evagoras* 40f., 76, *Antidosis* 304, *Panathenaicus* 204, and in general the frequent conjoining of *kallista* with *epitēdeumata*).

explicitly: so Isocrates' *aretē-logos* is easily more lasting and appropriate than the mere conspicuous consumption of athletic contests (4) and does something for a contemporary benefactor that epic and tragedy did only for ancient heroes (6). This conveniently elides the fact that media for praising the living and dead did exist (and even contests of praise-song in some rare instances[7]). Since *philosophia* is itself a field of contest, the passage inevitably suggests the possibility that Isocrates' innovative example—this festival occasion which displayed his unique didactic authority—will lead other orators to rival each other with *logoi* of praise, and we have to concede credit to Isocrates when we see that rival *epitaphioi logoi* were produced by *philosophia*-types in the following decades, a phenomenon for which we do not find a close parallel earlier, even in verse. Eventually, indeed, this type of contest came to seem so natural that some liked to read, in the Iliadic account of Patroclus' funeral games, not καὶ ῥ' ἥμονες ἄνδρες ἀνέσταν, "and the spear-thrower men stood up," but (by merging the rho of ἄρα with ἥμονες), "and the orator men [otherwise unattested ῥήμονες] stood up."[8]

Evagoras innovatively applies these themes to a new, biographical, kind of discourse, but they are drawn from the well-established terms of Isocrates' self-definition as orator and philosopher. The proem of the *Panegyricus*, published several years earlier,[9] had also combined the motifs of rhetorical competition and virtuous self-cultivation. Isocrates' claim is similar, too: he will supplant the traditional ceremonial *agōnes* of the body with an indefatigable labor-in-speech:

> I have often marveled that those who established panegyric festivals and set up athletic contests considered athletic success [*tas tōn sōmatōn eutukhias*] worthy of such great prizes, but established no such prize for those who work hard as private citizens for the public good and prepare their own lives [*tas hautōn psukhas*] so that they can benefit others. They should have given more thought to the latter, for even if the athletes acquired twice their current strength, there would be no greater benefit for the people, while if one person has good ideas, all who wish to share in those ideas would benefit. Nonetheless, I have not lost heart about these things or chosen to give up. Rather, I think that there is sufficient reward for me in the glory this discourse will bring, and so I have come to give advice about the war against the barbarians

---

7   Pernot 1993:47, esp. Lysander.
8   Plutarch *Table Talk* V 675a and some *Iliad* MSS: Pernot 1993:48.
9   Papillon 2004:24 ("published in 380 after ten years of composition").

and the need for unity among ourselves. I know that many who claim to be sophists have attempted this task, but I expect to speak so much better that people will think nothing has ever even been spoken on these matters before, and I consider those discourses most beautiful that treat the greatest subjects, best demonstrate the speaker's talent, and most help those who hear them. This is just such a discourse.

Isocrates *Panegyricus* 1–4
(trans. after Papillon 2004)

The claim of a transcendently original achievement echoes *Evagoras* (ὥστε τοῖς ἄλλοις μηδὲν πώποτε δοκεῖν εἰρῆσθαι περὶ αὐτῶν, *Panegyricus* 4 = περὶ δὲ τῶν τοιούτων οὐδεὶς πώποτ' αὐτῶν συγγράφειν ἐπεχείρησεν, *Evagoras* 8), as does the need to contrast it with the deficient efforts of intellectual rivals (τῶν προσποιησαμένων εἶναι σοφιστῶν, *Panegyricus* 3 = οἱ περὶ τὴν φιλοσοφίαν ὄντες, *Evagoras* 8).[10] The *Panegyricus*'s opposition between bodies and souls (*sōmata* vs. *psukhai*) has been taken up in the *Evagoras*'s contrast between martial and gymnastic contests and fame (the phrase *gumnikoi agōnes* occurs in the first sentence of both orations), and what is owed to *aretē*. (The idea is more fully applied to the royal addressee in *To Nicocles* 11, again in the contest of festival assemblies [*panēgureis*]: "Kings are required to train their souls as no athlete trains his body—for none of the public festivals offers the sort of challenge you [kings] undertake each day."[11]) Even the dejection one might feel about the world's mistaken priorities, over which Isocrates will prevail, is transferred from one speech to the other (οὐ μὴν ἐπὶ τούτοις ἀθυμήσας εἱλόμην ῥᾳθυμεῖν, *Panegyricus* 3 = νῦν δὲ τίς οὐκ ἂν ἀθυμήσειεν, *Evagoras* 6). The significant shift is from the many scores of references to the first-person-plural addressee of the *Panegyricus* to the second-person-singular address in *Evagoras* to Nicocles, the bereaved heir. In both cases Isocrates plants his care for virtue and the soul in what he hopes is fertile ground, but in *Evagoras* his didactic authority does not simply assert itself over all the rival policy proposals the Greeks might consider, but serves more subtly as a vehicle for immortalizing the father's virtue by transmitting it to the son (and the wider audience) for imitation.

Not many years after Isocrates' *Evagoras*, when Xenophon's son Gryllus died valiantly in the Battle of Mantinea in 362, Aristotle reports a flood of *enkōmia kai epitaphion* that sought to ingratiate their authors with Xenophon (soon to

---

[10]   Isocrates' assertion of his originality in *Panegyricus* is so strong as to elide all mention of "pan-egyric" predecessors such as Gorgias and Lysias' Olympic speeches.

[11]   Trans. Mirhady and Too 2000. Note the (rhetorically) performative dimension applied to the monarch.

be a practitioner of the genre with his *Agesilaus*), and Hermippus mentions that Isocrates was one of the encomiasts:

φησὶ δ᾽ Ἀριστοτέλης ὅτι ἐγκώμια καὶ ἐπιτάφιον Γρύλλου μυρίοι ὅσοι συνέγραψαν, τὸ μέρος καὶ τῷ πατρὶ χαριζόμενοι. ἀλλὰ καὶ Ἕρμιππος ἐν τῷ Περὶ Θεοφράστου καὶ Ἰσοκράτην Γρύλλου φησὶ ἐγκώμιον γεγραφέναι.

Aristotle says that a huge number of authors have composed an encomium or an epitaph in honor of Gryllus, partly also as a compliment to his father. And indeed, Hermippus declares in his work *On Theophrastus* that Isocrates, too, wrote a eulogy on Gryllus.

Diogenes Laertius 2.55 = Aristotle fr. 68 R³, F 38 Gigon
= Hermippus FGrHistCont 1026 F 34 ed. Bollansée 1999
(trans. Bollansée)

From *murioi*, from the base motivation of *kharizomenoi*, and from the subtitle of Aristotle's own *Gryllus—On Rhetoric*[12]—we can infer that Aristotle did indeed weigh in on the nature of rhetoric[13] and on the excesses and deficiencies of how the new kind of *epitaphios logos* was already being put to use. While the participation of Isocrates, the genre's founder, suggests that Aristotle's work was anti-Isocratean (perhaps in a dialogic way[14]), the two *philosophoi* were surely contesting the same basic claim we saw Isocrates stake in *Evagoras*: fitting praise of truly praiseworthy and virtuous qualities.[15] In any case, the fact that the myriad funeral orations for Gryllus provoked Aristotle to write his first work on the nature of rhetoric raises at least the possibility that these too, produced by school adherents experimenting with the new genre, self-consciously laid out important aspirations for what rhetoric could do, and how.

Six years after Gryllus' death, in 356, Isocrates has come to echo Aristotle's *murioi* with the fatigue he expresses in a letter to Archidamus of Sparta over

---

[12] Aristotle's *Gryllus* was discussed in connection with the Cephisodorus controversy in chap. 3.

[13] Aristotle sounds fairly Platonic in the report of Quintilian 2.17.14 = Aristotle fr. 69 R³, F 37 Gigon: *Aristoteles, ut solet, quaerendi gratia quaedam subtilitatis suae argumenta excogitavit in Grylo: sed idem et de arte rhetorica tris libros scripsit, et in eorum primo non artem solum eam fatetur, sed ei particulam civilitatis sicut dialectices adsignat.* "Aristotle, in his usual way, devised some arguments of characteristic subtlety [that rhetoric is not a *tekhnē*] in his *Gryllus*, for the sake of discussion; but he also wrote three books on the art of rhetoric and, in the first, not only admits it to be an art but says it is a part both of 'politics' and of 'dialectic'" (trans. Russell 2001). Cf. Blank 2007:14f.

[14] Perhaps in the dialogic way that *Phaedrus* is anti-Lysian: cf. D. S. Hutchinson and M. R. Johnson *per litteras* to Blank 2007:14n33.

[15] Cf. the "predictable lines" of Blank (2007:14).

the steady stream of encomia (presumably including Xenophon's *Agesilaus*) that continues several years after the death of his father:[16]

> Archidamus, knowing that many people are starting to praise you and your father and your family, I chose to leave this sort of discourse to others, since it was too easy to do. Instead I thought I would encourage you to take on the generalship.
>
> Isocrates *Epistle* 9.1 (trans. Papillon 2004)

Isocrates is here moving to dissociate himself from a kind of encomium that any practiced hand could accomplish, while working to reclaim the less easily counterfeited authority of his didactic posture to rulers: his present advice for the son is worth more than yet another praise of the father. Consonant with the permanent and traditional Greek association between commemorating the dead and instructing the living, this is an indication (together with Isocrates' many other efforts to cultivate his didactic authority) of what Isocrates also perceived as the limitations of the biographical plan.

The implicit possibility of a *contest* in funerary rhetoric is finally realized a few years later, in 352, in the funeral contests held for Mausolus, the philhellenic Carian dynast and imperfectly reliable Persian satrap of his country, by his widow and sister Artemisia. As we gather from Aulus Gellius and the *Suda*,[17] the *epitaphios logos* competitors were Theopompus of Chios, Theodectes of Phaselis, Isocrates of Apollonia, and Naucrates of Erythrae. Remarkably, all four of these orators can be attached to Isocrates' school through evidence that cannot be reduced to the Mausolus story, and they can be understood as carrying on their teacher's innovative practice. This is certainly preferable to Simon Hornblower's account of the Mausolus *agōn*, in which we are given to understand, following Pfister's old *Reliquienkult*, that these prose eulogies had gradually evolved from praise-song, without any specification or investigation of how deeply this event was situated in the scholastic milieu in which the phenomenon began.[18] Pernot more perceptively observes that Isocrates' innovation "announces the Hellenistic era": such close and friendly attention to sovereigns who intervene

---

[16] Pernot 1993:22.

[17] Aulus Gellius 10.18 = Theodectas 72 T 6 TrGF = Theopompus FGrHist 115 T 6b; *Suda*, s.v. Ἰσοκράτης, ι 653, and s.v. Θεοδέκτης, θ 138 = Theopompus FGrHist 115 T 6a; cf. "Plutarch" *Lives of the Ten Orators* 838b.

[18] Hornblower 1982. I also take issue with Hornblower's conclusion that Theodectes did not give a prose eulogy: see, *contra*, Zwierlein 1996:54 and Snell ad TrGF 72 T 6. (Pernot [1993:49n203] is noncommittal.)

in Greek affairs, a pattern seen in all these examples and more, with the exception of Gryllus, would only become more common.[19]

Yet, though I have tried to suggest how the Mausolus *agōn* brings together and crystalizes a number of important tendencies at work in its intellectual and historical environment, it must be admitted that it remained exceptional. Only from the first century BC are prose encomia well attested in *agōnes*, and these amount only to four good attestations, among many Hellenistic contests, and all of these at recurring festivals and not in the event of a death. Moreover, nothing remains of this later agonistic rhetoric, and the victors whose names we find inscribed are otherwise unknown to us.[20]

What we know about the careers of the Isocrateans who competed in this perfect-storm event confirms our impression of the school's wide interests: intellectual and professional versatility is characteristic of all of them. Theopompus seems to have practiced a more hot-tempered version of Isocrates' careful modulation between encomiastic praise and didactic correction. He praised Mausolus for oratorical glory in words that have perished, but his diagnosis of Mausolus in his *History* as a man who would do anything for money has fortuitously survived (F 299). Photius' *Life of Theopompus* records a fragment (F 25) in which Theopompus uses the same favorite money theme to compare Isocrates and Theodectes' dependence on paid rhetorical activities unfavorably with the self-sufficiency he and Naucrates of Erythrae enjoyed. Theopompus also wrote both encomia (F 257/T 8) and blame (*psogos*, T 8) of Alexander. Theopompus is famous to us as a historian, and he was also an impressive orator (F 25), but, just as Theodectes and Isocrates of Apollonia may have Platonic connections,[21] so too Theopompus (as we have seen) even wrote a work, *Against the Diatribē of Plato*, whose arguments against the Theory of Forms were serious enough to be cited in good philosophical company by Simplicius. As I have argued, these connections may help explain the savage treatment he receives in Speusippus' *Letter to Philip* alongside the elderly Isocrates and Isocrates of Apollonia, of whom he says (11), "You would quickly learn ... what Isocrates' educational system amounts to ... from the fact that he proclaimed his Pontic student as heir to his wisdom—a more loathsome fellow you, who have encountered many sophists, have never seen."[22] Indeed, it is important to remember that being a monarch meant dealing with loathsome sophists (however unfair this particular slur may be), and that

---

[19] Pernot 1993:22.

[20] Pernot 1993:48–50.

[21] μαθητὴς καὶ διάδοχος τοῦ μεγάλου Ἰσοκράτους, διακούσας δὲ καὶ Πλάτωνος τοῦ φιλοσόφου, *Suda*, s.v. Ἰσοκράτης, ι 653.

[22] Trans. Natoli 2004.

negotiating with intellectuals for their specific capital was a burden of policy and not a pastime.[23]

On the death of Aristotle's patron Hermias of Atarneus (on whom see just below) in 341, the philosopher's nephew Callisthenes composed a prose commemoration. The passage surviving in Didymus[24] proclaims the tyrant's *aretē* in his death at the hands of the Persian king. Andrew Ford rightly places this work in the context of scholastic encomium I have described here and well expresses the literarization of funerary rhetoric in this context by declaring the passage "equally suitable for performance as a eulogy and as a piece of artistic prose" (the alternative supplements *enkōmion* and *sungramma* to Didymus' fragmentary text), modes which are "of course not exclusive."[25] The apparently private and Peripatetic context of performance, long held probable, affords a valuable contrast to the more public and political negotiations of intellectual authority seen in the rest of this tradition. Such an intrascholastic occasion, with prose encomium, was already suggested by Wilamowitz, even before the discovery of Didymus with its evidence for Callisthenes' text, for Aristotle's closely related "Hymn to *Aretē*" and its more allusive assertion of Hermias' death for the sake of virtue.[26]

What about when Philip himself died in 336? We have fragmentary evidence suggesting some of the possibilities, with their attendant opportunities for accusations of loathsome sophistry. We have already mentioned the ambiguous title of Isocrates of Apollonia's work *On Not Performing a Taphos for Philip*, following in the wake of his necessarily political *Amphictyonic Speech*.[27] I am inclined to believe[28] that the younger Isocrates had not turned on Philip like Theopompus but was carrying on the idea of immortalization his teacher expressed in *Philip*

---

[23] I pass quickly over Speusippus' *Perideipnon Platōnos*, perhaps a eulogy for his uncle and teacher; for the connection between the topic of Plato's divine paternity in our report of this work (Diogenes Laertius 3.2) and the extravagance of contemporary prose eulogy in the wake of *Evagoras*, see Ford 2011:184n6. As Ford finds these two works "religiously bold," so Fredricksmeyer (1979:52n41) sees in Speusippus' Apollo/Heracles/Philip parallel at *Letter to Philip* 8 "the readiness of Philip's supporters to compare and associate him with the gods." Works that could be *epitaphioi* for Plato are attested by Speusippus (FGrHistCont 1009 FF 1–3 ed. Theys 1998), Clearchus (fr. 2 Wehrli), and Aristotle (Olympiodorus in Plato *Gorgias* = fr. 673 R³, F 708 Gigon).

[24] Col. 5.64–6.18 = FGrHist 124 F 2.

[25] Ford 2011:49f. Ford (2011:47f.) identifies the "persistent ethical norm" in the series of prose praises beginning with Isocrates' *Evagoras*; what I seek to add to the perspective of his survey is a picture of specifically interconnected scholastic rivals (claimants of *philosophia*), not just a "revolutionary time for prose" more generally.

[26] Ford 2011:45–51. For the possibility of continued performance in the *sussitia* of the Lyceum, Ford 2011:185n15.

[27] See chap. 3 above.

[28] With Sykutris (Bickermann and Sykutris 1928:74) and Natoli (2004:54f.), and against Fricel-Dana (2001–2003).

134.[29] Isocrates of Athens had offered the living Philip a share in *athanasia* midwifed by his own rhetorical fashioning of the ruler's significance in the world, and so his homonymous Pontic successor may well have memorialized the king in a way that looked insistently beyond the grave. But then, an anecdote from Plutarch's *Life of Demosthenes* shows how dyspeptically a Demosthenes would choke on that kind of encomium:

> Or how did it happen that, when [ca. 324 BC] Lamachus the Smyrnaean had written an encomium on Kings Philip and Alexander, in which many injurious things were said of Thebes and Olynthus, Demosthenes came forward and rehearsed with historical proofs all the benefits which the peoples of Thebes and Chalcidice had conferred upon Greece, and, on the other hand, all the evils of which the flatterers of the Macedonians had been the cause, and thereby so turned the minds of the audience that the sophist was terrified at the outcry against him and slunk away from the festival assemblage?
>
> Plutarch *Demosthenes* 9.1 = Lamachus of Smyrna FGrHist
> 116 T 1 (trans. after Perrin)[30]

Here, Lamachus of Smyrna is playing what is by now the banal and familiar game of prose eulogy for the deceased Philip and his living successor.

As politically irreconcilable as Demosthenes and Isocrates may have been, the anecdote reminds us of how strenuously Isocrates had worked to cast himself as something above the ingratiating flatterer. He didn't feel comfortable adding to the mass of encomia once they started to pour in from all quarters, and his form of address to Philip had left him open to attack by Speusippus for failing to take just the kind of obsequious line Lamachus is said to have pursued. Isocrates himself was always making compromises, and yet he fought against the trend that led to the empty conventions of panegyric and the excesses of "rhetorical history." His quasi-philosophical insistence on didactic independence and on the canons of virtue speaks about the unusual mix of literary ambitions and practices in his circle, which were very much of their time. Their future developments perhaps have more to do with the philosopher and historian's authority to judge lives and events than with any developments in oratory itself.

---

[29] "Keep in mind that we all have a body that is mortal, but we partake of immortality according to others' goodwill and the praise we receive and the reports that circulate about us and the memory we leave that lasts through time," trans. Papillon 2004. Cf. Isocrates' *praeteritio* at *Philip* 142f., where he places Philip's merit above his "demigod" ancestors but does not want to make them "seem less than those alive today."

[30] Cf. Pernot 1993:22.

Hermias of Atarneus and Theocritus of Chios

Hermias of Atarneus and his relations with Aristotle and Philip are much better known than many of the persons and traces of historical fact we must consider,[31] and accordingly I will focus only on the points most relevant to assigning him his place in our larger picture of scholastic networks and professional polemics, after a brief review of the other principal facts that are generally accepted. The tyrant Hermias supported a circle of philosophers from 347 to 344 that included Aristotle in addition to Erastus and Coriscus, two students of Plato who are addressed together with Hermias by the sixth Platonic epistle. For us, the defining event of Hermias' political career is his arrest and execution by the Persian authorities for treasonous complicity with Philip in 341,[32] by which time Aristotle had moved on to be Alexander's tutor after a short period in Mytilene. Aristotle was moreover allied to Hermias through his marriage to his niece and adoptive daughter, and the death of the "nursling of Atarneus" for the sake of *aretē* is notably remembered in Aristotle's famous hymn[33] as well as in verses spuriously attributed to him.

Hermias' association with the Academy begins but does not end with the Platonic *Epistle* VI.[34] This purports to be Plato's intervention to resolve any discord between the ruler and his philosopher neighbors (Erastus and Coriscus). The Academics are capable of being the trustworthy friends of Hermias, whose power (*dunamis*) they need if they are not to neglect wisdom in their life outside the Academy; Hermias, in turn, is admonished that his *dunamis* depends more on dependable friends (*philoi*) than on his supplies of wealth or war equipment.

---

[31] Jaeger 1948: chap. 5 ("Aristotle in Assos and Macedonia"); Wormell 1935; Düring 1957:272–283; Hammond and Griffith 1979:518–522; Trampedach 1994:66–70. Ford 2011:175n3 lists the primary sources.

[32] Hermias' death has occasioned much speculation about Aristotle's role in the politics of this time. Griffith's sensible discussion of this question (Hammond and Griffith 1979:518–522) concludes that while Aristotle was an available and obvious personal connection to Hermias, there is no reason to suppose that Aristotle's political utility in this capacity would have influenced his selection as Alexander's tutor.

[33] Aristotle fr. 675 R^3 = 842 PMG, which is a text that combines literary, theoretical and practical-philosophical influences. Ford 2011 now provides an exhaustive and wide-ranging study, taking as a point of departure Athenaeus' report (15.696a–697b, going back to a mixture of sources including Hermippus FGrHistCont 1026 F 30 Bollansée 1999 = fr. 48 Wehrli 1974) that Aristotle was accused in Athens of hymning a tyrant (presumably after Alexander's death in 323). For its place in the prose literary culture of the 340s, see above.

[34] On this letter see, in addition to the authors cited on Hermias in general, Isnardi 1955:262–265, Ford 2011:166–169 (who finds it acceptable as authentic and in any case accurate testimony of an undoubtedly real "network of friendship," apparently free of any later writer's agenda). Brunt (1993:292) discusses Plato *Epistle* VI but not at his usual standard ("the eleventh" Platonic letter for the sixth and "Corycus" for Coriscus). Jaeger (1948:111) considered Brinckmann's argument for the letter's genuineness convincing.

The three are thus urged each to do their part to create and maintain a single intertwining embrace of *philia* and to write to Plato for healing words if this is difficult.[35] A striking verbal repetition underscores that the process by which they will cement their bond to each other is the same as the philosophic mode of life that leads to the ultimate blessings:

> πάλιν εἰς τὴν προϋπάρχουσαν φιλότητά τε καὶ κοινωνίαν, ἣν ἂν μὲν <u>φιλοσοφῶμεν</u> ἅπαντες ἡμεῖς τε καὶ ὑμεῖς, ὅσον ἂν δυνώμεθα καὶ ἑκάστῳ παρείκῃ, κύρια τὰ νῦν κεχρησμῳδημένα ἔσται. ... καὶ χρῆσθαι συνθήκῃ καὶ νόμῳ κυρίῳ, ὅ ἐστιν δίκαιον, ἐπομνύντας σπουδῇ τε ἅμα μὴ ἀμούσῳ καὶ τῇ τῆς σπουδῆς ἀδελφῇ παιδιᾷ, καὶ τὸν τῶν πάντων θεὸν ἡγεμόνα τῶν τε ὄντων καὶ τῶν μελλόντων, τοῦ τε ἡγεμόνος καὶ αἰτίου πατέρα κύριον ἐπομνύντας, ὅν, ἂν ὄντως <u>φιλοσοφῶμεν</u>, εἰσόμεθα πάντες σαφῶς εἰς δύναμιν ἀνθρώπων εὐδαιμόνων.

> If all of us, you and we alike, according to our several abilities and opportunities, apply our wisdom [ἣν ἂν μὲν φιλοσοφῶμεν] to the preservation of this bond, the prophecies I have just uttered will come true. ... Adopt [this letter] as a just and binding law and covenant, taking a solemn oath—in gentlemanly earnest, but with the playfulness that is the sister of solemnity—in the name of the divine leader of all things present and to come, and in the name of the lordly father of this governor and cause, whom we shall all some day clearly know, in so far as the blessed are able to know him, if we truly live the life of philosophy [ἂν ὄντως φιλοσοφῶμεν].[36]

> 323b7–c3 and c8–d6 (trans. Morrow 1997, corrected)

Far from the Academy, some power (*dunamis*) will be needed to preserve the orientation of these men towards wisdom. This security comes from a universal *kurios patēr*, a god-monarch-philosopher who sanctions the bond that keeps them safe in the harsh world. Such an authority recalls the problematic of the Laws in *Crito*: it provides the basic social framework within which philosophy can be preserved in the brave new world apart from the Academy's "men of moderation and goodwill." For Erastus and Coriscus have been uprooted from this Athenian milieu. Hermias' role in Academic society is revealed in how he is here addressed together with the trained philosophers and given this solemn philosophical charge in common with them. This makes an obvious contrast

---

[35] The friendship is also mentioned at Didymus *Commentary on Demosthenes* col. 5.53f.

[36] For this common Platonic locution, see Plato *Sophist* 216c6, *Philebus* 57d1, and several passages in *Epistle* VII (326b4, 335d2, 340c2, 340d6). Cf. Epicurus *Vatican Gnomology* fr. 54.

with the two letters we have considered in which the philosophical guidance of Plato's student is recommended in a direct (and more politically down-to-earth) address to the monarch.

Additional important evidence of Hermias' implication in philosophical practice was already seen when we took up his role as a target of Theopompus' bitter anti-Platonic attacks in the previous chapter. But there are some other links to the Academy worth noticing. One tradition reaches us, through Strabo, that Hermias was the student of Plato in addition to Aristotle.[37] More worthy of our attention is the statement in Athenaeus (7.279e–f) that Speusippus paid Hermias' debts after his arrest. This is another indication of Hermias' specifically Academic connections, and the link back to Speusippus, the author of the *Letter to Philip*, also prepares us for that anti-Isocratean letter's anti-Platonic counterpart in Theopompus' savage blasts.

Theocritus of Chios is another obscure *rhētōr* of the Isocratean school, but unlike Isocrates of Apollonia and Theodectes, whose participation in both Isocratean and Platonic circles was notable, Theocritus is mainly remembered for a nasty attack on Hermias and on Aristotle's fond commemoration of him. Theocritus is said to have been the student of "Metrodorus the Isocratean."[38] Theocritus' intellectual-rhetorical insult of Anaximenes is cited by Athenaeus from Hermippus, so it was presumably reported in Hermippus' *On the Students of Isocrates* (as Wehrli assigns it).[39] This tussle could ultimately have had something to do with Anaximenes' teacher Zoïlus' authorship of such books as *Against Isocrates*. Like his fellow Isocratean and "political opponent" Theopompus,[40] he wrote history and had a special interest in the marvelous, his *epistolai thaumasiai*[41] calling to mind Theopompus' collection of *thaumasia* in his *Philippica*.[42]

---

[37] Strabo 13.1.57. This would seem to conflict with Plato *Epistle* VI 322e6–323a1, Ἑρμείας μοι ... ὅσα μήπω συγγεγονότι, a difficulty Novotný and Harward (cited by Wormell [1935:59]) solved by supposing "that Hermias visited Athens and associated with members of the Academy at a time when Plato was absent abroad." While this is not impossible, it is more likely that the alleged association with Plato has to do with the *Freundschaftsbund* with Plato's students in Assos. As suggested above, Plato's striking philosophical intimacy in *Epistle* VI may evince a more meaningful relationship than a known physical encounter would necessarily require.

[38] *Suda* s.v., θ 166, μαθητὴς Μητροδώρου τοῦ Ἰσοκρατικοῦ.

[39] Ἕρμιππος δέ φησι Θεόκριτον τὸν Χῖον ὡς ἀπαίδευτον μέμφεσθαι τὴν Ἀναξιμένους περιβολήν, FGrHistCont 1026 F 86, ed. Bollansée 1999 = fr. 78 Wehrli = Athenaeus 1.21c. Theocritus belonged "zu den Autoren, gegen deren Anschwärzungen Hermippos das Verhältnis des Aristoteles zu Hermias verteidigte" (Wehrli 1974:90).

[40] *Suda* s.v., θ 166, ἀντεπολιτεύσατο δὲ Θεοπόμπῳ τῷ ἱστορικῷ. I am not persuaded by the attempt by Teodorsson (1990) to reduce this division to the terms of class-based factions. For the tradition of Theocritus' execution by Antigonus the One-Eyed, see also Weber 1998–1999.

[41] *Suda* s.v., θ 166.

[42] FGrHist 115 FF 64–76; for other *mirabilia*, cf. FF 127, 267f., 270f., 274, 277f., 296, 343. Of course this literary topic can also point back to other influences, such as Ctesias.

Theocritus' style of participation in scholastic polemics is best seen in the "sarcastic comment on Aristotle's hymn and epigram" that he composed as an immediate response.[43]

Ἑρμίου εὐνούχου τε καὶ Εὐβούλου τόδε δούλου
    σῆμα κενὸν κενόφρων θῆκεν Ἀριστοτέλης,
ὃς διὰ τὴν ἀκρατῆ γαστρὸς φύσιν εἵλετο ναίειν
    ἀντ' Ἀκαδημείας Βορβόρου ἐν προχοαῖς.

For Hermias, the eunuch and slave of Eubulus
    empty-headed Aristotle made this empty tomb;
doing honor to his unrestrained belly, he chose to dwell
    at the mouths of the Slime River rather than in the Academy.[44]

These verses seem to have had an effect: their popularity can be seen in the fact that they reach us in four traditions.[45] Düring aptly appreciates the value of the ditty's clear attestation: "This contemporary evidence is extremely valuable, not only on account of the factual knowledge it affords, but also because it proves that the unfavourable biographical tradition was already strong in Aristotle's lifetime."[46] One of the sources, Didymus' fragmentary commentary on Demosthenes, also preserves Theopompus' similar but more obviously scholastic abuse of Hermias and thus is now the central document for the Hermias tradition.[47] This all comes under the heading "What those who have left a written record of Hermias of Atarneus say about him" (Περὶ Ἑρμίου τοῦ Ἀταρνείτου τί λέγουσιν οἱ τὰ περὶ αὐτὸν ἀναγράψαντες).[48]

It is the second half of the epigram I find most interesting, since here the criticisms being flung might be heard as professional in nature. The accusation of "incontinence of belly" (*akrateia gastros*) recalls, even more than any number of Platonic or Isocratean[49] passages, Theopompus' veritable obsession

[43] Düring (1957:277), pointing out that Didymus' introduction of the epigram (quoting Bryon's possibly near-contemporary pamphlet) with the words πρὸς ὅν (*Commentary on Demosthenes* col. 6.43) makes this certain.
[44] For the text, see Lloyd-Jones and Parsons 1983:355. See now the discussion in Ford 2011:35–41 (whose translation is adapted here), who does not, however, consider any Isocratean connections, calling Theocritus simply a "hostile source."
[45] Aristocles in Eusebius *Praeparatio evangelica* 15.2.12; "Bryon" in Didymus *Commentary on Demosthenes* col. 6.44ff.; "Ambryon" in Diogenes Laertius 5.11; Plutarch *On Exile* 10, 603c.
[46] Düring 1957:277.
[47] Milns (1994) argues that, at least in his account of Hermias at col. 5.51–63, Didymus' authority is not Hermippus (at least directly), but an earlier author (perhaps Theophrastus).
[48] Cf. Demosthenes *Fourth Philippic* 32, where the scholia identify ὁ πράττων καὶ συνειδὼς ἄπανθ' ἃ Φίλιππος κατὰ βασιλέως παρασκευάζεται as our Hermias.
[49] Cf. esp. *Antidosis* 221–224; also *Philip* 135.

in his *Philippica* with rulers and nations given over to pleasure (especially Philip and Athens), and with the anthropology of pleasure in Greek versus barbarian society.[50] But it is in the final barb that we most clearly sense Theocritus' professional odium: "He chose to dwell at the mouths of Borboros[51] instead of at the Academy." Here we could not be farther from the spirit of Antiphanes' smear on Theodectes, which was a satire of intellectuals. No doubt such a dig at Aristotle could have been rich. But Theocritus cannot afford to undermine the entire scheme of value in which the schools are competing for intellectual prestige, the political capital specifically restricted to those who have entered the field and accepted the worth of scholastic judgments. Theocritus' interest is rather in striking precisely where Aristotle can be hurt in these specific terms, and for this purpose Aristotle's (potentially) unseemly dissociation from the Academy to live under Hermias' protection offers the greatest polemical payoff, a strategy in which Theocritus need not take on the task of demolishing the Academics' right to respect in the narrow and wider worlds, but can actually turn the Academy's capital against Aristotle. This is in much the same way that a modern intellectual might better humiliate an opponent by saddling the exponent of a rival school of criticism with an insinuation that he or she falls short of the rival school's own intellectual standards. Why couldn't this pupil of Plato's have resisted the prospect of serving a eunuch slave? He was ill-natured. (Oh, and who are those Academics, now that you mention it, and what are they really up to?)

Isocrates' *Philip*

> What a splendid comparison this is—the Macedonian king and [Isocrates] the sophist!
>
> *On the Sublime* 4.2

The wise man's counsel to the monarch is one of the most perennial of didactic genres, but somehow addresses to the Macedonian ruler, made when Philip had not yet reached a final settlement with the Greek cities, possess an air of urgency

---

50   See e.g. FGrHist 115 FF 39f., 49, 62, 204.

51   Plutarch's explanation that this is a Macedonian river around Pella (otherwise unknown) is unlikely; as Düring (1957:381), says, "The river Borborus owes its existence to the fertile imagination of the author of this *ad hoc* interpretation." (Consequently, we must treat with caution Plutarch's corollary statement, that Theocritus' reproach is specifically ὅτι τὴν παρὰ Φιλίππῳ δίαιταν ἀγαπήσας.) It is probably not quite used as a common noun either (as Flower 1994:88, "in outpourings of slime"); rather, Aristotle has abandoned Academe for the vaguely exotic Filth River Delta (a suggestion now seconded by Vayos Liapis *per litteras* to Ford [2011:182n13]), which probably chimes in unison with Theopompus' attack on Hermias as *barbaros* (F 250), especially since Theocritus has already labeled Hermias as a eunuch and a slave.

and high stakes that is lacking in the stories of the Seven Sages. This may largely be due to the fact that we get to read real missives to the king, from an era whose political pressures are fully familiar to us through the surviving works of Demosthenes and other Athenian politicians. The orators' talk of plots and conspiracies has prepared our minds to see manipulations and machinations in any dealings between Philip and an Athenian party. Indeed, I will suggest that the unprecedented concentration of power and good fortune in Macedonian hands, among other factors more intellectual than political, led to some of the changes and accommodations that we might expect to develop in a world where the persuasion of a single man is of paramount importance. However, it seems that, even in these new political circumstances, a great deal of authority (and maybe even power) continues to attach to the wise man who speaks fearlessly in confidence of his own superior wisdom,[52] whether this is in tune with the older didactic tradition, or a phenomenon within "philosophical" culture, or both.

It is worthwhile to read alongside each other Isocrates' discourse *Philip* and the *Letter to Philip* of Speusippus, Plato's successor as head of the Academy. For we have, in these two texts, directly competing bids for influence with Philip from the same decade, the 340s. Isocrates made his address in 346, at the age of ninety, soon after the Peace of Philocrates, and Speusippus sent his letter (with its explicit attack on Isocrates' discourse) perhaps just three and a half years later—though these were eventful years that saw expanding Macedonian conquest and political control. In such times as these, Isocrates impressively maintains a more classically didactic stance, which dares not only to urge on Philip Isocrates' pet project of a Panhellenic campaign against Persia, but even to defend Athens' claim to Amphipolis. This didactic stance strongly contrasts with Speusippus' nakedly partisan intriguing, and I will look for the right context within which to account for these striking differences.

The most important generic cues in Isocrates' *Philip*, for my purposes, relate to Isocrates' expression of his own authority as a speaker. In an opening section that tackles the delicate and controversial matter of Amphipolis, he quickly establishes his ability to speak independently and impartially: "I tried not to give the same advice about this city and its territory as either your advisors or the rhetors here, but to differ as much as I could from their point of view" (Isocrates *Philip* 2). What is interesting to me here is that the very same claim that would pass as a commonplace in a discourse made for an Athenian audience—an impartial and uncorrupted stance that will allow the speaker to give fair advice to his fellow-citizens in the jury or Assembly—undergoes a transformation of meaning when addressed to Philip. Isocrates refuses to assign himself

---

[52] Cf. Cartledge 2009:98 on Isocrates' preoccupation with "speaking truth to monarchical power."

the limited perspective of an Athenian politician or of a Macedonian partisan. Symbuleutic discourse normally takes place within a single arena such as those from which Isocrates here detaches himself: it aims at the interest of a single sovereign entity, whether the *dēmos* or the king.[53] All of Isocrates' other deliberative works fit this model. If we insist on seeing the *Philip* as politics, we have to credit Isocrates, as many have, with a novel kind of politics, which is well enough. But in devising a *politikos logos* that claims to work outside of the normal arenas, Isocrates is reaching beyond politics, and towards the autonomous didactic authority of the wise man or of (to use the word popularized in Plato and Isocrates' schools) the philosopher. This is strikingly different, not only from the civic discourse practiced by Athenian politicians in Athens' interest, but also from Speusippus' assumption that it is right to pursue Philip's interests without qualms.[54]

Isocrates at one point expresses to Philip his frustration with the ordinary constraints of political action under the regime of a Greek *polis*: "I saw all the other men of good reputation living in cities with constitutions and laws such that it was impossible for them to do anything except what those laws and constitutions prescribed."[55] There is a tension here between a constitutional system and the supremely noble and useful action to which Isocrates wants to lead Philip. This could be taken as a statement of a political preference: laws are a hindrance, and absolute rule without them is more promising. And indeed, Isocrates hopes to see his pet project finally realized through Philip's power. But Isocrates insists on emphasizing not so much Philip's discretionary right over policy, but rather the obligatory force that the meritorious action—and Isocrates' advice!—ought to have *over* Philip. There are several indications that this is part of Isocrates' pursuit of a suprapolitical perspective and authority, what Isocrates would call philosophical.

First, Isocrates relates his students' criticism of the kind of address he proposes to send to Philip. This typically Isocratean device at once separates Isocrates from the normal political arena by evoking the scholastic milieu. The students' main point is that it is absurd for Isocrates to presume to send deliberative advice to someone as brilliantly successful in battle and politics as Philip: "You are on the verge of sending a discourse that will send advice [*sumbouleusonta logon*] to Philip ... Don't you think that [Philip] will ... conclude that the sender is quite confused [*diapseusthai*] about the power of his discourses

---

[53] Cf. Too 1995:149 on Isocrates' statement in *To Nicocles* 53 that "a good counselor [*sumboulos*] is the most useful and most tyrannical [*turannikōtaton*] of all possessions" for a ruler.

[54] Of course, Isocrates maintains that he *does* serve the interests of both parties—but it is this very premise that explodes the normal political assumptions, since the parties do not (conventionally speaking) belong to the same political community.

[55] Isocrates *Philip* 14.

[*logoi*] and his own wisdom [*dianoia*]?" (*Philip* 18, 21). The students suggest that Isocrates' presumption is gross self-deception about the power of *logoi* and his own intelligence. By rejecting this criticism, Isocrates clearly asserts the power of intelligence and *logoi* over even a ruler such as Philip.

Isocrates' students make their criticism in direct response to their teacher's proposal of a genre for his address:

> When I revealed to them that I was going to send you a discourse that would not make a display of my talent [*epideixis*] and would not praise [*enkōmiasomenon*] the wars that you have waged—for others will do this—but one that tried to encourage [*protrepein*] you toward deeds that were more fitting, more noble, and more advantageous for you than those you have now chosen ...
>
> *Philip* 17

It is interesting that they expect their teacher rather to make an epidictic display or an artful encomium. This more-than-political text, we are told in this passage, is not *epideixis*, but rather *protreptic*, and there is some reason to hear a resonance of the philosophical use of that term. Most immediately, what Isocrates says here: a *logos* that will attempt to urge Philip on *to nobler deeds than the ones he has currently chosen*. This echoes an important principle expressed in Isocrates' *To Nicocles*, a text that has been recognized as at the very head of the long European tradition of wise men's open advice to princes:[56] "Those who educate private citizens [*idiōtas*] benefit only them, but if someone turns those in charge of [*kratountas*] the people to virtue, he would benefit both those holding positions of authority [*dunasteias*] and their subjects" (*To Nicocles* 8). In short, urge on a ruler to *aretē*, and you will benefit both him and his subjects. Isocrates' *philosophia* is practical and focused on excellent actions (especially in public life). His discourse *Philip* is certainly based on the Macedonian king's special status and influence, but it nonetheless casts his royal addressee in the role of a student of Isocratean *philosophia*.[57]

This is confirmed when Isocrates uses a key term of his school's training, *kairos*, the occasion of life at which the most successful and talented students crystalize all their training into action:

---

[56] See Hariman 1995, Born 1936:99n1, and the discussion in this book's conclusion. Isocrates' mass of precepts in *To Nicocles*, for which he apologizes (40f.), should be read alongside the opening pages of *Laws* 5, where Plato does not scorn the genre.

[57] This is true even if the historical situation is now less conducive to philosophical idealization than it was for Isocrates' earlier, more purely didactic essay. The age has passed in which Plato and Isocrates' wisdom performances were not addressed at rulers holding immense power over Athens' fate.

Therefore, since all these cities have acted in this way, you should never have had a dispute with any of them. Nevertheless, we are all naturally more prone to do wrong than to do right, and thus we can rightly ascribe prior mistakes to a common failing, but from now on, you must be on your guard that nothing like it happens to you again. You must also consider what good you can accomplish for them to make it clear that you have done things that are both worthy of yourself and a worthy response to their prior actions. You now have a prime opportunity [*kairos*].

Philip 35f.

Here Isocrates, after didactically delivering some particularly harsh criticisms of Philip's political mistakes, seems to explain his license to do so by the urgency of exploiting the *kairos* that is now available to Philip.

Many other passages in *Philip* continue Isocrates' unrelenting focus on intellect, both Isocrates' and Philip's, and on the paradox by which the teacher and speaker has the authority to give strategic counsel to the military expert.[58] This is of a piece with Isocrates' elsewhere labeling his address to the Athenian jury in *Antidosis* as "instruction" (*Antidosis* 29), and seeing promise in Philip's successor's reputation for being *philosophos* (*Epistle* 5). In the *Philip*, Isocrates and Philip are teacher and student, roles that are emphasized by several framing references to an additional, scholastic audience. In the opening pages of the *Philip*, in a passage extolling Isocrates' project far above the trivialities of the epidictic usually peddled at Panhellenic gatherings, he says that this discourse aims to set a pattern or example for his students:

ἠβουλήθην ἅμα τοῖς πρὸς σὲ λεγομένοις καὶ τοῖς μετ' ἐμοῦ διατρίψασιν ὑποδεῖξαι καὶ ποιῆσαι φανερὸν ὅτι τὸ μὲν ταῖς πανηγύρεσιν ἐνοχλεῖν καὶ πρὸς ἅπαντας λέγειν τοὺς συντρέχοντας ἐν αὐταῖς πρὸς οὐδένα λέγειν ἐστὶν.

I wished at the same time to make a demonstration by example for my students and to make it clear to them that being an annoyance at Panhellenic gatherings and speaking to everyone who gathers together for them is tantamount to speaking to no one.

Philip 12

Midway through, Isocrates frets about the adequacy of his present arguments to the high purpose of "making others who are engaged in *philosophia* more

---

[58] See, for example, *Philip* 81f., 105, 122, 155.

adept" but takes comfort in the fact that others, presumably his students, will follow through on the pattern he has traced in outline (with the common sense of *hupodeixai* and *hupographein* further linking this to the passage just cited): "my discourse *Panegyricus*, which made others who are engaged in learning [*tous peri tēn philosophian diatribontas*] more adept ... But I still think I will sketch [*hupograpsein*] out a pleasant discourse for those who can fill in the details and complete it [*exergazesthai kai diaponein*]" (*Philip* 84f.). Finally, this scholastic frame is completed in the discourse's very last sentences, when Isocrates assigns to his plural "hearers" the right to measure his work against the standards of *kairoi* and exactitude:[59] "It is right for me to learn from you, my audience [*par' humōn tōn akouontōn*], whether these things have been written with timeliness [*tois kairois*] and accuracy [*tais akribeiais*]" (*Philip* 155).

Isocrates' *Philip* and Speusippus' *Letter to Philip*

Before proceeding to a full discussion of Speusippus' *Letter to Philip*, I would like to review it more briefly in the context of Isocrates' *Philip*. Speusippus' letter includes a totally destructive attack on Isocrates, accusing him of plagiarizing himself, speciously quoting him against himself several times,[60] and taking him to task for not writing encomiastically and gratifyingly enough about what the Greek cities owed Philip. Yet these are precisely the points on which Isocrates proudly and bravely asserts his right to be an independent teacher. Isocrates even presciently warns Philip against merely gratifying epistles masquerading as good advice. In one passage of the *Philip* he says that written discourses are always suspect, tending as they do towards showing off (*epideixis*) and profit-seeking (*ergolabia*), but he insists that *his* message treats seriously of pressing matters.[61] And at the end of the *Philip* Isocrates counsels the king that "the finest praise comes from those who think your nature is capable of even greater accomplishments and from those who do not only speak favorably about the

---

[59] Note also how both Isocrates and Speusippus compare themselves to Philip, but in tellingly different ways. Isocrates in his first letter to Philip—ἀλλὰ πλεῖστα πάντων ἐπιτετιμηκώς, οὔτ' εὖ παρὰ τοῖς πολλοῖς καὶ τοῖς εἰκῇ δοκιμάζουσιν φερόμενος, ἀλλ' ἀγνοούμενος ὑπ' αὐτῶν καὶ φθονούμενος ὥσπερ σύ (*Epistle* 2.22), "I am not well regarded by the common people and especially by those who form opinions casually, but just like you, I am misunderstood and envied," trans. Papillon 2004—takes as the grounds of equality and of his right to address Philip the potential positive opportunity for action (an ethical good). Speusippus, in contrast, casts himself as the unabashedly interested victim of an attack which is to be returned (see below). See Natoli 2004:96 for Philip and Plato juxtaposed "as the victims of unfair attack." (A further important point of comparison was to be use of historical exempla.)

[60] 4, 9, 14. See Natoli 2004:11n8 on the distinctiveness of this method.

[61] *Philip* 25: τοὺς μὲν περὶ σπουδαίων πραγμάτων καὶ κατεπειγόντων ῥητορεύεσθαι, τοὺς δὲ πρὸς ἐπίδειξιν καὶ πρὸς ἐργολαβίαν γεγράφθαι.

present."[62] Isocrates amply proves that this was no rank flattery by telling Philip that the road to greater accomplishments goes through his recognizing Athens' claim to Amphipolis.

Speusippus' first line of attack is to use Isocrates' didactic presumption against him by rereading him through the lens of what he takes to be the more appropriate, partisan, and encomiastic approach. This is complemented by Speusippus' complaint[63] that Isocrates' student, the historian Theopompus, is slandering Plato at the Macedonian court. And this despite the fact that Plato, through his student Euphraeus of Oreus, had been instrumental in laying down the conditions for Philip's rule (presumably a more tangible benefit than any conferred by Isocrates).[64] About Theopompus, we have seen that he wrote a work against Plato's teachings containing criticisms of the Theory of Forms. This corroborates our inference from Speusippus' attack on Isocrates' *Philip*—that the two Athenian schools of *philosophia* are rivaling each other in pursuit of Macedonian patronage and influence.

We are faced with the two texts—what are we to conclude about their real consequences in the political and philosophical arenas of their day?[65] A tempting assumption is that each text is somehow a natural expression of the moment of its composition—in other words, the change in political circumstances in the intervening years, and Philip's increasingly inarguable preeminence, have made Isocrates' confident authority look rash and inappropriate in hindsight, a product for consumption by a second, Athenian-civic, audience that no longer matters or exists in the same way. One scholarch savages the other by exploiting this historical gap. As stated, this is fallacious; and it turns out that there are other possible explanations of the difference, equally likely as the progress of political change over a certain number of years.

For example, we may point out the simple fact that Theopompus is there at Philip's court, criticizing Plato, years after Isocrates' *Philip*. This implies that Speusippus was not composing his letter from a position of strength.[66] Perhaps Isocrates' boldly authoritative protreptic was actually useful and pleasing for Philip to participate in. If this is so, it could be taken as a reassuring sign that a confident attempt to exert wisdom's mastery over the world's serious

---

[62] 153, trans. after Papillon, as mentioned by Natoli (2004:91).

[63] Speusippus *Letter to Philip* 12.

[64] On the argument around *euergesia*, see Natoli 2004:95–99.

[65] In the words of Hornblower (2004:85), who sees a problem similar to that of the social and propagandistic value of epinician poetry, "How far did Philip II of Macedon care what Isokrates wrote about him?"

[66] Other possible sources for sketching the further progress of the relationship between Isocrates and Philip are vexed by difficult issues of dating, but there is no contrary evidence. On the other hand, Schorn (2006) takes Speusippus' direct requests for Philip to intervene to help Antipater at the opening and close of his letter to indicate an expectant confidence.

issues, an exercise developed in the political and philosophical culture of democratic Athens, is showing that it has some legs, despite the desperate partisan savagery of Speusippus' letter, which paradoxically shows a withdrawal from truly political discourse.

And yet, after the death of Isocrates, the meager fragmentary remains of Plato and Isocrates' students seem to show an excess of precisely the empty polemical wrangling that is comparatively so hard to find in the vast Platonic and Isocratean corpuses. This raises the question of whether Speusippus' letter, even if in its moment it was an impotent attempt to remedy the Academy's political weakness, does not herald a new form of philosophical contest that prevailed within at least one mid-fourth-century circle of philosophical culture.

The generic complexity of this philosophical culture should be studied further (and below I will try to examine more closely and comparatively some of the specific devices employed by Speusippus' letter). Aristotle quotes Gorgias as having said, "You should kill your opponents' earnestness with jesting and their jesting with earnestness," a maxim that Niall Livingstone has rightly cited as a key to much of the philosophical polemics,[67] and whose spirit we have already applied in our refinement of Owen's views on philosophical polemics. Deadly ridicule can easily be traced back to Plato, who often employed jest to deliver serious blows. And Isocrates' *Busiris* presents us with an intact text devoted to this strategy, pulling in uproarious scenes from the comic stage[68] to poke at his rhetorical rival Polycrates. Likewise, Speusippus' attack on Isocrates as illegitimate parent to his own disgraceful works echoes the forensic litigant's smears of his opponent's parentage.[69] And it is a very similar imaginative repurposing of existing generic means that I have tried to present here: Isocrates' retooling of the politician's claim to evenhanded political judgment in order to develop his authoritative persona in a carefully constructed, new kind of frame that puts his advice into didactic, scholastic, and philosophic terms.

Speusippus' *Letter to Philip*

One has seen that Philip was not exactly a philistine. Certainly there is no evidence of his personal devotion to any area of literature or the arts that can be compared (for example) to Alexander's famous love of Homer. But there is no need, either, to dismiss his known connection with literary figures as purely utilitarian on both sides. Orators, historians, actors, philosophers addressed themselves to him. Were they all

---

[67] Aristotle *Rhetoric* 1419b4f., cited by Livingstone (2001:19n39), suggesting that Isocrates in *Busiris* demolishes Polycrates with (mock) seriousness and Plato with his humorous treatment.
[68] In particular the gluttony of Busiris and Heracles: Livingstone 2001:79.
[69] Cf. Owen 1983:14–17.

in it simply for the money? Was his time (and money) spent on them merely for the prestige or the propaganda? The men themselves are shadowy figures for us, mostly, one or two of them (whose personality can still make some impression) somewhat unpleasing. (I think especially of Speusippus and probably Callisthenes and Theopompus.) The greatest mind of the day, however, and one which gives an impression of suffering neither fools nor knaves gladly, was able evidently to put up with Philip.

G. T. Griffith, A History of Macedonia[70]

Among all the evidence, much of it fragmentary, from which we can reconstruct a historical picture of the Academic and Isocratean cohorts' status, relations, and corporate maneuvering for patronage during the lifetime of Philip, perhaps the most crucial document is a complete letter from Speusippus to Philip that is full of *prima facie* indications identifying it as an Academic intervention of 343/2 against the Isocrateans' growing critical mass of influence at the Macedonian court. (Most notably, the letter interrupts its extended tirade against Isocrates to denounce the anti-Academic machinations of Isocrates' alleged student Theopompus at Philip's court.) The potential evidentiary import of this text demands a careful assessment of its value. A completely new appraisal of the historical and discursive contexts and content of the Speusippean letter would be beyond the scope of this study; fortunately, the recent study of Natoli, the first attempt at such an appraisal since Bickermann and Sykutris's pathfinding 1928 edition and investigation, remedies this lack to a large extent and is a valuable new historical approach to the text.[71] Both of these thorough and careful reviews deemed the letter genuine. However, we still must ground our new assessment of the letter's plausibility and significance on a full and critical consideration of some of the arguments that were made over it in the wake of Bickermann and Sykutris. Most particularly, this means reviewing in some detail the arguments put forward by Lucio Bertelli in two articles that critiqued Bickermann's reasons for affirming two key aspects of the text's historicity: its purported date and its purported Speusippean authorship.[72]

This approach can lead to new positive results since Bertelli's arguments still stand as the most extensive criticism on several important points concerning the

---

[70] Hammond and Griffith 1979:620.

[71] Natoli 2004, Bickermann and Sykutris 1928. I often refer to Bickermann alone since he was responsible for the historical (as opposed to philological and textual) arguments; these in turn are the ones Bertelli took up and subjected to critical questioning (see further below).

[72] Bertelli 1976, 1977a.

document's immediate historical and scholastic contexts. We will see, however, that despite Bertelli's thoroughgoing skepticism of any attempt to forge too easy a reconciliation between the epistle's wide range of topics and the single historical moment in which Bickermann placed it, his eventual conclusions still explain the letter's indisputable anti-Isocratean intentions as issuing from a mid-fourth-century Academic writer. Thus we must realize that those scholars whose conception of the *Letter to Philip*'s spuriousness leads them to insist that it must be dissociated in our minds from the Academy of Speusippus' scholarchy cannot claim to be supported by Bertelli's investigations.[73]

In fact, most scholars who have considered the *Letter to Philip* have accepted that it is from Speusippus' pen,[74] a conclusion that I will also accept. But I will

---

[73] I make a point of this because scholars on both sides of the authorship question have taken notice of moments where it appears that Bertelli will be justifying such a dissociation ("una redazione di scuola," without any qualification, Bertelli 1977a:75; the counterfeit he suggests by interpreting an allusion to a recent historical event as an intentional *sphragis*, Bertelli 1976:280f., and by declaring the general hypertopicality of the letter as cause for suspicion, Bertelli 1976:284; in general the recurring intimations that Bickermann's chronology is coming unraveled made in Bertelli's first article, e.g. Bertelli 1976:287, which ends on a note of doubt and a diagnosis of "chronological irrationality," 300, with no hint of how far the second article's argumentation will go to rehabilitating the letter, even if un-Speusippean, as a valid historical document). They have (understandably) not always done justice to Bertelli's eventual conclusions characterizing what kind of "school" product is finally meant, which is not at all late rhetorical hackwork, but rather "una rielaborazione di scuola accademica pressoché contemporanea ai fatti, e non un 'patchwork' di un retore tardo," Bertelli 1977a:111 (cf. 106 for Bertelli's clarification that the chronological critique does not "automatically" exclude Speusippean authorship). It seems possible that at the time of his first publication, Bertelli did not yet envisage such a conclusion and therefore did not refrain from articulating suspicions he would eventually overrule. In any case, such a statement as that by Flower (who accepted the *Letter to Philip* as genuine)—that Bertelli judged the text a "school exercise" (Flower 1994:52n37)—shows how Bertelli left himself open to misunderstanding. Those who accept the authenticity of the epistle do so on Bickermann and Sykutris's authority, which is sound enough; if not unaware of Bertelli's work (e.g. Usener 1994), whose publication in the *Atti della Accademia delle Scienze di Torino* put it farther from notice than it deserved, they have rejected Bertelli's claim to have altered the framework of historical necessity put up by Bickermann (e.g. Trampedach 1994:94n10, "nicht überzeugend," cf. ibid. 138n100), without however directly identifying the weaknesses or inadequacies that make his conclusion unacceptable. It is scarcely an exaggeration to say that Bertelli's actual arguments have not been discussed at any length in print, but Isnardi Parente is a partial exception, as she includes the letter in her edition of Speusippus (unlike Tarán 1981) and offers the fullest discussion of the critical issues between Bertelli and Natoli, lingering briefly over a couple of his points (Isnardi Parente 1980:391–402, esp. 396f.).

[74] These also include Markle (1976) and, among writers after Bertelli, Isnardi Parente (1980) and Trampedach (1994). The most noticed recent dissent is that of Speusippus' editor Tarán, whose edition does not print the letter or discuss its problems in any detail. "The reader of this work who is interested … is hereby referred to my monograph *The Pseudo-Speusippean Letters* where he will find a critical edition" (Tarán 1981:xxiii, cf. 8, 182, 227; Tarán does not reject the more general tradition of hostility between Isocrates and Speusippus). The author has confirmed to me *per litteras*, however, that this project was never realized.

first subject Bertelli's reservations to the consideration they have not received, as they offer a most stimulating series of complications and provocations from which a more nuanced understanding can arise that accounts for what have been seen as untopical, ineffective, or un-Speusippean lapses.

Bertelli's faithful dedication to historical criticism was, in the end, destined only to illuminate small cracks in Bickermann's conclusions, but it is in these interstices that a revised set of assumptions about the nature of the scholastic groups and their rivalries can most profitably be applied. That Bertelli ended up strengthening the arguments for the letter's provenance from an Academic circle late in the first decade of Philip's reign only increases the value of this discussion, since our chief goal is to clarify and test the explanatory power of a revised view of the scholastic context within which such figures as Speusippus and Theopompus were operating—and these assumptions are of disproportionate importance in the small differences asserted by Bertelli (e.g. the implausibility of Speusippean authorship versus the plausibility of authorship by Heraclides Ponticus or Aristotle). Special attention must be paid to whether a consideration of the literary and generic affiliations of such personalities beyond the fields in which they have traditionally been placed (Academic philosophy, "rhetorical" historiography) will help explain their motivations or rhetorical strategies. Moreover, a fresh reading of the grounds for Bertelli's doubts will show that they do not require us to doubt the value of the *Letter to Philip* for a historical understanding of the position of Academics and Isocrateans vis-à-vis Philip's court.

Speusippus' *Letter to Philip* is a unique constituent of the corpus of so-called *Epistulae Socraticae*. Usually cited as *Epistula Socratica* 30,[75] it is the only letter in this group that has been generally regarded in recent times as genuine,[76] and it appears in the company of three spurious letters also attributed to Speusippus.[77] The source from which all known manuscripts of the *Epistulae Socraticae* derive is Codex Vaticanus graecus 64, a copy made in AD 1269/1270 from an original of indeterminate date but characterized by Sykutris, who devoted two studies to the collection, as "old, quite neglected, and riddled with errors."[78] The same manuscript not only contains letters ascribed to Aeschines but is also a very

---

[75] The most commonly used numeration is that of Orelli (1815), followed by Hercher (1873), but the letter is also sometimes cited as *Epistula Socratica* 28, after e.g. Köhler 1928.

[76] Some of the respects in which Speusippus' letter differs from the ones with which it is preserved are immediately striking. For example, while the doubtful authenticity of the corpus in general was already suggested by Bentley three hundred years ago on the basis of their not appearing in Athenaeus (Sykutris 1933:9), it is in Athenaeus (11.506e) that we find Carystius' citation of the Speusippean letter.

[77] 32, 33, 35 Orelli (1815).

[78] Sykutris 1933:7.

important witness for the Isocratean letters, all of which possess strong claims to authenticity, and which moreover have in common with Speusippus' letter that they are among the most important sources for the politico-scholastic alliance Isocrates sought to forge with the Macedonian court.[79]

A Philosopher at Court: Euphraeus in Carystius, the *Letter to Philip,* and Demosthenes

Our eventual goal is to fit the *Letter to Philip* into a larger historical understanding of the literary figures named or alluded to in it, the patterns of their interactions, the schools to which they belonged, the range of their intellectual and political motivations and strategies of self-presentation, and the criteria that made something topical and worth arguing over to such persons—for these are all matters bearing on the authenticity as well as the interpretation of the *Letter to Philip*, and ones on which Bertelli's arguments also deserve attention. Before proceeding to these questions, however, I will discuss the more basic issues surrounding the letter's authentically Speusippean textual tradition.[80] These issues were raised by Bertelli in an investigation founded on the reassessment of Carystius' apparent citation from the *Letter to Philip*, preserved in Athenaeus 11.506e. In this passage, Athenaeus sums up his several examples, all tending to illustrate Plato's alleged tendencies to engage in combative personal polemics:

> And this is Plato, of whom Speusippus says that he was most dear to Philip[81] and was responsible for his kingship. At any rate Carystius of Pergamum writes in his *Historica Hypomnemata*, "Speusippus,[82] learning that Philip[83] was speaking ill about Plato wrote in a letter something

---

[79]   Vaticanus graecus 64 is the basis of the "vulgate" for the Isocratean letters and the oldest source for them apart from Codex Urbinas (9th/10th cent. AD). Cf. Mathieu's remarks in Mathieu and Brémond 1962:163–183. See further Drerup 1901:358ff.

[80]   In particular, I wish to address first the issues surrounding the text of *Letter to Philip* 12, in which Theopompus and his attacks on Plato are denounced; this passage is (not coincidentally) both of central importance to our interest in scholastic politics and one whose apparent problems especially exercised Bertelli. It is in the context of the broader questions that Bertelli's larger concerns about the letter's chronological, stylistic, rhetorical, and intellectual range can best be answered. I do not mean to imply, however, that the latter are any less a part of Bertelli's fundamental argument concerning authenticity.

[81]   The manuscripts have two datives: (1) most dear *to Archelaus*, (2) *to Philip* the cause of his kingship (φίλτατον ὄντα Ἀρχελάῳ Φιλίππῳ τῆς βασιλείας αἴτιον γενέσθαι). For the deletion of Ἀρχελάῳ, see Gomperz 1882:112n11.

[82]   Our actual text of the letter does not preserve the sender's name, which depends on Carystius here.

[83]   Philip's name here in place of Theopompus' will be discussed below.

of this sort: 'as if people didn't know that Philip even got the beginning of his kingship through Plato.' For Plato dispatched to Perdiccas
Euphraeus of Oreus, who persuaded him to parcel out some territory
to Philip."[84]

Bertelli identifies two problematic discrepancies in Carystius that he interprets
as evidence for an original of which the *Letter to Philip* may be a recreation or
reelaboration. One of these discrepancies is a matter of expository technique
and verbal expression, and we will consider this at length before proceeding
to the other divergence, which concerns the facts, too, and which is the sole
point on which Bertelli finds corroboration outside the Athenaeus passage for
his view that Carystius constitutes an independent textual tradition.

To begin with, corresponding to Speusippus *Letter to Philip* 12, ὥσπερ οὐ
Πλάτωνος τὴν ἀρχὴν τῆς ἀρχῆς ἐπὶ Περδίκκου κατασκευάσαντος, we find in
Athenaeus-Carystius, ὥσπερ ἀγνοοῦντας τοὺς ἀνθρώπους ὅτι καὶ τὴν ἀρχὴν
τῆς βασιλείας Φίλιππος διὰ Πλάτωνος ἔσχεν, followed by the explanation about
Euphraeus quoted above. While recognizing that this is a paraphrase or a quotation from memory (introduced by Carystius with ἔγραψέ τι τοιοῦτον), Bertelli
suggests that two differences are significant.

First there is the fact that Carystius (not necessarily, however, the
Speusippean text he is citing, as I have noted) amplifies with details what in
Epistulae Socraticae 30 is merely an allusion—with Euphraeus' name and any
specific description of how Plato helped engineer Philip's ascent left unstated.[85]
If Bickermann was guilty of not offering a positive defense of the idea that
Carystius is unobtrusively expanding where Speusippus was diplomatically
allusive, such a defense is nonetheless not difficult to construct. The problem is
to reconcile those sources that present Euphraeus as Perdiccas' ally—whether
as political counselor, pedantic courtly *arbiter*, or theoretical tutor—with the
portrayal of Euphraeus as an anti-Macedonian martyr in Demosthenes' *Third*

---

[84] I have punctuated in line with the interpretation offered below; there is no way of knowing
precisely where Carystius' direct quotation of Speusippus comes to an end. Bertelli, in his consideration of the inconcinnities between Carystius and the *Letter to Philip* in the use of second and
third person (which, he points out, provoked Bernays to wonder whether the letter Carystius
cited was not in fact addressed to Philip), and in the distribution of direct and indirect speech,
bolsters his case that these are suspect with something of a *petitio principii*, declaring his conclusions more likely because the complete text of Speusippus' letter is "già sospetto per la sua stessa
natura di documento epistolare" (Bertelli 1977a:80).

[85] Bertelli (1977a:80) highlights this as a discontinuity. Cf. Bertelli 1976:286f., which expresses dis-
satisfaction (on chronological grounds—for the dating of the occupation of Oreus see ibid. n33)
with Isnardi Parente's reconciliation of the various accounts of Euphraeus' career in a manner
similar to what I propose, recognizing that Demosthenes and the author of the *Letter to Philip* are
both expending their rhetorical efforts to appropriate Euphraeus for their own purposes.

Philippic (59–61). In fact, the cumulative picture of Euphraeus' relations with Macedon yielded by all of our sources is basically coherent; while the elements that compose it show a great deal of partiality, they are not irreconcilable when the appropriate allowances are made. Demosthenes' account of Euphraeus' end is to be accepted in its essentials, and it easily justifies by itself Speusippus' tactful omission of the man's name in the *Letter to Philip*. But what were the circumstances that brought Euphraeus back to his native city, Oreus, and opposed him to Philip?

This is a question best answered through judicious use of a flawed source—namely, Carystius himself, who, in addition to his endorsement of the account by "Speusippus" that sees Euphraeus as instrumental in Philip's rise to power, relates how the incredible snobbery with which he excluded the ungeometrical and unphilosophical from the royal *hetairia*'s commensality brought about his arrest and execution once Philip took the throne.[86] The Academic's abuse of his courtly privileges is described in language that recalls Speusippus' assault on the position of the Isocratean Theopompus in the *Letter to Philip*. In each source, the learned courtier is slanderous (*blasphēmein*, *Letter to Philip* 12; *diabolos*, Athenaeus 11.508e), engages in meddlesome activity introduced by the predicative use of the *psukhr-* stem (παρ' ὑμῖν μὲν εἶναι πάνυ ψυχρόν, *Letter to Philip* 12; ψυχρῶς συνέταξε τὴν ἑταιρίαν τοῦ βασιλέως, Athenaeus 11.508e), and occupies his position at court through an injustice that must be or has been repaired by his elimination from account (ὑπὸ πάντων ἐξαλειφόμενος, *Letter to Philip* 12; λαβὼν ἀπέκτεινεν, Athenaeus 11.508e). If we are at all ready to accept that these charges could be made against Theopompus, in what was eventually a successful campaign to shore up the courtly influence of the wider Academic circle, then perhaps we can entertain the hypothesis that Carystius, too, has preserved the kernel of Euphraeus' situation. Carystius has the advantage of being the only source for Euphraeus' career that explicitly characterizes both his influence under Perdiccas and his disfavor under Philip. Even if this picture is colored with lurid tones, none of the other available information contradicts the basic idea of Euphraeus' abruptly altered position vis-à-vis the monarchy.

---

[86] ὅθεν, Φιλίππου τὴν ἀρχὴν παραλαβόντος, Παρμενίων αὐτὸν ἐν Ὠρεῷ λαβὼν ἀπέκτεινεν, ὥς φησι Καρύστιος ἐν Ἱστορικοῖς Ὑπομνήμασι (Athenaeus 11.508e). Besides Carystius' apparent generic tendency to serve up scandalous tales about philosophers, which will be addressed below, notice should be taken of how the story in Athenaeus passes from Euphraeus' lording it over the court in Macedon to his being arrested in Oreus, without any time frame or explanation for the transition. While it is possible that Euphraeus left his position at the Macedonian court before Perdiccas' death, we would certainly like to know why. Perhaps more likely is that the truth in Demosthenes' account, which presupposes a time of political (or merely quasi-political: see below) activities in Oreus during the reign of Philip, has been glossed over by Carystius, who may be more interested in Euphraeus' intemperate philosophical zeal than in the factional tendencies of the Macedonian court as the motive force of his story.

What, then, was Euphraeus' status at Perdiccas' court? For this period we have, in addition to the *Letter to Philip* and Carystius, another important independent source—the fifth Platonic letter.[87] This text, which purports to be Plato's recommendation of Euphraeus to Perdiccas, characterizes Euphraeus' potential role in the king's service:

πολλὰ μὲν γὰρ ὁ ἀνὴρ χρήσιμος, μέγιστον δὲ οὗ καὶ σὺ νῦν ἐνδεὴς εἶ διά τε τὴν ἡλικίαν καὶ διὰ τὸ μὴ πολλοὺς αὐτοῦ πέρι συμβούλους εἶναι τοῖς νέοις. ἔστιν γὰρ δή τις φωνὴ τῶν πολιτειῶν ἑκάστης καθαπερεί τινων ζῴων, ἄλλη μὲν δημοκρατίας, ἄλλη δ' ὀλιγαρχίας, ἡ δ' αὖ μοναρχίας· ταύτας φαῖεν μὲν ἂν ἐπίστασθαι πάμπολλοι, πλεῖστον δ' ἀπολείπονται τοῦ κατανοεῖν αὐτὰς πλὴν ὀλίγων δή τινων. ἥτις μὲν ἂν οὖν τῶν πολιτειῶν τὴν αὑτῆς φθέγγηται φωνὴν πρός τε θεοὺς καὶ πρὸς ἀνθρώπους, καὶ τῇ φωνῇ τὰς πράξεις ἑπομένας ἀποδιδῷ, θάλλει τε ἀεὶ καὶ σῴζεται, μιμουμένη δ' ἄλλην φθείρεται. πρὸς ταῦτ' οὖν Εὐφραῖός σοι γίγνοιτ' οὐχ ἥκιστα ἂν χρήσιμος, καίπερ καὶ πρὸς ἄλλα ὢν ἀνδρεῖος· τοὺς γὰρ τῆς μοναρχίας λόγους οὐχ ἥκιστ' αὐτὸν ἐλπίζω συνεξευρήσειν τῶν περὶ τὴν σὴν διατριβὴν ὄντων· εἰς ταῦτ' οὖν αὐτῷ χρώμενος ὀνήσῃ τε αὐτὸς καὶ ἐκεῖνον πλεῖστα ὠφελήσεις.

The man can be of service to you in many ways, but most of all in supplying what you now lack, for you are young and there are not many who can counsel young men about it. Constitutions, like species of animals, have each their own language—democracy one, oligarchy another, and monarchy still another. Many persons would say they know these languages [*phōnai*, cf. *Republic* 493b3–5], but for the most part, and with rare exceptions, they fall short of understanding them. The constitution that speaks its own language to gods and men, and suits its actions to its words [*phōnē*], always prospers and survives; but it goes to ruin if it imitates another. Now in this Euphraeus can perhaps be of most use to you, though he will be a manly aid in other respects as well; I believe that he can search out the words [*logoi*] appropriate to monarchy as well as any man in your service. Use him, then, for this,

---

87 This letter, though it may not be genuine, and though it has suffered from being pressed for insights it simply does not offer into the nature of the Academy's relationship with the Macedonian court, is nonetheless hardly explicable except as an Academic document; there is no obvious or economical explanation for its falsely placing the otherwise obscure Euphraeus in this general context. Another source relevant here is Harpocration s.v., who also identifies Euphraeus as a member of the Academy; this could derive from the Platonic text, though there must have been other available sources, including the one that lies behind Carystius' information.

and you will not only profit yourself but confer upon him a very great benefit.

Plato *Epistle* V 321d2–322a4 (trans. Morrow 1997)

This passage puts the emphasis squarely on Euphraeus' qualifications in political theory, despite its speaking of utility to a real monarch. Even Euphraeus' potential rivals in "searching out the *logoi* of monarchy"—whom we might easily imagine as products of a less philosophical and more conventional political *paideia*—are classed as "those connected with your *diatribē*," a word in which it is hard not to hear philosophical or scholastic connotations when it is applied to a serious pursuit.[88]

Though the Platonic epistle's appraisal of Euphraeus' likely functions is evidently partial, our other sources bestow some credibility on its idea of Euphraeus as something less (and something more) than the conventional politician imagined both by those who have scoured the record for evidence of a politically effective Academy and by those who, unable to accept the strange picture of court philosopher found in the Platonic letter and in Carystius, have placed all their stock in Demosthenes' conveniently opposite tribute to Euphraeus the principled enemy of Philip. The letter from "Plato" to Perdiccas, as Trampedach has said, is nonetheless credible as a "euphemistic" and "imprecise" confirmation of Carystius' savage portrayal of a philosopher gone amok.[89] These two accounts agree in making Euphraeus a philosopher at court, despite the wide gulf between the Academic source's sympathetic prospective and Carystius' contemptuous retrospective. Either or both of these would lead us to judge Euphraeus an ally of Perdiccas, and an example of a philosopher serving this role *as a philosopher*.

We need not imagine this alliance as exclusively "philosophical" in character, but we may suppose that the connection depended more on Perdiccas' personal approval than on conventional political credentials. Part of the reason for this is simply that Perdiccas did not most require dyed-in-the-wool partisans—the kind of factional propagandists made necessary only by Philip's ambitions in Greece.[90] The Speusippean *Letter to Philip* corroborates this view. Plato is defended from Theopompus' slander for two reasons given in parallel—his

---

[88] Bertelli (1977:108) associates Euphraeus' capacity for *logoi* in the Platonic epistle with Antipater's λόγοι δυνάμενοι τὴν σὴν ἀρχὴν ὠφελεῖν (*Letter to Philip* 8), but he takes this as evidence that both works are pastiches stitched together in an Academic workshop.

[89] Trampedach 1994:93; Trampedach does not accept it as genuine (ibid. 137n107).

[90] It was thus left for Speusippus to recommend a sycophantic toady, Antipater, to the Macedonian court. Plato died just a year before Isocrates' publication of the *Philip*, spared the possibly embarrassing opportunity to respond to the forces that provoked Speusippus to write his letter.

"having established the *arkhē* of your rule in Perdiccas' time" and what sounds like his repeated intervention (e.g. through Euphraeus?) to smooth out discord between Perdiccas and Philip (12, "as if Plato had not ... invariably borne it hardly if anything ungentle or unbrotherly arose between you"). Each service, here claimed as a benefaction to Philip, directly involved Perdiccas' affairs when Perdiccas was king. It is telling if the best praise Speusippus can give Plato is a diplomatically vague allusion to a service that may really have been rendered not for Philip's sake, and not for the sake of Macedonian rule per se, but in the course of a solicitous and personal concern for the affairs of the temperamentally quite different Perdiccas.[91] In other words, this allusion may have the defensive tone of, "Even if it didn't seem friendly to come between you and Perdiccas then, and even if it involved the offices of Euphraeus, a man I am loath to name since you may consider him as *psukhros* as the evil-tongued Theopompus about whom I have just warned you, consider in retrospect how necessary it all was to the eventual establishment of your present position." In any case, Demosthenes' tribute to Euphraeus' stance in Oreus confirms our impression that Euphraeus' understanding with Perdiccas meant that he was not destined to be a favorite of Philip—indeed, quite the opposite.

Bertelli responds with contradictory impulses to the body of evidence suggesting a relationship between Euphraeus and Perdiccas. On the one hand, he finds in it no sound basis for any important or continuing link between the Academy and Macedonian political affairs. On the other hand, he simultaneously depends on Carystius' "richer" account of such a link as evidence for an independent and superior textual tradition against which the *Letter to Philip* can be tested and found wanting.[92] These two purposes are at odds with one another, with the result that neither the utility of Carystius' information nor the authenticity of the Speusippean epistle is effectively impugned. It is quite appropriate to expose the extravagances of Carystius' tales, which Bertelli aptly calls, in the case of Philip or Parmenio's revenge on Euphraeus, "a flunked student's vendetta—exaggerated, to put it mildly."[93] But the critical weight rests on what are supposed to be the irreconcilable differences among the traditions for Euphraeus' career, and in Bertelli's exposition of these Carystius is esteemed

---

[91] For one explanation of how the very same *spoudaios* character traits that led to Euphraeus' swift execution upon Philip's rise to the throne may also have accounted for his being in a position to intervene in some discord between the two Macedonian brothers to Philip's benefit, see Griffith's comments in Hammond and Griffith 1979:206f. Griffith acknowledges the difficulty of identifying the occasion (ἀπομερίσαι) of Euphraeus' supposed benefaction with specific reference to Macedonian institutions; cf. Gomperz 1882:112n11: "Hardly more need be true than the one item, that Euphraeus, at the time of Philip's enfeoffment by Perdiccas, was staying at his court."

[92] See esp. Bertelli 1977a:80–82.

[93] Bertelli 1976:285. Cf. Natorp 1907 ("resentful").

as more reliable when he happens not to confirm a point in the *Letter to Philip* but is depreciated as a florid scandalmonger when his information discords with the other sources.

Thus Bertelli attaches value to the fact that there is no clear counterpart in Carystius to the *Letter to Philip*'s statement of Plato's directly and personally taking an interest in negotiating an ease to trouble between the royal brothers.[94] Yet we have seen above that this problematically personal intervention by Plato and his pupil can be used as a key to resolve Euphraeus' opposite situation vis-à-vis Perdiccas and Philip. Anyway, when Carystius goes beyond the *Letter to Philip* and spells out that it was Euphraeus through whose offices Philip's prospects for kingship were made easier, it is quite clear that Euphraeus is Plato's instrument (Εὐφραῖον γὰρ ἀπέστειλε τὸν Ὠρείτην πρὸς Περδίκκαν Πλάτων, ὃς ἔπεισεν ἀπομερίσαι τινὰ χώραν Φιλίππῳ, Athenaeus 11.506ef). In all fairness it is hard to see anything of significance in the *Letter to Philip* text (12, Πλάτωνος ... καὶ διὰ τέλους χαλεπῶς φέροντος, εἴ τι γίγνοιτο παρ' ὑμῖν ἀνήμερον ἢ μὴ φιλάδελφον) that is not explicitly or implicitly covered in this sentence of Athenaeus. Yet this is Bertelli's claim.[95] Given that our text of Carystius consists of the mere scraps Athenaeus has stitched into his own text, it is the extensive convergences with the *Letter to Philip* that should impress us rather than such a divergence as this. We must also be sure we are not discounting the possibility of other sources to which Carystius may have had access, which might make the "richness" of his information not simply a function of his usage of one fixed epistolary text.

As for the fifth Platonic letter, Bertelli acknowledges that challenging its Platonic authorship is not enough to dismiss its evidence, and he instead takes it as reliable information whose theoretical bent contradicts the heavy-duty, real-world kingmaking suggested in the *Letter to Philip* (12, τὴν ἀρχὴν τῆς ἀρχῆς ἐπὶ Περδίκκου κατασκευάσαντος), and to a lesser degree in Carystius' account of Euphraeus' courtly influence.[96] As I have also argued, it is very appropriate to emphasize the philosophical character of this text. But is the idea of Euphraeus as an expert in such *logoi* irreconcilable with the other sources? It must be

---

[94] Bertelli 1977a:82 and n22.

[95] Identifying the cited text of the *Letter to Philip* as "E," Bertelli (1977a:82) declares its absence in Carystius as more significant than Carystius' expansion to give a specific account of Euphraeus, which he has just been discussing: "Piuttosto è l'ultimo elemento (E) a suscitare non poche perplessità, non soltanto perché esso non ha riscontro in Caristio né è confermato da alter fonti, ma anche e soprattutto perché l'unico altro confronto che si può fare è con un documento molto sospetto quale l'ep. XXXI (Hercher) socratica, che per la sua genericità ad alcuni è sembrata un falso construito proprio su questa frase di ep. XXX." As for this second, supposedly weightier, reason for suspicion, it is really no positive reason at all, since the Socratic epistle in question has been almost universally regarded as a later, and thus irrelevant and possibly derivative, forgery (Bertelli's citation of Momigliano's transitory "impression of authenticity" notwithstanding).

[96] Bertelli 1977a:81.

remembered that the *Letter to Philip* limits itself to a brief allusion to what may well have been a complex and contentious episode in the inner workings of the Macedonian royal family. Speusippus, in addressing Philip, is trying delicately to rehabilitate the Academic name with a ruler who may well have been antagonized precisely by the intellectual impositions suggested by the prospective and retrospective versions furnished by the Platonic letter and Carystius. The recasting of what may be all too true in Carystius into political terms is a predictable part of the rhetoric of a letter that seeks to persuade a king that the terms of "justice" and "injustice" have been mistakenly applied (by his royal highness himself!) to the men of letters seeking favor at his court.

Finally, to get to the crux of Bertelli's objections to the Euphraeus–Perdiccas connection, we must consider the criteria by which he chose to rely on Demosthenes' portrayal, excluding any reading that tries to flesh out what we learn from the fifth Platonic letter in the light of Carystius' story of a flamboyant philosopher who negotiated Philip's status during his brother's reign. For Bertelli, the problem of Carystius' colorful excesses is compounded by the alleged fact that he garbles the story of Euphraeus' life—particularly, the story of his death.[97] This utter historical unreliability is essential to demonstrate if we are going to use Demosthenes' "anti-Macedonian" (anti-Philip, at least) Euphraeus to deny any "political" significance (in any sense) to the fifth Platonic letter. But it is on this point that Bertelli overreaches the most, appealing to Theodor Gomperz's 1882 article, "Die Akademie und ihr vermeintlicher Philomacedonismus," in support of his thesis that Carystius is "un ben cattivo lettore di Demostene."[98] Gomperz had indeed claimed that Carystius' account of Euphraeus' death could be rejected after a comparison to what Demosthenes says in the *Third Philippic*,[99] but it is critical to know what Bertelli does not tell us, that Gomperz was utterly unaware of the existence of the actual *Letter to Philip*; for him, any "letter of Speusippus" was known only through the reference to it in Athenaeus-Carystius.[100] When the *Letter to Philip* (whose somewhat different

---

[97] If Carystius, at the end of Bertelli's various challenges to his coherence, stands in some discredit, this is certainly not to the benefit of his argument doubting Speusippean authorship, which asks us to prefer Carystius' "independent" tradition of a Speusippean letter to that of the *Letter to Philip* itself. Any doubts as to whether Carystius can answer such expectations will be seen to be all the more costly once we have raised problems that cast doubt on whether the second pillar of this tradition proposed by Bertelli, Theopompus (FGrHist 115 F 294 = Diogenes Laertius 3.40), is in fact a parallel to Carystius at all (see below).

[98] Bertelli 1976:285.

[99] "Erweist sich ... Karystios durch seine dem Demosthenes widersprechenden Angaben über das Ende des Euphraios (Athen. 11, 508, E) als ein wenig genauer Kenner dieser Dinge" (Gomperz 1882:112).

[100] Bertelli's reaching back to Gomperz's polemical 1882 review of Bernays's *Phokion* indicates the strength of his dislike for the idea of Academic philo-Macedonism; yet Carystius, on whom

pedigree, and thus independent value, from the Carystian citation Bertelli himself has ably demonstrated) is taken into account, the formula is changed for evaluating fairly the historical evidence concerning Euphraeus' final days. I have already explained why an enmity between Euphraeus and Philip, following Philip's succession of Perdiccas, need not be regarded as a strange reversal of the Academic's sympathies; indeed, this would be an unsound "political" reading (mistaking enduring international factional commitments, rather than the more tenuous project of seeking scholastic influence and patronage, as the motive for a philosopher's encounters with statesmen).

If Carystius is not merely an aberrant text, we should look at its evidence for Euphraeus' end critically. The enmity between Euphraeus and Philip is a constant between Carystius and Demosthenes. So is the setting of Euphraeus' death at Oreus, an unexplained leap from the stories of Euphraeus at court[101] and thus a likely sign of Athenaeus' telescoping of his source narrative. The discrepancy is supposed to occur between Demosthenes' placement of Euphraeus' trouble in the context of the occupation of Oreus, and Carystius' implication that Parmenio took revenge swiftly on Euphraeus as soon as Perdiccas was out of the picture. Actually the text states only that Parmenio arrested and executed Euphraeus after that time, though the circumstantial participle does imply a connection.[102] Therefore, Carystius could be placing this execution at the same time as Demosthenes, in which case Parmenio could be identified, as some have suggested, as one of the leaders involved in taking Oreus whom Demosthenes does not identify.[103]

Even Demosthenes' version may ultimately make more sense if its character "Euphraeus" is more a philosopher than a political force. Even if its necessary priority is denied, its nature as public speech requires us to relate its various claims to what was arguable and potentially believable at the time of its delivery. Demosthenes' rhetorical motivations are every bit as palpable as Carystius'. Just as Speusippus is eager to claim Euphraeus' alleged benefaction in the name of Plato without bringing any residual odium too directly to mind,

---

Bertelli must depend more generally as a witness to the "truth" about Speusippus and Philip, affirms loud and clear an Academy that enjoyed, and worried over, friendly relations with Macedon. The more Carystius' alleged recklessness with major historical facts is called into question, the less easily we can dismiss Carystius as a source—not so hard to reconcile with the others—for the nature of the Academy–Macedon relationship.

[101] See above.

[102] Cf. the ease with which Griffith disposes of this problem with the proper solution: "The amusing inaccuracy of Carystius here (the capture of Oreus being about eighteen years later at least) implies a rare unpopularity of Euphraeus among the leading Macedonians" (Hammond and Griffith 1979:206.)

[103] Trampedach 1994:96f., citing articles by Brunt and Cawkwell published well in advance of Bertelli's work.

so too Demosthenes wishes to evoke the very convenient moment of Euphraeus' unyielding bitterness and endurance of his opportunistic countrymen's hatred when the Macedonian army was at the gates. This made for good rhetoric even if this crisis was an ironic vicissitude in the context of the Academic's whole life, including his probable relationship with Perdiccas (whose attachments were really not so great a concern to Demosthenes as he faced the challenges of the present moment in his *Third Philippic*). Moreover, as Trampedach has suggested, even at the end of Euphraeus' life, we need not understand Demosthenes as presenting us with a man who has become a conventional politician. Rather, we best appreciate Demosthenes' character-sketch when we consider Euphraeus' philosophical background:

> Yet Demosthenes described him as a lone fighter and not as the leader of a "party" or indeed of a "regime." (Against Brunt, who calls Euphraeus "the genuine democratic leader at Oreus" and Wirth, who speaks of the "Athens-friendly regime of Euphraeus"...) Euphraeus was obviously no politician at all in the narrow sense. He interfered when he saw the unity of the polis threatened by a clique willing to fight a civil war. This, and the civic courage with which he did it, could be understood as the product of a philosophical ethos. A long-term political program, however, that went beyond the preservation of the democratic status quo, is something Euphraeus seems not to have pursued.[104]

This is an attractive argument that Euphraeus never really crossed the line into the field of politics. While arising from a different point of view, these questions about the "political" adventures of someone like Euphraeus assist our developing understanding of how the inner-circle world of philosophers, with its intellectual and literary concerns, could seek to situate itself with reference to or even within courtly circles, but in a manner that does not really resemble naked political intervention.

Besides the question of implicit versus explicit reference to Euphraeus, Bertelli's second concern with the congruity of the *Letter to Philip* and Carystius as parallel texts is that the *grammatikos* Carystius has failed to preserve the rhetorical turn of τὴν ἀρχὴν τῆς ἀρχῆς, instead offering the more banal τὴν ἀρχὴν τῆς βασιλείας.[105] But this objection loses its force if we do not accept the premise that the true and original Speusippean text named Euphraeus and explicitly defined his contribution to Philip's career. For otherwise Carystius is trying to clarify what is unquestionably an obscure point in the *Letter to Philip*,

---

[104] Trampedach 1994:97.
[105] Bertelli 1977a:80.

and it is to that end that we should expect him to adapt the text, especially when he has clearly indicated the imprecision with which he is adducing it. Carystius, *grammatikos* or not, is quoted by Athenaeus as author of a historical work whose point is to describe Euphraeus' strange and precarious position as a philosophical courtier, and then his consequent demise. (It is necessary to consider together Athenaeus' two references to Carystius' discussion of Euphraeus' career in his *Historica Hypomnemata*—the one at 11.506ef and the one at 11.508e.)

So far, in analyzing the relationship between the *Letter to Philip* and Carystius' awareness of related events as preserved in Athenaeus, the issues have concerned rhetorical methods and motivations: what was stated implicitly or explicitly and why, and whether Euphraeus' role in Macedonian affairs was colored as more political or philosophical. These points have deserved so much of our attention because it is in regard to them that we possess the most extensive and interesting outside, parallel traditions for the politico-scholastic situation described in the *Letter to Philip*; this is apparent from a glance at the table[106] in which Bertelli lays out, in one column, what the Socratic epistle says about Theopompus at Philip's court, Philip's debt to Plato, and Plato's involvement in affairs between Philip and Perdiccas, and in another column, the points of comparison that can be drawn from Carystius. Taken as a whole, the numerous points of connection are more impressive than the discrepancies in emphasis noted so far, and we have explored the historical and rhetorical conditions that can explain the various expression of the same events in our different sources. But when it comes to one crucial name, Carystius differs factually from the *Letter to Philip*, and on this one point Carystius, on whose weaknesses as a historian Bertelli places such stress, is apparently echoed in a fragment of Theopompus himself, a contemporary of the events, a participant in the events (in our view[107]), and (especially in contrast to Carystius) a "fonte ben informata e certamente independente da ep. XXX."[108] This is the third column in Bertelli's table of sources, much shorter than the other two—since limited to this one point—but much weightier in the argument for the existence of a more trustworthy tradition in the light of which questions can be raised about the authenticity and authority of the parallel presentation found in the *Letter to Philip*.

Whereas the *Letter to Philip* 12 focuses on Theopompus' presence at Philip's court, Athenaeus' text, as we have seen, says that "Speusippus, learning that *Philip* was speaking ill about Plato wrote in a letter ..." (11.506e). Bertelli seeks a fourth-century corroboration of this version, and a crucial support for a

---

[106] Bertelli 1977a:79.

[107] One need not accept the *Letter to Philip* in order to place Theopompus at Philip's court; this is discussed below.

[108] Bertelli 1977a:78.

stream of tradition independent of the *Letter to Philip*, in a reported statement by Theopompus (F 294 = Diogenes Laertius 3.40, on the death of Plato), which has been variously interpreted as meaning that "according to Theopompus honors were paid to [Plato] by Philip" (trans. Hicks 1925) or that "according to Theopompus Plato was criticized by Philip" (Bertelli).[109]

Bertelli does not quote this in Greek but offers it in Italian, "Filippo, 'dal quale—dice Teopompo—Platone era criticato.'"[110] This interpretation seems to follow that of Bickermann, who referred to the text only in German, "Bei Theopomp stand, daß Philipp Plato gescholten hätte."[111] Despite their differences on whether Carystius was conflating what he had read in Theopompus and in the *Letter to Philip* (so Bickermann) or whether the accuracy of Carystius' hypothetical alternative version of our *Letter to Philip* is confirmed by Theopompus' independent information (so Bertelli), the two scholars concur that the Theopompus text agrees with Carystius' account and must be reckoned as related to it. But this interpretation is open to doubt.

Bickermann and Bertelli did not pause over the meaning that ἐπιτιμηθῆναι held for Theopompus. The passive of this verb with a personal subject seems to be attested only once elsewhere in Greek up to Theopompus' time.[112] Otherwise, outside of some papyri,[113] I have found no comparable passive in Greek before the first century BC.[114] Despite the poor attestation of grammatical parallels, we would have to understand that Theopompus meant "censured" in the absence of other documented possibilities. But there is a significant and relevant alternative model that he may have followed. Herodotus tells how the younger Miltiades, on inheriting the rule of the Chersonese when his brother Stesagoras was assassinated, manipulated his potential political enemies under the pretense of honoring his dead sibling: Μιλτιάδης δὲ ἀπικόμενος ἐς τὴν Χερσόνησον εἶχε κατ' οἴκους, τὸν ἀδελφεὸν Στησαγόρην δηλαδὴ ἐπιτιμέων

---

[109] καὶ ἐτελεύτα μὲν ὃν εἴπομεν τρόπον Φιλίππου βασιλεύοντος ἔτος τρισκαιδέκατον, καθὰ καὶ Φαβωρῖνός φησιν Ἀπομνημονευμάτων τρίτῳ. ὑφ' οὗ καὶ ἐπιτιμηθῆναί φησιν αὐτὸν Θεόπομπος.

[110] Bertelli 1977a:78.

[111] Bickermann and Sykutris 1928:37n2.

[112] Isocrates *Panathenaicus* 149, εἰκότως ἂν ἐπιτιμῴμην (where we might expect εἰκότως ἄν μοι ἐπιτιμῷτο). Theopompus was perhaps thirty-five when the elderly Isocrates began work on this oration. Another such present passive is not extant before Cassius Dio.

[113] P. Cair. Zen. 59314, 250 BC, lines 7f., τὸν δὲ Ἡρακλείδην νύκτα ἡμέραν ποιούμενος ἀπόστειλον, ἵνα μὴ ἐπιτιμηθῶμεν; P. Enteux. 79, 218 BC, line 8, ἐπιτιμηθεῖσα δὲ ὑπό τινων τῶν παρόντων.

[114] The next extant example of such an aorist passive after Theopompus would be Diodorus Siculus 11.40.2, ὁ μὲν Θεμιστοκλῆς ἀνακληθεὶς ὑπὸ τῶν ἀρχόντων καὶ ἐπιτιμηθεὶς (another aorist passive infinitive such as we find in Diogenes', or Favorinus', report of Theopompus occurs only in Galen *Adversus Lycum libellus* p. 239 Kühn; cf. a sole comparable example of the perfect passive, roughly contemporary, Polybius 7.12.9. (Around this time we start to see transitive usage in a distinct sense, "punish," e.g. Diodorus Siculus 3.67.2, but especially in Jewish writers, e.g. Josephus *Jewish Antiquities* 5.105, LXX 3 Maccabees 2:24; cf. Bauer 1979 s.v.)

("kept inside, ostensibly honoring his brother Stesagoras," 6.39.2). Though this usage is unusual, we will see that it is more appropriate to the context, and that it makes sense in terms of Theopompus' literary inclinations. But in strictly grammatical terms, the evidence on the other side is limited to one sentence. The fact that Herodotus uses the verb not in the passive, but with a personal direct object, and in a clearly distinct sense, marks his usage more definitely as a distinct one.[115] For the same reasons that modern lexica have been well aware of the unusual Herodotean usage as such, whereas the uncommon slippage into the personal passive has been less remarked,[116] the signal and clear example in Herodotus may have constituted more of a warrant for Theopompus. There is no question that Theopompus was extraordinarily well acquainted with Herodotus' book; he made numerous borrowings from it (sometimes adapting individual sentences to the narration of different historical facts) and wrote an *Epitome of Herodotus*. It seems to have been a very conscious literary emulation.[117]

Moreover, the context in which Diogenes Laertius quotes Theopompus makes it more likely that the meaning is that Plato died in the thirteenth year of the reign of Philip, "by whom Theopompus says he was honored." The aorist well befits a statement of what happened on the occasion of Plato's death;[118] the interpretation of Bickermann and Bertelli makes the reference to Philip's censure of Plato into a cryptic and unanchored indication of something in the past, and it makes the immediate passage an awkward pastiche of information verging on incoherence. The Herodotean passage relates specifically to a ruler's showing posthumous honor to a deceased notable, which is precisely the situation I propose Theopompus meant to describe.[119] On the other hand, we are not likely to find a parallel for ἐπιτιμάω referring to a postmortem rebuke.

In this small but coherent fragment of Theopompus, one word, ἐπιτιμηθῆναι, constitutes the heart of the predicate, and it is not likely to mean "criticato" or "gescholten." If we cannot positively or perfectly explain the text of Carystius

---

[115] Even in later sources such as the papyri, the active of ἐπιτιμάω takes a dative personal object with extreme (and apparently total) regularity. It is procedurally difficult to have the same degree of certainty in eliminating the possibility of additional occurrences of ἐπιτιμάω with a personal direct object, but it would be surprising if such examples had escaped the notice of modern lexicographers.

[116] For example, LSJ omits the lone Isocratean instance I have cited, giving Polybius as the first and only example of the personal passive.

[117] The nature of the *Epitome* (T 1, FF 1–4) is not perfectly clear, but it seems to have been an unprecedented kind of text. See Christ 1993 and the response in Flower 1997:253f.

[118] Note that Diogenes Laertius is likely taking the citation of Theopompus from the same passage of Favorinus' *Memorabilia* that stated how far into Philip's reign Plato had died.

[119] Translators have chosen the interpretation I justify here: Hicks 1925 (with a footnote citing Herodotus); Shrimpton 1991:257, "Theopompus says that he was held in honour by Philip [or, was honoured by Philip at his funeral]."

in the form that it has reached us, we can in any case reject the idea that Theopompus is an adequate basis for shifting the discussion to a place where "il problema da risolvere resta appunto questo: spiegare la variante di ep. XXX, 12, che al posto di Filippo introduce Teopompo come detrattore di Platone,"[120] since we lack reason to suppose that the *Letter to Philip* contains a "variant" that "introduces" the name of Theopompus. To the contrary, it is easier to explain the substitution, somewhere along the line,[121] of "Philip" for "Theopompus with his influence at Philip's court." Indeed, this could even be understood as a loose shorthand for the same factual situation. If Carystius and the *Letter to Philip* are related as textual witnesses, then Theopompus' name, as read in *Epistula Socratica* 30, is preferable as the *lectio difficilior*.

Contestants, Motivations, and Literary Modes in the *Letter to Philip*

In showing that there are not insuperable difficulties in the way of accepting the *Letter to Philip*'s standing as an original source grappling with the political valences of Euphraeus and Theopompus, we have deferred some more general questions concerning whether and how the letter is credible as a document that in fact arose among this cast of characters, with their relative positions and motivations. We are now ready to consider the participants in the drama that the epistle implies: where they were in their lives; their affiliations, interests (intellectual and "political"), motivations, and rivalries; and how the contents of the *Letter to Philip* would have been topical to them.

Speusippus' reasons for displacing the slandering Theopompus from his position at court, on which we have been focusing so far, are in fact but a brief tangent to his sustained attack on Isocrates as a historian, as a writer, and above all as a friend to Philip. The Academic philosopher is recommending to the monarch the useful qualities of the man bearing his letter, Antipater of Magnesia, a historian who creatively deploys mythological and political arguments so as not only to deny the construction put on Philip's actions by his enemies, but even to expound his shining beneficence to the Amphipolitans and Olynthians and his (mythologically based) legitimate claims to being regarded as Athens' citizen and benefactor and to hold rightful sway over the Delphic Amphictyony.[122]

---

[120] Bertelli 1977a:78. Cf. ibid. 100, where the question of what the "Philip" reading would actually mean is raised.

[121] Note that Carystius at this point is not yet directly quoting "Speusippus."

[122] For a consideration of how Isocrates' students Theopompus and Ephorus took up the challenge of defending Philip's conduct in the Third Sacred War, see Squillace 2010:72–75.

In so arguing, Antipater would show up the inadequacies of Isocrates' famous *Philip*, published in 346. This discourse had certainly invested Philip with heroic potential, but its task was more delicate, as it also sought to persuade the monarch, pressing him to realize his plans in Greece and abroad so as to prove wrong his enemies' ungenerous interpretations. Isocrates sought to make Philip feel the pressure of such inimical views without being seen as putting his own weight behind them. This job was nobler but more difficult, and it left him wide open to the sniping of an Antipater. For Isocrates had used the same legendary web of connections between Philip's family and the Greek *poleis* cited by Antipater, but to urge the king to treat his *philoi* with gentleness and restraint, not to justify an imperious sense of entitlement. Thus, if Argos is Philip's fatherland (*patris*, *Philip* 32), then this is reason for the king to show her as much care (*pronoia*) as he would to his own ancestors, and if Heracles is honored by the Thebans, Spartans, and Athenians (33f.), then this is a debt to be repaid:

> Therefore, seeing that these cities have each and all shown such a spirit, no quarrel should ever have arisen between you and any one of them. But unfortunately we are all prone by nature to do wrong more often than right; and so it is fair to charge the mistakes of the past to our common weakness. Yet for the future you must be on your guard to prevent a like occurrence, and must consider what service you can render them which will make it manifest that you have acted in a manner worthy both of yourself and of what these cities have done. And the opportunity now serves you; for you would only be repaying the debt of gratitude which you owed them, but, because so much time has elapsed, they will credit you with being first in friendly offices. And it is a good thing to have the appearance of conferring benefits upon the greatest states of Hellas and at the same time to profit yourself no less than them. But apart from this, if anything unpleasant has arisen between you and any of them, you will wipe it out completely; for friendly acts in the present crisis will make you forget the wrongs which you have done each other in the past.
>
> Isocrates *Philip* 35–37 (trans. Norlin 1928–1929)

After an interval of only a few years, Antipater would feel free to argue that the bonds between Philip and these *poleis* had precisely the effect of entitling him not to use the cautious sense of responsibility that Isocrates here demands. In comparison, Isocrates' performance of didactic authority commands respect.

Does the difference lie in the writer or in the rapidly changing political situation? Let us consider briefly what had transpired in the meantime. Demosthenes went from the guarded vigilance of *On the Peace* to the *Second Philippic*'s clear note of warning (in 344), while Philip had to counter such suspicions as Demosthenes had planted during his embassy to Argos and Messene with proposals for autonomy under a Common Peace (*koinē eirēnē*). Isocrates in 344 wrote a letter to Philip pursuing the program of the *Philip*,[123] but any further political efforts in this direction are conspicuously absent from his work until the dying gasp of his final letter to the king,[124] which defied the hope-crushing event of Chaeronea. In the changed moment that produced Speusippus' *Letter to Philip*, a new standard of loyalty, and a higher pitch of praise, could be demanded.[125]

Consequently, the Isocratean and Speusippean texts are separated not only by a gap in political perspectives and methods, but by a concomitant generic shift brought about through the radically altered positions assumed by writer and royal addressee. The terms of this relationship were changeable as unipolar power eclipsed the relevance of the wider arena of political opinion, which had required a more sophisticated (and authoritative) negotiation of the transaction on the orator's part. Rolf-Bernhard Essig has seen Isocrates as the proper starting point for a history of the "open letter" that continues on to Grass by way of Luther and Zola. This perspective helps us recognize how the symbuleutic writer's tendency simultaneously creates a representation of himself and effects a change in his addressee, a process exemplified in the *Philip*, and in stark contrast to the terms of Speusippus' answer:

> The unusually self-assured position that Isocrates takes up in the text can be clearly recognized in comparison with another open letter, which was written by Speusippus as a sort of "Anti-*Philip*." In it there is not one admonitory word, no advice addressed to Philip; here it is praise and panegyric to the great Macedonian that predominates above all—Speusippus practices harsh criticism only on his rival Isocrates.[126]

On the level of how and where the polemical wording is being focused, it is interesting to note that whereas for Isocrates (*Philip* 37) Philip himself can and must do away with (*dialuseis*) anything that is unpleasant (*aēdes*) between him and the Greek *poleis*, Speusippus (*Letter to Philip* 12) is arguing that since Plato helped prevent anything ungentle (*anēmeron*) from internally unsettling the Macedonian polity, his attacker Theopompus should justly be obliterated from the consciousness of the larger courtly and international audience (ὑπὸ πάντων

---

[123] Isocrates *Epistle* 2.

[124] Isocrates *Epistle* 3.

[125] Bearing in mind the limitations of this explanatory framework, which I have suggested above, it is possible that Speusippus erred in sensing such a decisive shift in the requirements determining the usefulness of philosophers and writers to the king.

[126] Essig 2000:38.

ἐξαλειφόμενος).[127] Where Isocrates was able to speak of Philip's own missteps (πεπλημμελημένων), Speusippus' boldness is in declaring Theopompus' enjoyment of the king's favor to be an abusive injustice (ἀδικῶς δὲ τῆς παρὰ σοῦ χορηγίας τυγχάνων).

But if Isocratean politics, with its multiple audiences and its carefully constructed admonitory authority, was perhaps less relevant in 343/2 BC, then we must explain the motives of Speusippus' urgent counterblast, which is savage in its determination to discredit Isocrates, even if it considers challenging the orator in his own political terms to be unnecessary. With the turning of the political tide, Speusippus' efforts might appear not only ugly but gratuitous. But this is so only if we accept the surface appearance of the *Letter to Philip* as concerned with a merely personal target, the man Isocrates. In fact, the nonagenarian Isocrates can have consumed Speusippus' scheming mind only in terms of the influence he projected beyond himself, as master of a school. The elderly Isocrates himself—"Isocratean" precisely in that no extrapolation of his personal political evolution would ever have gotten him to the point of giving an answer to Antipater's sycophantic slanders in their own terms[128]—was not the one on whom Speusippus so keenly wanted his epistle to inflict political damage. But younger products of Isocrates' school such as Theopompus, "Isocratean" in scholastic-political affiliation, were easily versatile and varied enough among themselves to take up arms and fight Speusippus on equal terms. This is why the tangent attacking Theopompus is so important: it lets us solidly fill out the analogy whereby Speusippus aggressively engages the ancient Isocrates just as Theopompus goes after the dead scholarch Plato.[129] While there are many detailed issues of "topicality" raised by the

---

[127] "Obliterate" or "erase": Speusippus again uses the vocabulary of texts to define the struggle for King Philip; likewise the erasure will be effected by comparative reading to Theopompus' disadvantage (*paranagnōnai*).

[128] Although Isocrates' political "negotiations," as we describe them here, have so often been disadvantageously compared to the policy of Demosthenes, his political frankness and independence compare favorably to the coarser politics of the next generation. This parallels the prominence of overt polemics among Plato and Isocrates' pupils (despite the limited quantity of evidence for their work), beside which the textual traces of an alleged feud between Plato and Isocrates are unimpressive.

[129] Thus Bertelli (1977a:83f.), in noticing the marked contrast between Isocrates' circumspection and Theopompus' recklessness in directing their criticisms of the rival Platonic *paideia* to the Macedonian court ("La mancanza di cautela da parte dello storico fa uno strano contrasto con le critiche molto circospette e cautelose avanzate da Isocrate nella breve lettera ad Alessandro giovane, *Ep.* V, contro l'impostazione eristico-dialettica data da Aristotele all'educazione del giovane principe"), has noticed an important phenomenon, but one that is not best made to serve (as in Bertelli's argument) as evidence to dismiss the report of Theopompus' slandering Plato at court as a false intrusion into the *Letter to Philip*, since the dissonance between the styles of teacher and student can be resolved along the lines I argue here. For Bertelli's further

letter's specific references to the international politics of the preceding years, it is the topicality of Isocrates himself that stands as the most glaring and extreme indicator of how the author's universe of friends and enemies, ascendance and oblivion, works along the chain of literary and philosophical education, and not according to the terms of ordinary political currency. The focus on Isocrates in the epistle (from whatever post-343 Academic circle one believes it issues) is one of the most important indirect testimonies to the influence of a larger, lasting Isocratean movement.[130] In the end, the *Letter to Philip*, by deeming the Isocrateans to be an important target worth going after so strenuously, calls its own message into question, only reinforcing our impression of the scholastic prestige enjoyed by Isocrates and his school.[131]

While situating the *Letter to Philip* in relation to Isocrates' and Philip's political programs is relatively straightforward, evidence illuminating the letter's place in Speusippus' life is more elusive. As it happens, the *Letter to Philip* is Speusippus' only fairly secure appearance in the historical tradition during the years of his scholarchy (347–339).[132] We can draw some confirmation of the philosopher's epistolary activities from the list of works in Diogenes Laertius (4.4f.), which includes *Letters to Dion, to Dionysius, to Philip*.[133] There are important hints that Plato's nephew Speusippus, who heads the main list of his students (*mathētai*),[134] carried on publicly a quite personal relationship with Isocrates.

---

thoughts on the letter's abruptly personal focus and narrowly scholastic perspective, see Bertelli 1977a:101, where he labels the descent into freely broadcasting specious arguments a "trahison des clercs."

[130] One of Bickermann's most important arguments for the letter's authenticity (or at least its attachment to the 340s BC or very soon thereafter) is that it is so alive to the importance of Isocrates as a specifically political writer. On other considerations, the letter must have been written in either the fourth century BC or ca. the first century AD, and it is hard to imagine anyone putting together the political drama in the latter period: "This period, however, had completely lost any understanding of Isocrates as a political writer of the day. His value was rather only as a teacher and rhetor, whose writing appeared to be σχεδὸν ἐναντία τῇ τῶν πολιτικῶν [virtually the opposite of political discourse]. His *inanis sermonis elegantia* ["empty elegance of style," Cicero *De oratore* 3.141, see chap. 3] was conceived as just the opposite of political discourse and activity. On the other hand, he was highly praised and extolled as a moralist: one must only read Dionysius' appreciation. How, then, could a forger in that time, for whatever purpose he may have worked to produce the document either as prosopopoeia or as an alleged autograph of the fourth century, arrive at this conception of Isocrates—completely out of joint for his contemporaries—as a journalist in the service of Macedonia?" (Bickermann and Sykutris 1928:36f.).

[131] Compare the continued political topicality of Aristotle in Athens after his death, Ford 2011:67.

[132] Trampedach 1994:138, avoiding the straw men handled by Tarán (1981:5n14).

[133] Thus Dionysius and Philip both seem to have had letters addressed to them by Isocrates and Speusippus alike. To this list we may juxtapose Speusippus' accusation that Isocrates recycled his *Philip* from material previously peddled to Dionysius and others (*Letter to Philip* 13). For Isocrates' other appeals to monarchs, cf. Ostwald and Lynch 1994:599f., Frolíková 1979.

[134] Diogenes Laertius 3.46.

A controversial sentence forms part of a list of Speusippean "firsts" preserved by Diogenes Laertius: "And [Speusippus] was the first to disclose the so-called 'secret' material from Isocrates' school, as Caeneus [Aphareus?] says" (καὶ πρῶτος παρὰ Ἰσοκράτους τὰ καλούμενα ἀπόρρητα ἐξήνεγκεν, ὥς φησι Καινεύς [Ἀφαρεύς Gigante], 4.2).[135] The interest of this statement has been somewhat obscured by its being used, perhaps overambitiously, to claim that Speusippus must have received some education at Isocrates' school; it is apparently the only basis for this oft-repeated factoid about Speusippus' life.[136] We need not bite at this tantalizing possibility. More clearly, the sentence does provide an additional reflection of ancient traditions about the hostility between Speusippus and Isocrates. Hermann Usener has made a very plausible suggestion for the occasion on which Speusippus' divulged the *aporrēta*: his work *Pros ton Amarturon*, listed by Diogenes Laertius (4.5).[137] This was Speusippus' entry in the rhetorical controversy that had already resulted, at least, in Antisthenes' *Pros ton Isokratous Amarturon*,[138] or *Reply to Isocrates' Speech Without Witnesses*.[139] When Isocrates alluded to this controversy at the end of the *Panegyricus*,[140] he was denouncing as futile such efforts as Antisthenes' and Speusippus'.

This episode is informative quite apart from the question of Speusippus' specific relations with Isocrates. First, it demonstrates that Speusippus, often depicted as a hardcore philosophical theorist, was involved in a heated rhetorical controversy.[141] Second, the mention of *aporrēta*, whatever they concerned, suggests esoteric doctrines in the Isocratean circle that may provide a comparandum with the educational practices of the Platonic Academy.[142] Finally,

---

[135] This Caeneus is not otherwise known. The testimonium is discussed by Gigante (1969), Isnardi Parente (1980:211), and Tarán (1981:181f.). Gigante suggests reading Ἀφαρεύς for Καινεύς; Aphareus is Isocrates' adopted son and the one who actually spoke in his place in the *Antidosis* lawsuit, cf. "Plutarch" *Lives of the Ten Orators* 838b-c, 839c, Dionysius of Halicarnassus *Isocrates* 18.

[136] It is the only text offered to show this by Stenzel (1929:1636). I am unsure where the notion of Speusippus' having passed through Isocrates' school first appears; Stahr (1830–1832:II.286f.) makes the inference on this basis, citing Casaubon and Menage's annotations to Diogenes Laertius.

[137] Usener 1880, cited by Gigante (1969:48).

[138] Cf. Diogenes Laertius 6.15. The translation of Hicks 1925 (*A Reply to the Anonymous Work*) obscures the connection.

[139] The reference may be to Isocrates' *Against Euthynus* of 303/2—the dispute over this famous case had legs—to which Isocrates himself will refer as *hē parakatathēkē* (*Panegyricus* 188). Cf. Gigante 1969. However, it is immaterial to my argument whether the extant Isocratean speech is the one meant.

[140] Isocrates *Panegyricus* 188, quoted, translated, and discussed below.

[141] A conclusion can be drawn here much more securely than from the title *Pros Grullon* (Diogenes Laertius 4.4); see Tarán 1981:194f. (questioning its existence) and Blank 2007:14n32 (stressing that we know nothing about it). Speusippus' *Tekhnōn elenkhos* (Diogenes Laertius 4.5) was surely a response to rhetorical treatises and methodology (cf. Tarán 1981:195).

[142] Cf. Too 1995:174ff.

whatever the circumstances under which secret Isocratean teachings may have come into Speusippus' possession, this story provides a useful context for recognizing less overt points of continuity between Isocrates and Speusippus. For example, Bertelli considered connections between historical *exempla* in Isocrates, the *Letter to Philip*, and Aristotle's *Rhetoric* and found it significant that an Isocratean set of *paradeigmata* (Alcibiades, Conon, Dionysius, Cyrus: *Philip* 58–67) was picked up by Aristotle, in *Rhetoric* and elsewhere, as recurrent *topoi* in a partial form (Alcibiades and Dionysius together) that is also employed by the author of the *Letter to Philip*.[143] Indeed, Bertelli found this striking enough that he used it as support for the unlikely hypothesis of Aristotelian authorship of the epistle.[144] But it is a more likely possibility that the intermediate source through which Aristotle sometimes imbibed Isocratean rhetoric was, if not Speusippus himself, then at least Academic discussions of rhetoric to which Speusippus was also party.[145]

The other character in the *Letter to Philip*'s dramatic moment is Theopompus, and since our fuller evidence for his literary career has allowed us to evaluate the range of his possible connections to Isocratean *paideia* and scholastic politics as a separate question, we will consider here only a few of the points most relevant to his involvement in these events. One of these relevant facts is Theopompus' presence at the Macedonian court in the first place. Bertelli, after dismissing quite hastily the evidentiary value of the intimate sketches of courtly life in Theopompus' *Philippica*, states that the *Letter to Philip* is the sole positive evidence for the historian's stay at the royal court.[146] This is not quite true, since Sozomen also preserves the tradition that Philip was Theopompus' patron.[147]

---

[143] See now Natoli 2004:146. Oliver (1968:25) says, "In order to know the truth one must have information, sometimes called *historia*. For example, when Speusippus criticizes Isocrates for getting a simple fact wrong, he criticizes the *historia* of Isocrates [11]."

[144] Bertelli 1977a:110.

[145] Diogenes Laertius 4.5 reports (citing Favorinus *Memorabilia* 2) that Aristotle bought Speusippus' *biblia* for the sum of three talents.

[146] In a note citing a host of twentieth-century scholars who have addressed the "biographical" formulation of the *Philippica* (Bertelli 1977a:83n26), Bertelli claims, "Per la permanenza di Teopompo alla corte di Filippo ... non abbiamo tuttavia altra testimonianza *positiva* oltre quella di ep. XXX," which, he complains, is pressed into a circular demonstration of authenticity.

[147] οὐ τοιοῦτοι (sc. as Theodosius II behaved towards writers) Κρητῶν οἱ πάλαι ἐγένοντο περὶ τὸν ἀοίδιμον ἐκεῖνον Ὅμηρον, ἢ Ἀλευάδαι περὶ Σιμωνίδην, ἢ Διονύσιος ὁ Σικελίας τύραννος περὶ Πλάτωνα τὸν Σωκράτους ἑταῖρον, ἢ Φίλιππος ὁ Μακεδὼν περὶ Θεόπομπον τὸν συγγραφέα (*Church History* preface 5). This testimonium is omitted by FGrHist. E.g. Griffith accepts it as evidence (Hammond and Griffith 1979:521n2), without, however, citing Boehnecke (1864:477n3), who seems first to have adduced this text. Note that while Boehnecke's broader suggestion of the utility to Philip of Theopompus' earlier writings (and thus of Theopompus' attractiveness as a royal client) may be supportable on the basis of other sources, Boehnecke errs in maintaining this on the basis of the *Trikaranos*, written by Anaximenes of Lampascus and falsely attributed to Theopompus.

The connection of Theopompus to Isocrates through Speusippus' joining of the two in the polemics of the *Letter to Philip* raises another contentious issue, the traditions naming Theopompus as one of Isocrates' students. So many scholars have resisted accepting this tradition—usually by casting their doubt on the phenomenon of "rhetorical history" that such a relationship has been held to imply[148]—that the association conveyed by the *Letter to Philip* has been challenged either by disputing the reliability of the letter as a source or by interpreting the letter so as to limit its significance on this point. Bertelli follows the scholarly tradition whereby the Isocratean influence evident in Theopompus' and Ephorus' works is used to argue that the biographical testimonia have concretized into discipleship what is actually purely literary (not personal or scholastic) influence. He thus considers the implication of a closer attachment, in the Theopompus passage of the *Letter to Philip*, to be a reason for doubting the authorship of Speusippus in 343/2 BC. If the significant connection between Isocrates and his alleged pupils is merely stylistic, then the "Isocratean historical school" could not have existed at this date, simply because Theopompus and Ephorus' literary careers had not yet produced the works that show their literary affinity to Isocrates.[149] This interpretive problem is purely the result of insisting that a knowable and publishable connection as suggested by the *Letter to Philip* would have required an indirect literary influence—when the hypothesis of a student's known connection to a school explains this so much more easily. This is not to beg the question, for dislocating the letter's representation of Theopompus from its general context (the 340s) creates the unsolvable problem of how such an intrusion or distortion became joined to the letter. Bertelli offers no explanation of how this would have happened, and if he did, it would probably have further strengthened the idea of a scholastic connection, since targeting Theopompus in this way would have to be the motivated act of a later Academic writer (say, Heraclides Ponticus or Aristotle)—and this motivation would have had to come from scholastic interest, since it could hardly have been influenced by the encrustations of Ciceronian criticism doubted by Bertelli and others. In sum, the objections raised on this point only focus our attention on the positive evidence for school polemics—and thus school associations—provided by *Letter to Philip* 12.[150]

---

[148] In the previous chapter I questioned the accuracy of this modern and somewhat artificial construct.

[149] Bertelli 1977a:92f. and nn62f. Bertelli considers "Ephorus' and Theopompus' stylistic and thematic dependence on Isocrates" to be an "undeniable fact."

[150] The effort of Bertelli (1977a:92f.) to undermine the other sources for the teacher–pupil relationship centers on the statement in Photius' life (*Library* 120b30 = T 3a) that "Isocrates the Athenian" was a contemporary (*sunakmasai*) of Theopompus. This "would exclude" such a relationship. But this is absolutely impossible given that their births are separated by more than

The overall arguments and concerns of the *Letter to Philip* give us a good deal of information about its author's intellectual interests or competencies, even if this is far from its purpose. The picture thus formed can then be checked against other sources for our knowledge of Speusippus, both to see if it meets a basic threshold of compatibility and, if so, to ask what we might positively learn from it about Speusippus. We have already touched on Speusippus' rhetorical interests, and with these we may associate the criticism of Theopompus as "frigid" (*psukhros*, *Letter to Philip* 12), which may be taken in its literary critical sense, and the criticism of Isocrates' various "excuses" (*prophaseis*).[151] More controversial are the evident historical interests of the author of the *Letter to Philip*: do these exclude the philosopher Speusippus? Historical arguments, after all, make up the majority of the epistle, and not all of them are owed to Antipater—Isocrates even comes in for criticism where his version of the foundation of Cyrene disagrees with Herodotus (11).[152] There is no certain way to draw a line separating the literary curiosity we would expect of Plato's nephew and student from the degree of historical erudition that would be puzzling if uncorroborated, but we may certainly admit that the *Letter to Philip* shows a keen interest in Greek political history. Perhaps the most important point is the obvious one, that the letter does not show us *historia* for its own sake guiding Speusippus as a writer; rather it simply shows that researches were undertaken by or for Speusippus wherever they might be useful to please his potential patron (Philip was everyone's potential patron by 343/2) and to undermine his enemies. The epistles to Dion and Dionysius also in the Speusippean corpus list may likewise have occasioned historical digressions—these would seem to be dictated more by the addressee than by the author of such

---

fifty-five years. Bertelli actually cites the parallel testimonium naming instead "Isocrates of Apollonia" (*Suda* s.v. Θεοδέκτης, θ 138) to say that his reading is "confirmed" by sources that "substitute the Athenian Isocrates." Rather, it is plainly the famous Isocrates whose name has displaced that of his obscure pupil. The problems here go back to Jacoby, whose authority later writers have accepted too automatically on this point: see the discussion in chap. 3.

[151] Cf. Bertelli 1977a:84ff. and 108. The former, an apparent instance of literary criticism (*pace* Flower 1994:19n31; the insistence on reading *psukhros* as a predicate in its own right is sound, but there is not sufficient evidence for preferring the exclusive sense "disagreeable"), again leads Bertelli, who considers it without reference to a scholastic context, to object that Theopompus' literary fame was insufficient to attract such hostile notice in 343/2 (p. 90). The audience that Bertelli feels is implied by the wish to see the historian "erased by everyone" (*Letter to Philip* 12) could be not the wider literary public, but the other participants in the specialized scholastic field, among whom such insults did not require extensive individual familiarity.

[152] Bertelli 1977a:109, pointing out that the reference to Damastes of Sigeum, mentioned together with Herodotus at *Letter to Philip* 4, would predate any other testimonium for the fifth-century writer. But, since Damastes is also known to have written e.g. a work *On Poets and Sophists*, I am reluctant to agree that this is particularly strong evidence for Speusippus' specifically historiographical curiosity.

letters.[153] As head of the Academy, Speusippus need not have concocted on his own whatever was not ready in Antipater's propaganda; it would be strange if he spared any efforts to call on all available resources in his campaign against the rivals of his school.

For Bertelli, who seems certain that the epistle is a "pezzo" assembled in an Academic *officina* (much like certain Platonic epistles),[154] the historical arguments of the *Letter to Philip* require us to look for an Academic whose qualifications provide a better fit to the text's contents. This is an illuminating, if perhaps unnecessary, exercise. Bertelli identifies Heraclides Ponticus and the young Aristotle as the candidates who fulfil his condition of historical learning.[155] The former is certainly an interesting character—and Bertelli should have mentioned that he seems to have begun his association with the Academy as Speusippus' personal pupil,[156] which complicates any conclusion that sees his role as sole author—though how well he deserves his reputation for historical interests is open to doubt.[157] As for the suggestion of Aristotle, I would just like to note that Bertelli's arguments, which might be persuasive if we really had to exclude Speusippean authorship, deserve close attention from anyone inclined to attribute the *Letter to Philip* to a late writer or one only indirectly concerned with the matters it raises.

The *Letter to Philip* as Evidence for School Politics

Having established some reasonable parameters for the circle of the *Letter to Philip*'s author, associates, and rivals, we may next consider the unique glimpses afforded by the letter into the methods and habits of these creatures of *skholē* as such. To begin with, it provides a specific image of what actually took place in a fourth-century school—in this case Speusippus' Academy—when the matter of the day's discussion was not to expound Academic doctrine, but to read Isocrates' *Philip*. Speusippus has barely greeted Philip and explained that he is writing to recommend Antipater, the historiographer and bearer of the letter, when he begins on the subject of Antipater's worthiness as a propagandist:

---

[153] "Una conoscenza non superficiale della storia macedone prima di Filippo" (Bertelli 1997a:109) is what we would expect in a targeted communication from a man whose pursuit of courtly favor was well attested.

[154] Bertelli 1977a:108.

[155] Bertelli 1977a:110.

[156] Ἀθήνησι δὲ παρέβαλε πρῶτον μὲν Σπευσίππῳ (Diogenes Laertius 5.86).

[157] The polymathy suggested by the many headings under which his *dialogoi* are listed (*ēthika*; *phusika*; *grammatika*; *mousika*; *rhētorika*; *historika*, see Diogenes Laertius 5.86–88) has rightly impressed scholars. But it should be noticed that the two works actually listed in the final category (*Peri tōn Puthagoreiōn* and *Peri Heurēmatōn*) hardly evoke a concern with political history.

δικαίως δ' ἂν αὐτῷ βοηθήσειας διὰ πολλὰ καὶ διότι, παρ' ἡμῖν ἀνα-
γνωσθέντος ἐν διατριβῇ τοῦ σοὶ πεμφθέντος ὑπ' Ἰσοκράτους λόγου, τὴν
μὲν ὑπόθεσιν ἐπήνεσεν, τὸ δὲ παραλιπεῖν τὰς εἰς τὴν Ἑλλάδα γενομένας
εὐεργεσίας ὑμῶν ἐνεκάλεσε.

There are many reasons why you would do right to help him, and in
particular because when the discourse sent to you by Isocrates was
read out among us in school he praised the subject it proposed but
laid to its charge its omission of the benefits you and your family have
brought about for Greece.

Speusippus Letter to Philip 1

This occasion, on which Antipater, gathered with other Academics, laid out
guidelines for a more obsequious follow-up to Isocrates' *Philip*, is mentioned
only incidentally but gives valuable evidence for Academic practice under
Speusippus. The phrase "when Isocrates' speech was read among us at school"
lets us imagine the philosophers (at a time when historians of philosophy will
assure us of the Academy's philosophical seriousness) hashing out a rhetorical-
political criticism of Isocrates' political discourse.[158] The scholastic motivations
for this intervention are transparent.

The passage sits beside few others as evidence for the interested rereading
and misreading (or, more charitably, critical reading) of rival schools' texts
within the walls of a school. We can add to this evidence from Isocrates' own
works that helps us understand how he elicited organized attention and
responses in rival scholastic circles. Isocrates' *Panathenaicus* has been widely
appreciated for its very deliberate and sophisticated presentation of debate
within Isocrates' school, in the form of his student's challenge that he has been
unfair to Sparta. Less remarked is what Isocrates has to say, closer to the beginning of this discourse, about the readings to which his instructive discourses are
subjected *outside* the confines of his own school.[159] Isocrates refers to those who
have been, for the audience of their students, "abusing my discourses, reading
them in the worst possible manner side by side with [*paranagignōskontes*] their
own, dividing them [*diairountes*] at the wrong places, mutilating them [*katakni-
zontes*], and in every way spoiling their effect" (*Panathenaicus* 17, trans. Norlin
1928–1929). Many of these complaints could be applied to Antipater's use of
Isocrates' *Philip*, as described in Speusippus' letter. The technical language here
could also very appropriately cover what Speusippus says was argued *en diatribēi*

---

[158] See Alexiou 2010:179 (on Isocrates *Evagoras* 74: διαδοθέντας ἐν ταῖς εὖ φρονούντων διατριβαῖς,
"published in the *diatribai* of men of good sense") for the modern literature on the dissemination
of Isocrates' discourses, among which see esp. Usener 1994.

[159] Usener (1994:54f.) independently makes this same connection.

(for example, παραναγιγνώσκοντες, otherwise a term for adducing the law in forensic contexts[160]). In fact, Speusippus uses just this word when telling Philip how Antipater's reading from his *Greek History* will silence and supplant the pretension of Theopompus' savage frigidity.[161] This is another good reminder of how writerly and intellectual are the terms in which Speusippus criticizes Isocrates and his school—a bit surprising given that he is addressing King Philip.

Certainly *these* misreaders, or rather interested and polemical *re*readers, of Isocrates' texts are in no danger of being taken seriously as philosophers. But they suggest that we are missing something about Speusippus' Academy if we cannot explain why it, too, was engaged in the interested and polemical rereading of Isocrates' even *less* philosophically significant discourses. Given the exiguity of evidence for the actual practice and procedure of discussion in the Academy, I think we have to allow this convergence of interests and methods some weight in forming our total impression of the Academy's place in its world. Isocrates was felt to be a necessary reference point for defining this. Of course I am not suggesting that the early Academy was not also the context for the creation of the philosophical doctrines that have been the focus of historians of philosophy; I am simply suggesting that the importance of the purely philosophical aspect for our own retrospective disciplinary history should not blind us to the possibility that in Speusippus' time the Academy was in addition a place for something else, perhaps something less familiar from our knowledge of the later Hellenistic schools.

Moreover, there are some reasons to believe that the opponents to be seen behind the proem of *Panathenaicus* are "a group within the Academy associated with Aristotle." Even while rejecting chronologically strained biographical attempts to make Aristotle himself one of the smart alecks whose slanders and sophistries are located at the Lyceum[162] in *Panathenaicus* 16–33, Roth argues convincingly that the catholic flavor of "those who say they know everything" (18) and the literary-rhapsodic interests on display fit Aristotle, that they are supported by other signs that point to Aristotle's influence, and that it was no accident that Aristotle founded his school in this place a few years later.[163]

With this in mind, we can coordinate the additional evidence to take the measure of Speusippus' engagement with Isocrates' projects. As I have

---

[160] Note, however, Socrates' use of it in a description of law court procedure meant to contrast with the proper conditions of philosophical conversation at *Theaetetus* 172e3.

[161] *Letter to Philip* 12.

[162] Besides the "sophists" and rhapsodes mentioned by Isocrates among frequenters of the Lyceum, we can add Socrates and the older sophists (several references in Plato and Diogenes Laertius 9.54), as well as Isocrates himself (anonymous *Life of Isocrates*, line 117 in Mathieu and Brémond's Budé edition [1962]).

[163] See Roth 2003:85–90.

mentioned, the fragmentary records of Speusippus' output mention letters to Dion and Dionysius, who would be a second monarch addressed by both Speusippus and Isocrates, giving additional point to Speusippus' accusations of self-plagiarism on Isocrates' part. Then there is the direct personal entanglement between the two school-generals in the rhetorical controversy over Isocrates' *Amarturos*, a conflict for whose like we can scarcely find evidence between Isocrates and Plato. Isocrates at the end of *Panegyricus* seems to give his counterblast to this pattern of his opponent's critical engagement with his literary works:

χρὴ ... τοὺς δὲ τῶν λόγων ἀμφισβητοῦντας πρὸς μὲν τὴν παρακαταθήκην καὶ περὶ τῶν ἄλλων ὧν νῦν φλυαροῦσιν παύεσθαι γράφοντας, πρὸς δὲ τοῦτον τὸν λόγον ποιεῖσθαι τὴν ἅμιλλαν καὶ σκοπεῖν ὅπως ἄμεινον ἐμοῦ περὶ τῶν αὐτῶν πραγμάτων ἐροῦσιν, ἐνθυμουμένους ὅτι τοῖς μεγάλ' ὑπισχνουμένοις οὐ πρέπει περὶ μικρὰ διατρίβειν, οὐδὲ τοιαῦτα λέγειν ἐξ ὧν ὁ βίος μηδὲν ἐπιδώσει τῶν πεισθέντων.

and those who engage in dispute over discourses ought to cease writing against my *Deposit* speech and about the rest of their nonsense, but instead direct their contest to *this* discourse and consider how to speak better than I about these matters, bearing in mind that it is not fitting for those who promise great things to invest their *diatribē* over small matters or to speak the kind of discourse that will cause no improvement to the lives of those persuaded.

Isocrates *Panegyricus* 188f.

I have made a point of translating this passage boldly,[164] especially since the existing English translations are confused and even contradictory. The important point that emerges from my interpretation is that Isocrates is deriding his fellow intellectuals for how they have spent their intellectual and scholastic energies (I take διατρίβειν in the technical sense of "school activity") on polemics against him. Cleverly, despite the fact that Isocrates' philosophical attackers probably would have portrayed his novel early forensic production as a very small-minded pursuit, all of this is couched in terms of finding suitably lofty and morally consequential subjects for discourse and debate.

So it seems there may have been a considerable overlap between Isocrates and Speusippus' schools' *interests*[165] during this period. A valuable confirmation of this commonality and rivalry of interests would be to find not only destruc-

---

[164] After Gigante 1969.
[165] Their "interests" converge in both of the word's senses.

tive polemics, but cases where scholastic capital (the very stuff we allege is getting fought over) really works as a common currency between both schools. To use an analogy: if Professor X is the bitter rival of Professor Y, then, whatever the uglier and less professional factors involved, we'd want some confirmation that there really is some definable common currency of professional recognition: for example, if they are both philologists, seeing both of their conjectures admitted in autonomous editions, or seeing Y forced to recognize X's merits, might convince us that they really are philologists battling over real philological capital. Importantly, this "interest in disinterestedness" (whether embraced with or without ulterior motivations) opens up the possibility that you can have not only relationships of enmity or politics by other means, but philology for its own sake.[166] The examples of "crossover" between the schools, discussed in chapter 3, provide evidence for something of this kind. When the Isocratean/ Academic/mathematician Helicon is recommended as a philosophical expert in the thirteenth Platonic epistle,[167] then, as in the *Letter to Philip* and Isocrates' *Philip*, we may start from the premise that criteria of intellectual excellence matter to the monarch. We also recall the propagandistic potential of such titles ascribed to Isocrates of Apollonia as *Amphictyonic Speech* and *On Not Performing a Taphos for Philip*. When Speusippus nastily dismisses such a writer,[168] he feels the need to attack in specifically intellectual and writerly terms. This should be compared to his dismissal of Theopompus as "frigid," also discussed above, in what could otherwise be seen as a political quarrel.[169]

In conclusion, this range of evidence shows people we might not have expected to do so trading in intellectual capital, thus broadening our picture of the period's literary and intellectual culture. If we read carefully the texts addressed to King Philip—Speusippus' letter and Isocrates' *Philip*—we see Philip himself participating in these school-intellectuals' discourses. There is even some evidence that Philip used some of these intellectuals' rhetoric in his own diplomatic self-presentation to the Greek cities.[170] What is repeatedly striking is the sense that intellectual currency proved so convertible and bankable in the "real world."

---

[166] I make use of Pierre Bourdieu's terms of analysis, esp. Bourdieu 1998.

[167] Recall also the similar fifth epistle.

[168] The "Pontic student" in *Letter to Philip* 11.

[169] "Frigid": *psukhros* (*Letter to Philip* 12). Compare Isocrates, *To Nicocles* 24, on the difficulty of *sprezzatura*: "you will find that those who are dignified are cold [*psukhrous*], and those who wish to appear urbane are base." If not the language of literary criticism, we have the language of conscious and critical self-fashioning.

[170] See Wendland 1910 on how "Demosthenes" *Philip's Letter* 12.19 (summer 340) quotes Isocrates *Philip* 73, and compare Hegesippus' attack on Philip as "schooled" ("Demosthenes" 7.23, *didaskalos*, Natoli 2004:54).

The *Letter to Philip*'s own mode of address adds still more to our understanding of the process of interscholastic encounter. While it is doubtful that Speusippus published an "open letter" in the manner of Isocrates' *Philip*,[171] it is not of strictly private interest either. In any case, it is problematic to identify its wider audience as "the public" simply defined. Its crass polemics, whose contrast to the diplomatic niceties of Isocrates' open letter we have already considered, render impossible any intention to address and persuade the public of the Greek *poleis*. The *Letter to Philip* is not the kind of "politics" that Isocrates ostensibly—and plausibly—offered in the public interest; it is scholastic "politics" conducted narrowly against the interests of Isocrates and the Isocrateans (e.g. Theopompus), and this is what defines the range of readers for whom it was intended (or whom it reached with effect, whether through the agency of Speusippus or of Philip). It is perhaps the unfamiliar nature of such an address that has caused modern readers to ignore the letter (as not pertaining to philosophers' philosophical differences), or else has tempted them into the position (completely untenable after Bertelli's thorough questioning of Speusippean authorship) that its literary and scholastic obsessions are best explained as issuing from a later Atticizing workshop. It is precisely its uncommon authentic glimpse into the specialized politics of intellectuals that makes Speusippus' letter so valuable.

In this less familiar form of combat, therefore, when we see that the relevance of a work of Isocrates is still felt well after politicians have ceased to speak in terms of the political conditions that produced it, this is not a sign of precious antiquarian curiosity. The canons of topicality applicable to the *Letter to Philip* are not the same as those we observe in, say, the work of Demosthenes. If there is some continuity joining Isocrates' *Against the Sophists*, produced perhaps in Speusippus' boyhood, to the *Letter to Philip* a half-century later,[172] this is not a stress on the consistency of the latter's text but another testimony to the longevity and variety of the school polemics. But even the central fact of the letter, its intense concern with Isocrates' *Philip* of three years earlier, has been found objectionable.[173] Speusippus is indeed "rekindling a polemic" at a time when Isocrates would have been embarrassed to bring it up. But this is precisely because he seeks to exploit the gap between the present moment and the one that had produced Isocrates' political overture to the Macedonian king, viciously

---

[171] Natoli (2004:20–22) argues for a private letter; Bickermann and Sykutris (1928:18) argue for an open letter, but based on the interpretation of *empodōn* rejected here (see n4 to the translation of §5 above, p. 136).

[172] Bertelli 1977a:105.

[173] "Per esempio al B[ickermann] non è sembrato affatto strano, proponendo come data di redazione l'inverno 343/42, che 'Speusippo' riaccenda la polemica contro il *Filippo* di Isocrate a distanza di tre anni dalla sua pubblicazione" (Bertelli 1977a:101).

rereading Isocrates out of context, as we have discussed above. Bertelli's most emphatic doubt about the authenticity of the *Letter to Philip* is that it reads as if the "Amphictyonic question" of 346 and the "Olynthiac question" that had been settled in 348 are still current events.[174] While in these cases the link to Isocrates is not as direct, this apparent problem can still be resolved if we adjust for the nature of school polemics, in which the rhetorical use that has been made of a historical moment with outstanding literary (and only consequently, political) effect is what determines topicality. The historical facts on which the *Letter to Philip* focuses are those that literarily and polemically have shown their value in reputation-building and propaganda-validation. It is the textual chain of argument, not the factual thread of history, that Speusippus' twists and turns are following. Griffith has a more satisfactory explanation of how less current elements came to be included in the letter, spelling out the possible terms in which what was interesting to scholarchs could be translated into capital that mattered to Philip:

> [Speusippus], through his tame historian Antipater of Magnesia, had gone to no small trouble scouring the life and hard times of the god Heracles to find just those things there that might be of use to Philip *at just this particular moment.* By a staggering coincidence they did find them; at Amphipolis, at Potidaea, at Torone, at Ambracia. At all these places, *three of them so much in the news as Speusippus wrote,* Heracles in his travels had found nasty men in charge and had replaced them with nice men ... In every case, Speusippus is careful to record, these rulers received their places from Heracles as *parakatathēkē.* The places belonged to Heracles (Ἡρακλειδῶν οὖσαν, brays Speusippus, three times in fifteen lines). Speusippus really has put in his thumb here, and pulled out plum after plum. ... The main object of Speusippus in his letter, it seems, was to damage Isocrates in Philip's eyes, and to a lesser degree to damage Theopompus who was in Macedonia at this time; and since Isocrates' *Philip* (the object of attack) was some three and a half years old by now, Speusippus probably did well *to add to his letter some material of topical interest smelling less of the lamp and the dust of academic vendetta.* Philip cared presumably as little as any other man

---

[174] "Il meno che si possa dire di fronte a una tale 'farrago' di riferimenti è che la lettera non fu scritta di getto per e in una circostanza particolare: essa si presenta piuttosto come una rubrica in cui sono concentrati avvenimenti e polemiche disposti in un arco di tempo che va dal 346—se non prima: vd. infatti la 'questione di Olinto'—al 341 almeno" (Bertelli 1977a:107). As for the attacks on political positions taken by Isocrates after 343/2 that Bertelli alleges to exist in the *Letter to Philip* ("al 341 almeno"), perhaps it is enough to emphasize that Bertelli himself has to refer to them as "subtle allusions."

of good sense just what Isocrates or Theopompus might once have said about Plato. But he did care about the Heracles thing in general, and in particular he may have reflected that a researcher who could find the evidence for declaring him, Philip, an Athenian citizen by virtue of his Heraclid descent, might reasonably be expected to find the evidence for anything. The researcher no doubt had been Antipater of Magnesia. But the crooked "proof" that Philip had never attacked Olynthus (Olynthus must have attacked him) must be all Speusippus' own work. Starting from an assumption that a known fact (Philip's attack on Olynthus) was really an open question, he shows that it cannot be a genuine fact, by adducing in evidence certain other facts that would speak against it if it were an open question. This is a crook writing, whether for money or merely in order to surpass Isocrates in being of use to Philip.

Hammond and Griffith 1979:514f. (emphases added)

This is an excellent starting point, if it does need to be supplemented by our earlier discussions in some respects. First, we require an explanation that will really render intelligible how much of "the lamp and the dust" there still is in the *Letter to Philip*. Second, we must be wary of exaggerating the effectiveness of the letter as purely political rhetoric. It is something of a stretch when Griffith turns to imagine just how painful a public relations "deafening silence" it would take to make Philip welcome the prospect of having this letter put in front of a general reading public as an effective counterblast "from an Athenian pen," under the theory that "Anything is better than silence, even a *Pravda* or a Speusippus."[175] In fact, we cannot laugh away the fact that the *Letter to Philip* is all too *Pravda*-like not to have been addressed first and foremost to the nomenklatura.

Thus Speusippus' letter, in renouncing the kind of rhetoric that would belong in the politics practiced in the *poleis*, signals the altered rules by which a new cohort of intellectuals will contend for their positions, while at the same time it sends us back to the texts of Isocrates and even Plato, not only to measure the differences that allowed those earlier writers to luxuriate in political *ideas* worthy of the name, but also to search for whatever first sprouts of this new scholastic politics may be discovered.

It cannot be overemphasized how unsatisfactory it is to take the crass attacks and displays of interest that feature in this new "politics" as evidence for a sudden growth of the philosophers' interest in honest-to-goodness, down-and-dirty, nakedly political politics. The game in its transformed state is not as simple as this. Thus the fact that Isocrates' writings can be correlated with an actual policy such as the one his former student Androtion brought before the

---

[175] Hammond and Griffith 1979:515.

Assembly in 344,[176] coupled with the fact that the *Letter to Philip* is a response to what Isocrates wrote, does not mean that it is right to take Speusippus' letter as a newer act undertaken in the same framework of political action—for example, in concert with the policy event of Androtion's exile.[177] This kind of construction leads us to see Speusippus as playing the same game as any Athenian politician, but on the team of those colluding to bring about Athens' subjection to Philip. Evidence for such connections is scarce, and Markle, who makes this argument, is forced to suppose a common, and political, class interest of Isocrates and Speusippus "on the assumption that the latter shared his uncle's opposition towards democracy."[178] Here Plato is dragged in, a man even harder to lay in the procrustean bed of conventional, factional politics. The question arises whether Isocrates is more easily caricatured as motivated by the basest kind of political interests precisely because of the complexity of the position with which he straddled the territories of ideas and kingdoms. Markle's distaste for Isocrates' "selfishness which he conceals behind a tiresome moral posturing that 'the best' should rule"[179] is in response to the very fact that Isocrates was more than merely a political actor. The anger with which Markle blames the intellectuals for what he alleges is their (perhaps decisive) contribution to the defeat of Athens at Chaeronea cannot be justified by what we actually know of Speusippus' life and work. The *Letter to Philip* is not the "smoking gun" that damns its author as a treasonous political actor; rather, absent any traces of Speusippus' direct participation in Athenian politics, conspiracy with Athenian politicians, or identification with a traditional political faction, the *Letter to Philip* demonstrates the remarkable fact that its author acted through the epistle and other scholastic activities, not through conventional political means. The letter itself is less a turning to "gross material interests" in the thick of Athens' souring political affairs than a flight into a specifically scholastic mode of social existence.[180]

---

[176] Markle 1976:89–91.

[177] Markle 1976:92–97. On Androtion's exile, FGrHist 324 T 14. Note that Markle, writing just before the publication of Bertelli's articles, accepts the letter on Bickermann and Sykutris's authority, and on their terms.

[178] Markle 1976:98.

[179] Markle 1976:98.

[180] Cf. Essig (2000:42), who sees an early example of a modern *Intellektuellenproblematik*: "In order to help their own utopias achieve greater effectiveness through a pact with the monarch's power, Isocrates and Speusippus alike turn their backs on democracy and on the welfare of their native city." Pina Polo and Panzram (2001) also discuss the political propaganda of the *Letter to Philip* in terms of the "violent polemic between Isocrates' followers and an Academy disposed to be friendly to Macedon."

Conclusion
Isocrateanism in the Renaissance

THE CONTROVERSIES AND CONTESTS OF THE ISOCRATEAN PERIOD left their mark, directly and indirectly, on later European culture. In the immediate, Hellenistic, wake of this period, we may well wonder whether the names "Isocrates," "Plato," and "Aristotle" still carried with them traces of their significance in the highly interested struggles—sometimes collaborative, sometimes polemical—of earlier fourth-century intellectuals. For how many Hellenistic Greek readers and writers (or adherents of schools with their own positions on these debates) did these contentious texts complicate the reception of Plato, Aristotle, and Isocrates as mere literary or philosophical classics, as they did for the later authors who conveyed their titles and concerns to us, and so provided the evidence for much of the present study?

Rhetorical and philosophical *paideia* continued to help define the horizons of intellectual, literary, and political culture. Cicero defined the philosophical inheritance in terms of eloquence, necessitating an important place for Isocrates. This same framework can be applied before and after his time, in antiquity and beyond, yielding a partial but compelling vision of the practical wisdom tradition. By way of conclusion I will make this point by assaying the remarkable vitality of the Isocratean project in the Renaissance. This follows naturally from the previous chapter's exploration of the dynamics of Isocrates' princely addresses, a field in which we can see the reception of Isocrates in his truest colors, in an area where he was comfortably preeminent. Isocrates' easy acceptance among Renaissance writers can remind us that the same urgent issues of the fourth century BC that dominated Isocrates' career and defined his claim to be in the mainstream of "philosophy"—virtuous self-formation and public political performance—were perennially relevant through later antiquity and beyond. Even when the anxiety about this courtly doctrine's place vis-à-vis "pure philosophy" returns—as in one of Isocrates' most attentive students, Castiglione—it is against the backdrop of an essentially Isocratean model of political culture.

Erasmus, Machiavelli, Castiglione

Isocrates' princely didactics became newly interesting to the generation of Erasmus (*The Education of a Christian Prince*, or *Institutio principis christiani*, 1516), Machiavelli (*The Prince*, 1513, published 1532), and Castiglione (*The Book of the Courtier*, 1528). Erasmus had presented his Latin translation of Plutarch's *How to Tell a Flatterer from a Friend* in manuscript to Henry VIII of England in 1513.[1] From this area of attention grew *The Education of a Christian Prince*, published in Basel in 1516, dedicated to the future Holy Roman emperor Charles V, and bound together with an expanded set of four appropriate Plutarchan essays[2] and a reprint of Erasmus' *Panegyricus* to Archduke Philip of Austria. Completing the volume, and placed at its opening, was a Latin translation of Isocrates' *To Nicocles* (*Isocratis praecepta de regno administrando ad Nicoclem regem*). Thus the book was a compendium of ancient and modern truth-telling to princes and a reassertion of the venerable genre of the mirror for princes, or *speculum principis*, with Isocrates at its head.[3] Erasmus' dedicatory letter makes clear the close connection between the privileged ancient work and its modern counterpart: "We have presented Isocrates' precepts on administering a kingdom, in emulation with which we have added our own."[4] The whole stood as "a manifesto for the crucial role of a 'philosopher' (or professional educator) in the administration of a properly run state," a role to be closely identified with the capacities of Erasmus himself.[5]

When Erasmus' volume was published, Machiavelli had composed *The Prince* but had likely not yet written its dedication to Lorenzo II de' Medici.[6] Although

---

[1] Clough 1981:199. Erasmus sent Henry a copy of the first edition of *Institutio principis christiani*, in which the dedication of this piece to the English king is retained, in 1517. The first reference to the *Institutio principis christiani* is in a letter of May 1515 (Levi 1986:xxvi).

[2] In Erasmus' intitulation: *Quo pacto possis adulatorem ab amico dignoscere*, *Quo pacto quis efficiat ut ex inimicis capiat utilitatem* (*How One May Derive Advantage from One's Enemies*), *In principe requiri doctrinam* (*Learning Is Needed in a Prince*, now known as *Ad principem ineruditum*), *Cum principibus maxime philosophum debere disputare* (*A Philosopher Ought to Converse Especially with Princes*).

[3] On the genesis of this work in its historical context, and its use of Isocrates as a model, see Herding 1966. Erasmus' only other Isocratean translation was of the *To Demonicus* (*Paraenesis ad Demonicum*, 1517).

[4] *Isocratis de regno administrando praecepta, Latinitate donavimus: ad cuius aemulationem adiecimus nostra.* The saturation of both works with commonplace precepts (which Isocrates defends at *To Nicocles* 40f.) is indeed at the heart of their generic connection (Born 1936:43n91).

[5] Jardine 1997:xx.

[6] For the consensus date of the dedication (September 1515–September 1516), see Landon 2005:121f. I would be inclined to narrow this further to after the May 1516 publication of Erasmus' book, a consideration I believe has been neglected because of the widespread but erroneous date of 1515 for Dirck Martens's unauthorized Louvain edition of Erasmus' work (given in such Machiavellian studies as Gilbert 1977:479n82), when in fact it followed in August 1516 (see

To Nicocles and some other Isocratean works had been known in Latin before this time,[7] Erasmus' modern and Christian contribution to the genre in rivalry with the pagan classic gave it a heightened relevance to Machiavelli's project, and it is notable that the dedication is the most certain and conspicuous locus in *The Prince* of Isocratean imitation.[8] The opening words of *To Nicocles* set a model that Machiavelli will follow closely in his dedication:

> It seems to me, Nicocles, that those accustomed to bring to you, who are kings, garments, bronze, wrought gold, or any other such possession which they themselves need and you have in abundance are evidently not giving gifts but trading, and they are much more skilled at selling these things than those who are acknowledged as traders. I thought that the finest, the most useful, and above all, the most fitting gift for me to give you and you to receive would be if I were able to define what sorts of activities you should aspire to and which ones you should avoid in order to govern your city and kingdom in the best possible way.[9]
>
> *To Nicocles* 1f. (trans. Mirhady and Too 2000)

> It is a frequent custom for those who seek the favor of a prince to make him presents of those things they value most highly or which they know are most pleasing to him. Hence one often sees gifts consisting of horses, weapons, cloth of gold, precious stones, and similar ornaments suitable for men of noble rank. I too would like to commend myself to Your Magnificence with some token of my readiness to serve you; and I have not found among my belongings anything I prize so much or value so highly as my knowledge of the actions of great men, acquired

---

Herding 1974:101). Machiavelli could have selected Lorenzo as the dedicatee before or after the death of the originally intended dedicatee, Giuliano de' Medici, in March 1516 (Burd 1891:169).

[7] Up to and including Erasmus, we have eleven editions of *To Demonicus* in Latin, eight of *To Nicocles*, two of the *Encomium of Helen*, and one each of *Nicocles* and *Evagoras*. All these works and a few others are also known in manuscript translations, with the earliest *To Nicocles* by Carlo Marsuppini dating to 1430. See Mandilaras 2003:123–131. A fuller Latin version did not appear until Johannes Lonicerus's 1529 *Orationes*, by which time Petrus Mosellanus's 1519 Latin *On the Peace* had also appeared. For the reception of Isocrates in the fifteenth and sixteenth centuries, see the thorough study and collection of texts by Gualdo Rosa (1984). For the lost medieval version of *To Demonicus*, known under the title *Liber exhortacionum* to such writers as Geremia da Montagnone (ca. 1250–ca. 1350) and Walter Burley (ca. 1275–ca. 1345), see Sabbadini 1905:219.

[8] Burd 1891:171–173, (A. H.) Gilbert 1938:12, 17, (F.) Gilbert 1977:479n82 ("no possible doubt"). For less certain echoes throughout the work, cf. Burd 1891:230, 335, 347–350, 366.

[9] Azoulay (2010) discusses Isocrates' emphatic application to himself of the terms of gift-exchange and guest-friendship (*xenia*).

through long experience of contemporary affairs and extended reading in antiquity.

Machiavelli, *The Prince*, dedicatory epistle
(trans. Robert M. Adams)

Isocrates' confidence in the princely-didactic role, which never left him, stands out in clear relief against the exile's humbler assertion of his doctrine's value. The verbal echoes are close and striking. Both authors begin their texts by contrasting their own approach to the prince with the courtiers' being "accustomed" to offer costly but superficial gifts.[10] Both declare their own most precious gift to be their authoritative judgment ("define," "knowledge") about kingly "actions" or "activities."[11] Machiavelli also sounds an Isocratean note in his defense of his book's unornamented style:

> This work of mine I have not adorned or loaded down with swelling phrases or with bombastic and magnificent words or any kind of meretricious charm or extrinsic ornament, with which many writers dress up their products, because I desire either that nothing shall beautify it, or that merely its unusual matter and the weight of its subject shall make it pleasing.

dedicatory epistle (trans. Allan Gilbert)

Here Machiavelli is *less* apologetic for the severity of his style than Isocrates (who blames his old age). Burd, despite his caution and general rejection of arguments for Machiavelli's unproven knowledge of Greek, accepted this as an imitation of Isocrates' *Philip* 27f.,[12] a work not known to have existed in Latin translation until Lonicer's *Orationes* (1529). I was independently struck by the resemblance in thought between Machiavelli's words and this passage.[13] Isocrates makes the same points in the same order as Machiavelli: no measured cadences or richly embroidered surface (*eurhuthmiais kai poikiliais kekosmēkamen*),

---

[10] Isocrates' first words οἱ μὲν εἰωθότες ... ἄγειν ... = Machiavelli's first words *Sogliono il più delle volte coloro ... farsegli incontro con quelle cose ...*

[11] Compare Isocrates' ἡγησάμην δ' ἂν γενέσθαι ταύτην <u>καλλίστην δωρεὰν</u> ... εἰ δυνηθείην <u>ὁρίσαι ποίων ἐπιτηδευμάτων</u> ὀρεγόμενος καὶ τίνων ἀπεχόμενος ἄριστ' ἂν καὶ τὴν πόλιν καὶ <u>τὴν βασιλείαν διοικοίης</u> with Machiavelli's *Desirando ... offerirmi ... con qualche <u>testimone della servitù</u> ... non ho trovato ... cosa quale io abbia <u>più cara</u>, o tanto stimi, quanto <u>la cognizione delle azioni degli uomini grandi</u>.*

[12] Burd 1891:173, xii–xiv. See Triantafillis 1878 for a less cautious exploration of the connections between *The Prince* and Isocrates' *Philip*.

[13] This is the same passage that I have suggested was the butt of Speusippus' mockery, when in *Letter to Philip* 4 he gleefully seizes on the superannuated Isocrates' admission that "discoursing rhythmically" (*to eurhuthmōs dialekhthēnai*) is a young man's game.

despite the gratifying effects of such devices in the hands of those who learned them from the younger Isocrates (*tous logous hēdious an ... poioien*), but rather a strict attention to the facts (*praxeis*) worthy of his royal addressee's attention. When Machiavelli goes on to excuse the presumption of his laying down rules for princes (*presunzione se un uomo di basso ed infimo stato ardisce discorrere e regolare i governi dei principi*), he perhaps echoes Erasmus' preemptive answer to charges of fawning or impertinence (*adulationis vel procacitatis*) on the grounds of his sixteen-year-old dedicatee's youth and relative inexperience (*admodum adolescens, et nuper inauguratus imperio*), and both are grappling with the problems of princely didactics on which they could take so many lessons from Isocrates: the pitfalls and vulnerabilities of such speech, set against its nobility and high opportunities.

In Castiglione's seminal dialogue on Renaissance courtliness, *The Book of the Courtier*, the prince's subordinate attendants have come into their own: their teaching of princes is of interest, but their fashioning of themselves is of no less interest, and this process of courtly self-realization, self-empowerment,[14] and performance is at the center of the *Courtier* (though, just as oratory was no "ordered art" for Isocrates, Castiglione too denies that courtliness could be taught through precepts[15]). Castiglione's attention to *abito* (Latin *habitus*) also depends upon the idea of virtue as a state (*hexis, habitus*) in Aristotle's ethics, so that some of the connections I have suggested between Isocrates and Aristotle in chapter 1 may have seemed evident to him. While Castiglione certainly took great interest in the publication of Erasmus' 1516 collection and paraphrased the *Education of a Christian Prince* and the accompanying Plutarchan essays at several points as he developed the 1513–1516 draft version of the *Courtier* into its finished form,[16] it seems likely that Castiglione had also encountered Isocrates in the original Greek on more intimate terms.

Castiglione's father Cristoforo's library (largely bequeathed to his son[17]) had been overwhelmingly devoted to the Greek and Latin classics, and he sent his son in 1494 to Milan to be given an education in Latin and Greek by the eminent humanists Giorgio Merula and Demetrius Chalcondyles.[18] Chalcondyles' editio princeps of Isocrates had just been published in 1493. Evidence from Baldassare

---

[14] For all the ideology of the courtiers' power and duty to sway the prince, we must not forget the "constraints of despotism" (Javitch 2002:319–328) within which their power of self-fashioning was limited.

[15] "In these books we shall not follow any set order or rule of distinct precepts" (I 1, though the emphasis is on the use of the dialogue form); "it is almost proverbial that grace is not learned" (I 25).

[16] See Scarpati 1983; the redactions concerned are in Courtier IV 4–48.

[17] Rebecchini 2002:115n96.

[18] Rebecchini 2002:110.

Castiglione's library, which focused on Latin and Greek to the exclusion of vernacular literature, indicates that he "probably continued to keep up and improve his [Greek] reading skills until the end of his life" with an assiduity "by no means common, even among men of letters."[19] Isocrates, then, may well have had a significant place in Castiglione's childhood education and lifelong study, and is one of the possible backgrounds for the courtier's education and performance in the *Cortegiano*.

Book IV of Castiglione's *Courtier* opens with a lament for the loss in death of three supremely promising gentlemen from the court of Urbino, Gaspar Pallavicino, Cesare Gonzaga, and Roberto da Bari. This occasions a programmatic reflection on this court's success in producing great men; if those who died had remained among its excellent company and praiseworthy manners, they too could have expected a meteoric rise in the world. Castiglione delivers this reflection, which announces the theme of his work's final book, through a figure closely copied from Antonius' admiration of Isocrates' school in Cicero's *De oratore* 2.94:

> Ecce tibi exortus est Isocrates, magister rhetorum omnium, cuius e ludo, tanquam ex equo Troiano, meri principes exierunt; sed eorum partim in pompa, partim in acie illustres esse voluerunt. Atque et illi, Theopompi, Ephori, Philisti, Naucratae, multique alii naturis different, voluntate autem similes sunt et inter sese et magistri, et ei, qui se ad causas contulerunt, ut Demosthenes, Hyperides, Lycurgus, Aeschines, Dinarchus, aliique complures, etsi inter se pares non fuerunt, tamen omnes sunt in eodem veritatis imitandae genere versati, quorum quamdiu mansit imitatio, tamdiu genus illud dicendi studiumque vixit.

> Then behold! there arose Isocrates, the Master of all rhetoricians, from whose school, as from the Horse of Troy, none but leaders emerged, but some of them sought glory in ceremonial, others in action. And indeed the former sort, men like Theopompus, Ephorus, Philistus, Naucrates and many more, while differing in natural gifts, yet in spirit resemble one another and their Master too; and those who betook themselves to lawsuits, as did Demosthenes, Hyperides, Lycurgus, Aeschines, Dinarchus and several others, although of varying degrees of ability, were none the less all busy with the same type of imitation of the truth,[20]

---

[19] Rebecchini 2002:115–117.

[20] I have modified the translation of this phrase; as Douglas (1973:106n32) observes, a simple reference to the "reality" of *verae causae* is difficult.

and as long as the imitation of these persisted, so long did their kind of oratory and course of training endure.

(trans. Sutton and Rackham)

For truly there did not come forth from the Trojan horse so many lords and captains as from this court have come men singular in worth and most highly regarded by all. Thus, as you know, messer Federico Fregoso was made Archbishop of Salerno; Count Ludovico, Bishop of Bayeux; signor Ottaviano, Doge of Genoa; messer Bernardo Bibbiena, Cardinal of Santa Maria in Portico; messer Pietro Bembo, secretary to Pope Leo; the Magnifico rose to the dukedom of Nemours and to that greatness in which he now finds himself. Signor Francesco Maria della Rovere also, Prefect of Rome, was made Duke of Urbino: although much greater praise may be given the court where he was nurtured because in it he became such a rare and worthy lord in all manner of virtue, as we now see, than because he achieved the dukedom of Urbino; nor do I believe that this is in small part due to the noble company which he continually kept there, where he always saw and heard laudable manners.

The Book of the Courtier IV 2 (trans. Singleton[21])

As Isocrates' school nurtured literary and political leaders alike, so the court of Urbino is the nursery of ecclesiastic and temporal lords; as Isocrates' students are unified in a shared form of "imitation," so the example of the Urbino court's "laudable manners" deserves no small credit for della Rovere's dukedom.

Why, though, should the school of Isocrates serve Castiglione as the type of the court of Urbino? The true answer must be sought in the Isocratean coloration in Castiglione's picture of the ideal courtier as "his prince's instructor" (IV 47), a major topic of the final book he has introduced with the Isocratean Trojan horse.[22] When Castiglione constructs Plato and Aristotle as "courtiers,"

---

[21] I regularly cite *The Book of the Courtier* in Singleton's translation from Javitch 2002.

[22] Gaylard (2009:89–95) has noticed the echo and taken the "Trojan horse" as an ambivalent and threatening figure, but her premise that "to readers of Cicero, Isocrates epitomizes inane Greek oratory" and served "as a punching bag in ancient Rome" is at odds with Cicero's acceptance of Isocrates as a stylistic model (see chap. 3 above, where I have also taken a somewhat different perspective on Isocrates' "empty elegance of style," *inanem sermonis elegantiam*, in *De oratore* 3.141, and Gaines 2009 on Cicero's overall admiration of Isocratean "sophistic"). I am unpersuaded that Castiglione would have taken this dismissive phrase at face value as the key of his (hidden) interpretation of Isocrates, given his direct knowledge of Isocrates as an author and the admiration of his age for Isocrates precisely as a model of the political relevance of humanistic education.

he may be combining his direct knowledge of Isocrates (whose texts provided a far clearer example of courtly address than anything to be found in the works of Plato and Aristotle) with the same Ciceronian testimony I have made use of for its striking picture of a confrontation between Isocrates and Aristotle around the intersection of eloquence and wisdom. Castiglione, for whom Isocrates was no cipher, would have been better equipped than many to read Cicero deeply in this way.

Castiglione paid close attention to Isocrates' remarks in *To Nicocles* about the monarch's difficulty in gaining the benefit of his subjects' frank speech (*parrhēsia*). Ottaviano announces the princely-didactic subject of book IV by insisting that "the aim of the perfect Courtier" is to seek the truth without fear of the prince's displeasure and "when he sees the mind of his prince inclined to a wrong action ... to oppose him and in a gentle manner avail himself of the favor acquired by his good accomplishments" (IV 5).[23] This topic draws inspiration from the proem to *To Nicocles* (specifically, from the passage that immediately follows the opening quoted as the model of Machiavelli's dedication). The imitation is most closely literal in Ottaviano's statement of the problem that "among their friends there are few who have free access to them, and those few are wary of reprehending them for their faults as freely as they would private persons, and, in order to win grace and favor often think of nothing save how to suggest things that can delight or please their fancy" (IV 6). This is directly modeled on Isocrates' assertion that "The majority of people do not come near them [=*turannoi*], and those who do have intercourse with them do so with a view to winning favor" (οἱ μὲν γὰρ πλεῖστοι τῶν ἀνθρώπων αὐτοῖς οὐ πλησιάζουσιν, οἱ δὲ συνόντες πρὸς χάριν ὁμιλοῦσιν, *To Nicocles* 4).[24] Of course, in each case the speaker has the ready solution to this difficulty: not only that the courtier, in the mold of Isocrates, stand fearlessly ready to use his authority in service of the truth,[25] but also that the prince submit graciously to instruction.

---

[23] Compare *To Nicocles* 28: "Consider trustworthy not those who praise everything you say or do, but rather those who censure your mistakes. Grant freedom of speech to those who have good sense, so that you may have persons to examine alongside you those matters about which you are in doubt" (Πιστοὺς ἡγοῦ μὴ τοὺς ἅπαν ὅ τι ἂν λέγῃς ἢ ποιῇς ἐπαινοῦντας, ἀλλὰ τοὺς τοῖς ἁμαρτανομένοις ἐπιτιμῶντας. Δίδου παρρησίαν τοῖς εὖ φρονοῦσιν, ἵνα περὶ ὧν ἂν ἀμφιγνοῇς ἔχῃς τοὺς συνδοκιμάσοντας).

[24] See Colclough 2005:64.

[25] Compare *Courtier* I 44 for the Magnifico Giuliano's warning that the courtier's dazzling accomplishments he has sketched must not lead him to be shipwrecked by the Siren song of praise and "get the mistaken notion that he knows something he does not know." This is given the vague support of ancient books "written to show how the true friend is to be distinguished from the flatterer" (with primary reference to the Plutarchan essay conjoined by Erasmus with the *To Nicocles*).

As Isocrates proceeds to elaborate upon the tasks and qualities that belong to the ruler, so Ottaviano continues to diagnose the fault of princes who in their erroneous efforts to establish their authority render themselves unable to be schooled (IV 7).

From this beginning, book IV of the *Courtier* leads up to Ottaviano's conclusion that "we might perhaps say that to become his prince's instructor was the goal of the Courtier" (IV 47). This is supported with copious ancient exempla derived from Cicero's *De oratore* on the marriage of oratory and philosophy, as for example Phoenix's job of making Achilles a "speaker of words and a doer of deeds" (*Iliad* 9.443 in *De oratore* 3.57).[26] For Cicero this leads towards the example of Aristotle as Isocrates' rival and model of wisdom-cum-eloquence (3.141), which we have considered at length. This must be in Castiglione's mind as Ottaviano continues, "Nor do I think that Aristotle and Plato would have scorned the name of perfect Courtier, for we clearly see that they performed the works of Courtiership to this same end—the one with Alexander the Great, the other with the Kings of Sicily" (IV 47, cf. I 25).[27] These examples are in *De oratore* 3.139–141, together with Isocrates as the teacher of Timotheus. Given the suppression of Isocrates' name where it was clearly in focus in the Trojan Horse simile, Castiglione's omission of Isocrates here may be part of a pattern.[28] Yet despite Castiglione's deployment of the superior prestige of philosophy at this point,[29] it is hard not to notice how Isocrates' addressees—Timotheus in *Epistle* 7[30] or Philip in *Philip*—serve so much more concretely and effectively as examples of the essence of the courtier as Castiglione is defining it. There is perhaps a hint of the mismatch between Aristotelian philosophy (as ordinarily

---

[26] Note the presence nearby (3.59f.) of Isocrates, as the example of those who *taught* the twofold wisdom (in action and in oratory), in distinction to Socrates, who scorned oratory despite his great eloquence and learning.

[27] Their philosophical orientation is made relevant through their knowledge of the prince's nature; cf. Isocrates' concern with propriety of fitting discourse to its hearer, whether theoretically (e.g. *Against the Sophists* 10–18), or in the specific context of his princely addresses.

[28] Isocrates' name occurs only in the passing reference at *Courtier* I 37.

[29] The names "Plato" and "Aristotle" were evidently precisely what was required to persuade signor Gasparo, who, when Ottaviano pauses, replies, "I certainly did not expect our Courtier to be honored so; but since Aristotle and Plato are his companions, I think no one henceforth ought to despite the name. Still, I am not quite sure that I believe that Aristotle and Plato ever danced or made music in their lives, or performed any acts of chivalry" (IV 48). The last part of this gestures towards the fragility of the conceit of Plato and Aristotle as courtiers; Isocrates may have been no more of a knightly lutenist, but he certainly puts much less of a strain on Castiglione's conception of the courtier.

[30] It is interesting that Castiglione mentions Timotheus' father, and Isocrates' and Plato's student, Clearchus, as the type of the fearful and friendless tyrant (IV 24). Could some awareness lie behind this of the astonishing and disappointing change in his student that Isocrates regrets at *Epistle* 7.12?

and less imaginatively known to Castiglione and to us) and perfect courtliness in the counterexample of Callisthenes:

> And Aristotle was the author of these deeds of Alexander, employing the methods of a good Courtier: which is something that Callisthenes did not know how to do, even though Aristotle showed him; for he wished to be a pure philosopher and an austere minister of naked truth, without blending in Courtiership; and he lost his life and brought infamy instead of help to Alexander.

Courtier IV 47

The same could not be said of those students who issued forth from Isocrates' Trojan horse! Looking just below the surface, we find Castiglione celebrating the Ciceronian (and Isocratean) idea of the unity of rhetoric and philosophy, as he inquires into human matters whose truths cannot be had by dividing the two.

Elizabeth and Isocrates: "To Meet Every Contingency of Life"

In the following generation, Isocrates' relevance to the modern world was discovered in England, in terms largely dependent on these European appropriations.[31] Sir Thomas Elyot had already alluded to *To Nicocles* in his *Boke named the Governour* (as I have quoted for an epigraph in the previous chapter[32]), and he translated this Isocratean work in its entirety and published it as *The Doctrinall of Princis* in 1533. Castiglione also became popular in sixteenth-century England, both through Sir Thomas Hoby's English translation of 1561 and through Bartholomew Clerke's Latin translation, commissioned by Thomas Sackville (*De Curiali sive Aulico*, 1571).

In a 1550 letter to Johannes Sturm, Roger Ascham reports that he has served as Queen Elizabeth's tutor in Greek and Latin for the previous two years. Isocrates not only occupies a leading position in the queen's studies but does so because of his relevance to her royal responsibilities: "She used to give the morning of the day to the Greek Testament, and afterwards read select orations of Isocrates and the tragedies of Sophocles. For I thought that from these sources she might gain purity of style, and her mind derive instruction that would be of value to

---

[31]   Erasmus' literary gifts to Henry VIII did not bring him the position he sought as the royal Latin secretary and were recognized only with the "disappointing reward" of £20 (Jardine 1997:xx–xxiv). Compare how Castiglione's *Ad Henricum Angliae Regem epistola de vita et gestis Guidubaldi Urbini Ducis* (also interesting as a specimen of Isocratean eulogistic biography), reaching the English court around the time of Henry VII's death, apparently "lay forgotten in the Royal Library" (Clough 1967:778f.).

[32]   The reference is to *To Nicocles* 36, a passage that may also be in Erasmus' mind at *The Education of a Christian Prince* i (Jardine 1997:15).

her to meet every contingency of life."[33] Ascham's *The Schoolmaster* gives further information about how Elizabeth would have engaged in double translation from Greek to Latin and back into Greek, a method whose success she proves:[34]

> And a better and nearer example herein may be our most noble Queen Elizabeth, who never took yet Greek nor Latin Grammar in her hand after the first declining of a noun and a verb, but only by this double translating of Demosthenes and Isocrates daily without missing every forenoon, and likewise some part of Tully every afternoon, for the space of a year or two, has attained to such a perfect understanding in both the tongues, and to such a ready utterance of the Latin and that with such a judgement as they be few in number in both the universities, or elsewhere in England, that be in both tongues comparable with her Majesty. And to conclude in a short room, the commodities of double translation ...

The historian John Bale's catalogue, contemporary with Elizabeth, recorded the Latin incipits of translations in the queen's hand of both *To Nicocles* and *Nicocles*.[35]

The image of Elizabeth practicing double translation of Isocratean sentences and seeking their "value to her to meet every contingency of life" makes a fitting coda to this episode in Isocratean reception. Isocrates' royal *paideia*, and its core principle of the monarch as the philosopher's willing auditor, has stamped humanistic education so definitively that Elizabeth, freshly on the English throne in her mid-twenties, directs a student's attention to these discourses in their ancient tongue. In some ways, the Renaissance triumph of scholastic values was the fulfillment of Isocrates' dream to operate his authority on the conduct of state. At the same time we may question what the royal adoption of

---

[33] Letter of April 4, 1550, Giles 1865:191f., lxiii. Sturm had not yet published his commentary on Aristotle's *Rhetoric*, but Ascham knew it in manuscript; in this same letter he praises the *Rhetoric* as Aristotle's best work (in which he would have found the approving use of many examples from Isocrates) and Sturm's explication of it (Giles 1865:184), giving us another example (to be compared with Castiglione) of Aristotle viewed through a "Ciceronian" or even "Isocratean" lens. In fact, Ascham seconds the chorus of praise Joachim Périon had received for "joining Cicero with Aristotle," whom he judged to need the rhetorical embellishment (*Joachimi Perionii in coniugendo Cicerone cum Aristotele et voluntatem multi probant ... Quanquam ut ipse quoque existimo, praeclaram Aristotelis doctrinam et minus ornatam videri ...*, Giles 1865:185f.). Where Cicero and Aristotle are joined, I would contend, Isocrates is there among them.

[34] Ascham justifies the approach with an idiosyncratic interpretation of a loose quotation from Pliny the Younger *Letter* 7.9.2: Pliny's *vel ex Graeco in Latinum vel ex Latino vertere in Graecum* is quoted as *ex Graeco in Latinum et ex Latino vertere in Graecum* and taken to mean double translation.

[35] Poole and Bateson 1902:157. In Elizabeth's 1563 *Sententiae*, most of the Isocratean gnomes are from Stobaeus' *Admonitiones de Regno* (4.7.28–41), but at least one, adapted from *To Nicocles* 19, seems independent: see Mueller and Scodel 2009:357.

this form of authority really means. Isocratean counsel, with all its insistence on success by virtue versus the tyrant's empty trappings, may have held significant cultural importance for both Elizabeth and Philip of Macedon, but any moderation or softening may have been more in the presentation than in the (more Machiavellian) practice of their authoritarian rule. The difficulties that encumbered Isocrates' project did not disappear in later times, even as his idealistic aspirations were given new life.

Bibliography

Aalders H. Wzn., G. J. D. 1978. "Die Meropes des Theopomp." *Historia* 27:317–327.

Abernathy, C. L. 2003. *Akribeia: Isocrates and the Politics of Persuasion.* MA thesis, University of Virginia.

Acosta-Hughes, B., and S. A. Stephens. 2011. *Callimachus in Context: From Plato to the Augustan Poets.* Cambridge.

Alexiou, E. 2007. "Rhetorik, Philosophie und Politik: Isokrates und die *homologoumene arete." Rhetorica* 25:1–14.

———. 2010. *Der "Euagoras" des Isokrates: Ein Kommentar.* Berlin.

Allan, D. J. 1953. "Fragmenta Aristotelica." *Philosophical Quarterly* 3:248–252.

Allen, J. 1994. "Failure and Expertise in the Ancient Conception of an Art." In Horowitz and Janis 1994:81–108.

Angeli, A. 1997. "Filosofia e retorica nella polemica antiaristotelica di Epicuro (Philod., Rhet. VIII coll. 41,12–LIV 17 Sudhaus, II, pp. 57–59)." *Rudiae* 9:5–27.

Arnim, H. von. 1898. *Leben und Werke des Dio von Prusa. Mit einer Einleitung: Sophistik, Rhetorik, Philosophie in ihrem Kampf um die Jugendbildung.* Berlin.

Athanassiadi, P., ed. 1999. *Damascius: The Philosophical History.* Athens.

Ax, W. 2005. "Quintilians Darstellung der peripatetischen Rhetoriktradition." In Knape and Schirren 2005:141–152.

Azoulay, V. 2007. "Champ intellectuel et stratégies de distinction dans la première moitié du IVe siècle: De Socrate à Isocrate." In Couvenhes and Milanezi 2007:171–199.

———. 2010. "Isocrate et les élites: Cultiver la distinction." In Capdetrey and Lafond 2010:19–48.

Balla, C. 2004. "Isocrates, Plato, and Aristotle on Rhetoric." *Rhizai* 1:45–71.

Barber, G. L. 1993. *The Historian Ephorus.* 2nd ed. Text and translation ed. M. C. J. Miller. Chicago.

Barker, A. 1984. *Greek Musical Writings* I. Cambridge.

———. 2007. *The Science of Harmonics in Classical Greece.* Cambridge.

Bauer, W., W. F. Arndt, and F. W. Gingrich. 1979. *A Greek-English Lexicon of the New Testament and Other Early Christian Literature.* 2nd ed. Chicago.

Baxandall, M. 1980. *The Limewood Sculptors of Renaissance Germany.* New Haven.

Bertelli, L. 1976. "L'epistola di Speusippo a Filippo: Un problema di cronologia." *Atti della Accademia delle Scienze di Torino, Classe di Scienze Morali, Storiche e Filologiche* 110:275–300.

———. 1977a. "La lettera di Speusippo a Filippo: Il problema dell'autenticità." *Atti della Accademia delle Scienze di Torino, Classe di Scienze Morali, Storiche e Filologiche* 111:75–111.

———. 1977b. *Historia e methodos: Analisi critica e topica politica nel secondo libro della «Politica» di Aristotele.* Turin.

Berti, E. 1962. *La filosofia del primo Aristotele.* Padua.

———. 1997. "Les écoles philosophiques d'Athènes et les princes de Chypre." *Diotima* 25:15–20.

Bickermann, E., and J. Sykutris. 1928. *Speusipps Brief an König Philipp: Text, Übersetzung, Untersuchungen.* Berichte über die Verhandlungen der Sächsischen Akademie der Wissenschaften zu Leipzig: Philologisch-historische Klasse 80:3. Leipzig.

Bignone, E. 1936. *L'Aristotele perduto e la formazione filosofica di Epicuro* I–II. Florence.

Blank, D. 2007. "Aristotle's 'Academic Course on Rhetoric' and the End of Philodemus, *On Rhetoric* VIII." *Cronache Ercolanesi* 37:5–47.

———. 2009. "*Philosophia* and *technē*: Epicureans on the Arts." In Warren 2009: 216–233.

Blass, F. 1892. *Die Attische Beredsamkeit* II. 2nd ed. Leipzig.

Boehnecke, K. G. 1864. *Demosthenes, Lykurgos, Hyperides und ihr Zeitalter* I. Berlin.

Bollansée, J., ed. 1998. "Andron of Ephesos." In Bollansée et al. 1998:122–167.

———, ed. 1999. *Hermippus of Smyrna.* Die Fragmente der griechischen Historiker continued IVA-3. Leiden.

Bollansée, J., J. Engels, G. Schepens, and E. Theys, eds. 1998. *Biography: The Pre-Hellenistic Period.* Die Fragmente der griechischen Historiker continued IVA-1. Leiden.

Bons, J. A. E. 1996. *Poietikon Pragma: Isocrates' Theory of Rhetorical Composition.* Nijmegen.

Born, L. K., ed. 1936. *The Education of a Christian Prince, by Desiderius Erasmus.* New York.

Botley, P. 2004. *Latin Translation in the Renaissance: The Theory and Practice of Leonardo Bruni, Giannozzi Manetti, and Erasmus.* Cambridge.

Bourdieu, P. 1991. "Le champ littéraire." *Actes de la recherche en sciences sociales* 89:3–46.

———. 1998. *Practical Reason: On the Theory of Action.* Cambridge.

Brancacci, A. 2008. *Musica e filosofia da Damone a Filodemo: Sette studi.* Florence.

Branham, R. B., and M.-O. Goulet-Cazé, eds. 1996. *The Cynics: The Cynic Movement in Antiquity and Its Legacy.* Berkeley.

Broadie, S. 1991. *Ethics with Aristotle.* Oxford.

Brown, W. E. 1955. "Some Hellenistic Utopias." *Classical Weekly* 48:57–62.

Brun, P. 2007. "Les *epieikeis* à Athènes au IVᵉ siècle." In Couvenhes and Milanezi 2007:141–154.

Brunt, P. A. 1993. "Plato's Academy and Politics." *Studies in Greek History and Thought* 282–342. Oxford.

Burd, L. A., ed. 1891. *Il Principe, by Niccolò Machiavelli.* Oxford.

Burk, A. 1923. *Die Pädagogik des Isokrates als Grundlegung des humanistischen Bildungsideals, im Vergleich mit den zeitgenössischen und den modernen Theorien dargestellt.* Diss., Würzburg.

Capasso, M., ed. 1992. *Papiri letterari greci e latini.* Papyrologica Lupiensia 1. Galatina.

Capdetrey, L., and Y. Lafond, eds. 2010. *La cité et ses élites: Pratiques et représentation des formes de domination et de contrôle social dans les cités grecques.* Bordeaux.

Carney, E., and D. Ogden, eds. 2010. *Philip II and Alexander the Great: Father and Son, Lives and Afterlives.* Oxford.

Cartledge, P. 2009. *Ancient Greek Political Thought in Practice.* Cambridge.

Cassio, A., ed. 1991. *L'inno tra rituale e letteratura nel mondo antico.* AION 13. Rome.

Celentano, M. S., ed. 2003. *Ars/Techne: Il manuale tecnico nelle civiltà greca e romana.* Alessandria.

Chiesara, M. L., ed. 2001. *Aristocles of Messene: Testimonia and Fragments.* Oxford.

Christ, M. 1993. "Theopompus and Herodotus: A Reassessment." *Classical Quaterly* 43:47–52.

Chroust, A.-H. 1964. "Aristotle's Earliest Course of Lectures on Rhetoric." *Antiquité classique* 33:58–72.

———. 1965. "Aristotle's First Literary Effort: The *Gryllus*—A Lost Dialogue on the Nature of Rhetoric." *Revue des études grecques* 78:576–591.

———. 1966. "What Prompted Aristotle to Address the *Protrepticus* to Themison?" *Hermes* 94:202–207.

Clough, C. H. 1967. "Federigo Veterani, Polydore Vergil's 'Anglia Historia' and Baldassare Castiglione's 'Epistola . . . ad Henricum Angliae regem.'" *English Historical Review* 82:772–783.

———. 1981. "A Presentation Volume for Henry VIII: The Charlecote Park Copy of Erasmus's *Institutio principis christiani.*" *Journal of the Warburg and Courtauld Institutes* 44:199–202.

Colclough, D. 2005. *Freedom of Speech in Early Stuart England.* Cambridge.

Cooper, J. M. 1986. "Plato, Isocrates, and Cicero on the Independence of Oratory from Philosophy." *Proceedings of the Boston Area Colloquium in Ancient Philosophy* 1:77–96.

———, ed. 1997. *Plato: Complete Works*. Indianapolis.

Couvenhes, J.-C., and S. Milanezi, eds. 2007. *Individus, groupes et politique à Athènes de Solon à Mithridate*. Tours.

Cuomo, S. 2007. *Technology and Culture in Greek and Roman Antiquity*. Cambridge.

Depew, D. 2004. "The Inscription of Isocrates into Aristotle's Practical Philosophy." In Poulakos and Depew 2004:157–185.

des Places, E. 1964. *Lexique de la langue philosophique et religieuse de Platon*. Paris.

de Vries, G. J. 1971. "Isocrates in the *Phaedrus*: A Reply." *Mnemosyne* 24:387–390.

Diels, H. 1866. *Über das dritte Buch der Aristotelischen Rhetorik*. Berlin.

Diggle, J., ed. 2004. *Theophrastus: Characters*. Cambridge.

Dillon, J., and T. Gergel. 2003. *The Greek Sophists*. London.

Di Matteo, T. 1997. "Isocrate nella Retorica di Filodemo." *Cronache Ercolanesi* 27:121–136.

Douglas, A. E. 1973. "The Intellectual Background of Cicero's Rhetorica: A Study in Method." *ANRW* III.1:95–138.

Drerup, E. 1901. "Die Vulgatüberlieferung der Isokratesbriefe." *Blätter für das Gymnasial-Schulwesen* 37:348–361.

———, ed. 1906. *Isocratis Opera Omnia* I. Leipzig.

Düring, I. 1957. *Aristotle in the Ancient Biographical Tradition*. Studia graeca et latina gothoburgensia 5. Göteborg.

———. 1961. *Aristotle's Protrepticus: An Attempt at Reconstruction*. Studia graeca et latina gothoburgensia 12. Göteborg.

Einarson, B. 1936. "Aristotle's Protrepticus and the Structure of the Epinomis." *Transactions of the American Philological Association* 67:261–285.

Engels, J., ed. 1998. "Philiskos of Miletos." In Bollansée et al. 1998:356–375.

———. 2003. "Antike Überlieferungen über die Schüler des Isokrates." In Orth 2003:175–194.

Erler, M. 1993. "Il *Panatenaico* d'Isocrate e la critica della scrittura nel *Fedro*: «aiuto» e «senso nascosto»." *Athenaeum* 81:149–164.

Essig, R.-B. 2000. *Der Offene Brief: Geschichte und Funktion einer publizistischen Form von Isokrates bis Günter Grass*. Würzburg.

Eucken, C. 1983. *Isokrates: Seine Positionen in der Auseinandersetzung mit den zeitgenössischen Philosophen*. Berlin.

Ferguson, J. 1975. *Utopias of the Classical World*. London.

Ferrario, M. 2007. "Il confronto tra retorica e filosofia nell'opera 'Sulla retorica' di Filodemo." In Palme 2007:215–220.

Flower, M. A. 1994. *Theopompus of Chios: History and Rhetoric in the Fourth Century BC*. Oxford.

———. 1997. Postscript to paperback edition of Flower 1994.

Ford, A. 1993. "The Price of Art in Isocrates: Formalism and the Escape from Politics." In Poulakos 1993:31–52.

———. 2011. *Aristotle as Poet: The Song for Hermias and Its Contexts*. Oxford.

Fortenbaugh, W. W., and D. C. Mirhady, eds. 1994. *Peripatetic Rhetoric after Aristotle*. New Brunswick, NJ.

Fredricksmeyer, E. A. 1979. "Divine Honors for Philip II." *Transactions of the American Philological Association* 109:39–61.

Fricel-Dana, M. 2001–2003. "L'orateur Isokratès d'Apollonia du Pont, le successeur d'Isocrate." *Studii Clasice* 37–39:41–63.

Frolíková, A. 1979. "Isokratovy výzvy panovníkům (Epist. Socr. XXX, 13)." *Listy filologické* 102:82–86.

Gaines, R. N. 1990. "Isocrates, Ep. 6.8." *Hermes* 118:165–170.

———. 2009. "Cicero and the Sophists." In Pernot 2009:137–151.

Garver, E. 1994. *Aristotle's Rhetoric: An Art of Character*. Chicago.

———. 2004. "Philosophy, Rhetoric, and Civic Education in Aristotle and Isocrates." In Poulakos and Depew 2004:186–213.

———. 2006. *Confronting Aristotle's Ethics: Ancient and Modern Morality*. Chicago.

Gaylard, S. 2009. "Castiglione vs. Cicero: Political Engagement, or Effeminate Chatter?" *Italian Culture* 27:81–98.

Giannantoni, G., ed. 1990. *Socratis et Socraticorum Reliquiae* I–IV. Naples.

Giannini, A. 1961. "La figura del cuoco nella commedia greca." *Acme* 13:135–217.

Gibson, S. 2005. *Aristoxenus of Tarentum and the Birth of Musicology*. New York.

Gigante, M. 1969. "ΑΦΑΡΕΥΣ in Diogene Laerzio IV 2?" *La Parola del Passato* 24:47–49.

———. 1999. *Kepos e Peripatos: Contributo alla storia dell'aristotelismo antico*. Naples.

Gilbert, A. H. 1938. *Machiavelli's Prince and Its Forerunners: The Prince as a Typical Book de Regimine Principum*. Durham, NC.

Gilbert, F. 1977. *History: Choice and Commitment*. Cambridge, MA.

Giles, J. A., ed. 1865. *The Whole Works of Roger Ascham* I.i. London.

Gill, M. L., and P. Pellegrin, eds. 2006. *A Companion to Ancient Philosophy*. Oxford.

Gomperz, T. 1882. "Die Akademie und ihr vermeintlicher Philomacedonismus." *Wiener Studien* 4:102–120.

Gribble, D. 1999. *Alcibiades and Athens: A Study in Literary Presentation*. Oxford.

Gualdo Rosa, L. 1984. *La Fede nella "Paideia": Aspetti della fortuna europea di Isocrate nei secoli XV e XVI*. Rome.

Guthrie, W. K. C. 1975. *A History of Greek Philosophy* IV. Cambridge.

Habicht, C. 1988. *Hellenistic Athens and Her Philosophers*. David Magie Lecture. Princeton.

Halliwell, S. 1997. "Philosophical Rhetoric or Rhetorical Philosophy? The Strange Case of Isocrates." In Schildgen 1997:107–125.

Hammond, N. G. L., and G. T. Griffith. 1979. *A History of Macedonia* II. Oxford.

Harder, R. 1930. "Prismata." *Philologus* 85:250–254.

Hardie, W. F. R. 1980. *Aristotle's Ethical Theory*. 2nd ed. Oxford.

Hariman, R. 1995. *Political Style: The Artistry of Power*. Chicago.

Haskins, E. V. 2004. *Logos and Power in Isocrates and Aristotle*. Columbia, SC.

Heitsch, E. 1993. *Platon: Phaidros*. Göttingen.

Hercher, R., ed. 1873. *Epistolographi Graeci*. Paris.

Herding, O. 1966. "Isokrates, Erasmus und die Institutio principis christiani." In Vierhaus 1966:101–143.

———, ed. 1974. *Institutio principis christiani*. Opera Omnia Desiderii Erasmi Roterodami IV 1. Amsterdam.

Hicks, R. D., ed. 1925. *Diogenes Laertius: Lives of Eminent Philosophers* I–II. Cambridge, MA.

Hirsch, U. 1993. "Ἀκρίβεια—Platons Verständnis der ἐπιστήμη und die hippokratische Medizin." In Wittern and Pellegrin 1993:149–157.

Hirzel, R. 1892. "Zur Charakteristik Theopomps." *Rheinisches Museum für Philologie* 47:359–389.

Hoche, R., ed. 1864. *Nicomachi Geraseni Pythagorei Introductionis Arithmeticae Libri II* I. Leipzig.

Hoffmann, P. 2006. "What Was Commentary in Late Antiquity? The Example of the Neoplatonic Commentators." In Gill and Pellegrin 2006:597–622.

Hornblower, S. 1982. *Mausolus*. Oxford.

———. 2004. *Thucydides and Pindar: Historical Narrative and the World of Epinikian Poetry*. Oxford.

Horowitz, T., and A. I. Janis, eds. 1994. *Scientific Failure*. Lanham, MD.

Horstmanshoff, M., ed. 2010. *Hippocrates and Medical Education: Selected Papers Presented at the XIIth International Hippocrates Colloquium, Universiteit Leiden, 24–26 August 2005*. Leiden.

Hubbell, H. M. 1920. "The Rhetorica of Philodemus." *Transactions of the Connecticut Academy of Arts and Sciences* 23:243–382.

Hutchinson, D. S. 1988. "Doctrines of the Mean and the Debate concerning Skills in Fourth-Century Medicine, Rhetoric, and Ethics." *Apeiron* 21:21–52.

Hutchinson, D. S., and M. R. Johnson. 2006. "*Protrepticus* and *Antidosis*." Paper presented at the Pacific Division Meeting of the American Philosophical Association, Portland. Version published online, dated February 8, 2006.

———. 2009. "Aristotle, *Protrepticus*: Provisional Reconstruction." Online publication dated Nov. 8, 2009.

———. 2010. "Aristotle, *Protrepticus*: Provisional Reconstruction." Online publication dated Aug. 31, 2010.

Innes, D. C. 2007. "Aristotle: The Written and the Performative Styles." In Mirhady 2007:151–168.

Irwin, T. 1985. *Aristotle: Nicomachean Ethics*. Indianapolis.

Isnardi, M. 1955. "L'Accademia e le lettere platoniche." *Parola del Passato* 10: 241–273.

Isnardi Parente, M., ed. 1980. *Speusippo: Frammenti*. Naples.

Jacoby, F. 1923–1958. *Die Fragmente der griechischen Historiker*. Berlin.

Jaeger, W. 1948. *Aristotle: Fundamentals of the History of His Development*. 2nd ed. Oxford.

Jardine, L., ed. 1997. *Erasmus: The Education of a Christian Prince*. Cambridge.

Javitch, D., ed. 2002. *Baldesar Castiglione: The Book of the Courtier. The Singleton Translation*. New York.

Jebb, R. C. 1893. *The Attic Orators from Antiphon to Isaeus* II. 2nd ed. London.

Johnson, R. 1959. "Isocrates' Methods of Teaching." *American Journal of Philology* 80:25–36.

Joly, R. 1994. "Platon, Phèdre et Hippocrate: Vingt ans après." *Glane de philosophie antique: Scripta minora* 32–54. Brussels.

Jouanna, J. 1999. *Hippocrates*. Trans. M. B. DeBevoise. Baltimore.

———. 2002. *Hippocrate: La nature de l'homme*. Berlin.

Jowett, B., trans. 1921. *Politica*. In Ross 1910–1952, vol. 10.

Kalischek, A. E. 1913. *De Ephoro et Theopompo Isocratis Discipulis*. Diss., Münster.

King, J. E., trans. 1945. *Cicero: Tusculan Disputations*. Rev. ed. Cambridge, MA.

Kleve, K., and F. Longo Auricchio. 1992. "Honey from the Garden of Epicurus." In Capasso 1992:211–226.

Knape, J., and T. Schirren, eds. 2005. *Aristotelische Rhetorik-Tradition*. Stuttgart.

Köhler, L. 1928. *Die Briefe des Sokrates und der Sokratiker*. Philologus Suppl. 20:2. Leipzig.

Landon, W. J. 2005. *Politics, Patriotism, and Language: Niccolò Machiavelli's "Secular Patria" and the Creation of an Italian National Identity*. New York.

Laplace, M. 1988. "L'Hommage de Platon à Isocrate dans le *Phèdre*." *Revue de Philologie* 52:273–281.

Levi, A. H. T., ed. 1986. *Collected Works of Erasmus* 27. *Literary and Educational Writings* 5. Toronto.

Livingstone, N. 2001. *A Commentary on Isocrates' Busiris*. Mnemosyne Suppl. 223. Leiden.

Livingstone, N.. 2007. "Writing Politics: Isocrates' Rhetoric of Philosophy." *Rhetorica* 25:15–34.

Lloyd-Jones, H., and P. Parsons. 1983. *Supplementum Hellenisticum*. Texte und Kommentare 11. Berlin.

Lo Presti, R. 2010. "The Physician as Teacher: Epistemic Function, Cognitive Function, and the Incommensurability of Errors." In Horstmanshoff 2010: 137–167.

Lord, C. 1978. "On Damon and Music Education." *Hermes* 106:32–43.

Luraghi, N., ed. 2001. *The Historian's Craft in the Age of Herodotus*. Oxford.

Luzac, J. 1809. *Lectiones atticae*. Leiden.

Lynch, J. P. 1972. *Aristotle's School: A Study of a Greek Educational Institution*. Berkeley.

Malhomme, F. 2009. "L'harmonie du savoir: Du modèle rhétorique au modèle musical." In Pernot 2009:215–247.

Mandilaras, B. G., ed. 2003. *Isocrates: Opera omnia* I. Munich.

Mansfeld, J. 1980. "Plato and the Method of Hippocrates." *Greek, Roman, and Byzantine Studies* 21:341–362.

Mansion, S., ed. 1961. *Aristote et les problèmes de méthode*. Symposium Aristotelicum 2. Louvain.

Markle, M. M., III. 1976. "Support of Athenian Intellectuals for Philip: A Study of Isocrates' *Philippus* and Speusippus' *Letter to Philip*." *Journal of Hellenic Studies* 96:80–99.

Martano, A. 2007. "Teodette di Faselide, poeta tragico: Riflessioni attorno al fr. 6 Snell." In Mirhady 2007:187–200.

Matelli, E. 2007. "Teodette di Faselide, retore." In Mirhady 2007:169–186.

Mathieu, G., and E. Brémond, eds. 1962. *Isocrate: Discours* IV. Paris.

Menchelli, M. 2007. "Un commentario neoplatonico come introduzione alla lettura di Isocrate nella scuola neoplatonica." Νέα 'Ρώμη 4:9–23.

Milns, R. D. 1994. "Didymaea." In Worthington 1994:70–88.

Mirhady, D. C., ed. 2007. *Influences on Peripatetic Rhetoric: Essays in Honor of William W. Fortenbaugh*. Leiden.

Mirhady, D. C., and Y. L. Too, trans. 2000. *Isocrates* I. Austin, TX.

Momigliano, A. 1971. *The Development of Greek Biography: Four Lectures*. Cambridge, MA.

Moraux, P. 1951. *Les listes anciennes des ouvrages d'Aristote*. Louvain.

Morgan, K. A. 2003. "The Tyranny of the Audience in Plato and Isocrates." In Morgan 2003a:181–213.

———. 2003a. *Popular Tyranny*. Austin, TX.

Morrow, G. R., trans. 1997. "Letters." In Cooper 1997:1634–1676.

Mueller, J., and J. Scodel, eds. 2009. *Elizabeth I: Translations, 1544-1589*. Chicago.

Mulvany, C. M. 1926. "Notes on the Legend of Aristotle." *Classical Quarterly* 20:155–167.

Murray, G. 1946. "Theopompus, or the Cynic as Historian." In *Greek Studies*, 149–170. Oxford.

Murray, O. 2001. "Herodotus and Oral History." In Luraghi 2001:15–44.

Natali, C. 1994. "La 'Retorica' di Aristotele negli studi europei più recenti." In Fortenbaugh and Mirhady 1994:365–382.

———. 2001. *The Wisdom of Aristotle*. Trans. G. Parks. Albany, NY.

Natoli, A. F. 2004. *The Letter of Speusippus to Philip II*. Historia Einzelschriften 176. Stuttgart.

Natorp, P. 1907. "Euphraios (2)." RE 6:1190.

Nehamas, A., and P. Woodruff, trans. 1995. *Plato: Phaedrus*. Indianapolis.

Nicolai, R. 2004. *Studi su Isocrate: La comunicazione letteraria nel IV sec. a.C. e I nuovi genere della prosa*. Rome.

Niese, B. 1909. "Wann hat Ephoros sein Geschichtswerk geschrieben?" *Hermes* 44:170–178.

Nightingale, A. W. 1995. *Genres in Dialogue: Plato and the Construct of Philosophy*. Cambridge.

———. 2004. *Spectacles of Truth in Classical Greek Philosophy: Theoria in Its Cultural Context*. Cambridge.

Nilsson, M. P. 1951. *Cults, Myths, Oracles, and Politics in Ancient Greece*. Lund.

Nix, G. E. 1969. *Aristotle's Protrepticus and Isocrates*. Diss., University of Chicago.

Noël, M.-P. 2009. "Painting or Writing Speeches? Plato, Alcidamas, and Isocrates on Logography." In Pernot 2009:91–107.

Norlin, G., trans. 1928–1929. *Isocrates* I–II. Cambridge, MA.

Ober, J. 1998. *Political Dissent in Democratic Athens: Intellectual Critics of Popular Rule*. Princeton.

———. 2004. "I, Socrates...: The Performative Audacity of Isocrates' *Antidosis*." In Poulakos and Depew 2004:21–43.

Oliver, J. H. 1968. "The Civilizing Power: A Study of the Panathenaic Discourse of Aelius Aristides against the Background of Literature and Cultural Conflict, with Text, Translation, and Commentary." *Transactions of the American Philosophical Society* 58:1–223.

Olson, S. D., trans. 2006. *Athenaeus: The Learned Banqueters* I–II. Cambridge, MA.

Orelli, J. K., ed. 1815. *Socratis et Socraticorum Pythagorae et Pythagoreorum quae feruntur epistulae*. Leipzig.

Orth, W., ed. 2003. *Isokrates: Neue Ansätze zur Bewertung eines politischen Schriftstellers*. Trier.

Ostwald, M., and J. P. Lynch. 1994. "The Growth of Schools and the Advance of Knowledge." *Cambridge Ancient History* VI, 2nd ed., 592–633. Cambridge.

Owen, G. E. L. 1961. "Logic and Metaphysics in Some Early Works of Aristotle." In Mansion 1961:163–190.

———. 1965. "The Platonism of Aristotle." *Proceedings of the British Academy* 51:125–150.

———. 1983. "Philosophical Invective." *Oxford Studies in Ancient Philosophy* 1:1–25.

Palme, B., ed. 2007. *Akten des 23. Internationalen Papyrologen-Kongresses*. Vienna.

Papillon, T. L., trans. 2004. *Isocrates* II. Austin, TX.

Pearson, L., and S. Stephens, eds. 1983. *Didymi in Demosthenem Commenta*. Stuttgart.

Pernot, L. 1993. *La rhétorique de l'éloge dans le monde gréco-romain* I–II. Paris.

———, ed. 2009. *New Chapters in the History of Rhetoric*. Leiden.

Pickard-Cambridge, W. A., trans. 1928. *Topica*. In Ross 1910–1952, vol. 1.

Pina Polo, F., and S. Panzram. 2001. "Mito, historia y propaganda política: La carta de Espeusipo a Filipo II de Macedonia." *Gerión* 19:355–390.

Pinto, P. M. 2003. *Per la storia del testo di Isocrate: La testimonianza d'autore*. Bari.

Poole, R. L., and M. Bateson, eds. 1902. *Index Britanniae scriptorum quos ex variis bibliothecis non parvo labore collegit Ioannes Baleus, cum aliis*. Oxford.

Poster, C. 1997. "Aristotle's *Rhetoric* against Rhetoric: Unitarian Reading and Esoteric Hermeneutics." *American Journal of Philology* 118:219–249.

Poulakos, T., ed. 1993. *Rethinking the History of Rhetoric: Multidisciplinary Essays on the Rhetorical Tradition*. Boulder.

Poulakos, T., and D. Depew, eds. 2004. *Isocrates and Civic Education*. Austin, TX.

Rackham, H., trans. 1942. *Cicero: De oratore* I–II. Cambridge, MA.

Rebecchini, G. 2002. *Private Collectors in Mantua, 1500–1630*. Rome.

Reinhardt, K. 1873. *De Isocratis aemulis*. Bonn.

Reinhardt, T., and M. Winterbottom, eds. 2006. *Quintilian: Institutio oratoria, Book 2*. Oxford.

Ries, K. 1959. *Isokrates und Platon im Ringen um die Philosophia*. Diss., Munich.

Romm, J. 1996. "Dog Heads and Noble Savages: Cynicism before the Cynics?" In Branham and Goulet-Cazé 1996:121–135.

Ross, W. D., ed. 1910–1952. *The Works of Aristotle* I–XII. Oxford.

———, trans. 1925. *Ethica Nicomachea*. Ross 1910–1952, vol. 9.

———, trans. 1952. *Select Fragments*. Ross 1910–1952, vol. 12.

———, ed. 1955. *Aristotelis fragmenta selecta*. Oxford.

Roth, P. 2003. *Der Panathenaikos des Isokrates: Übersetzung und Kommentar*. Munich.

Rowe, C. J., ed. 1986. *Plato: Phaedrus*. Warminster.

Russell, D. A., trans. 2001. *Quintilian: The Orator's Education* I–V. Cambridge, MA.

Sabbadini, R. 1905. *Le scoperte dei codici latini e greci ne' secoli XIV e XV* I. Florence.

Scarpati, C. 1983. "Dire la verità al principe (Sulle redazioni di *Cortegiano* IV 4–48)." *Aevum* 57:428–449.

Schiefsky, M. J. 2005. *Hippocrates: On Ancient Medicine*. Leiden.

Schildgen, B. D., ed. 1997. *The Rhetoric Canon*. Detroit.

Schlatter, F. W. 1972. "Isocrates, *Against the Sophists*, 16." *American Journal of Philology* 93:591–597.

Schorn, S. 2006. Review of Natoli 2004. *Gymnasium* 113:472–474.

Schuhl, P. M. 1946–1947. "Platon et l'activité politique de l'Académie." *Revue des études grecques* 44–45:46–53.

Schwartz, E. 1907. "Ephorus." RE 6:1–16.

Shackleton-Bailey, D. R., trans. 1999. *Cicero: Letters to Atticus* I–IV. Cambridge, MA.

Shields, C. 2007. *Aristotle*. London.

Shorey, P. 1909. "Φύσις, Μελέτη, Ἐπιστήμη." *Transactions of the American Philological Association* 40:185–201.

Shrimpton, G. S. 1991. *Theopompus the Historian*. Montreal.

Slings, S. R. 1999. *Plato: Clitophon*. Cambridge.

Solmsen, F. 1929. *Die Entwicklung der aristotelischen Logik und Rhetorik*. Neue philologische Untersuchungen 4. Berlin.

Sonnabend, H. 1996. *Die Freundschaften der Gelehrten und die zwischenstaatliche Politik im klassischen und hellenistischen Griechenland*. Hildesheim.

———. 2002. *Geschichte der antiken Biographie: Von Isokrates bis zur Historia Augusta*. Stuttgart.

Squillace, G. 2010. "Consensus Strategies under Philip and Alexander: The Revenge Theme." In Carney and Ogden 2010:69–80, 260–264.

Stahr, A. 1830–1832. *Aristotelia* I–II. Halle.

Steidle, W. 1952. "Redekunst und Bildung bei Isokrates." *Hermes* 80:257–296.

Stenzel, J. 1929. "Speusippos." RE 3A:1636–1669.

Stuart, D. R. 1928. *Epochs of Greek and Roman Biography*. Berkeley.

Sudhaus, S., ed. 1896. *Philodemi volumina rhetorica* II. Leipzig.

Sullivan, R. G. 2001. "*Eidos/Idea* in Isocrates." *Philosophy and Rhetoric* 34:79–92.

Sykutris, J. 1933. *Die Briefe des Sokrates und der Sokratiker*. Studien zur Geschichte und Kultur des Altertums 18:2. Paderborn.

Tarán, L. 1981. *Speusippus of Athens: A Critical Study with a Collection of the Related Texts and Commentary*. Leiden.

Teichmüller, G. 1881–1884. *Literarische Fehden im vierten Jahrhundert vor Chr.* I–II. Breslau.

Tell, H. 2011. *Plato's Counterfeit Sophists*. Hellenic Studies 44. Washington, DC.

Teodorsson, S.-T. 1990. "Theocritus the Sophist, Antigonus the One-Eyed, and the Limits of Clemency." *Hermes* 118:380–382.

Theys, E., ed. 1998. "Speusippos of Athens." In Bollansée et al. 1998:212–239.

Tindale, C. W. 2010. *Reason's Dark Champions: Constructive Strategies of Sophistic Argument*. Columbia, SC.

Too, Y. L. 1995. *The Rhetoric of Identity in Isocrates: Text, Power, Pedagogy.* Cambridge.

Trampedach, K. 1994. *Platon, die Akademie und die zeitgenössische Politik.* Stuttgart.

Triantafillis, C. 1878. *Nuovi studii su Niccolò Machiavelli "Il Principe."* Venice.

Tulli, M. 1990. "Sul rapporto di Platone con Isocrate: Profezia e lode di un lungo impegno letterario." *Athenaeum* 76:403–422.

Usener, H. 1880. "Abfassungszeit des platonischen Phaidros." *Rheinisches Museum für Philologie* 35:131–151.

Usener, S. 1994. *Isokrates, Platon und ihr Publikum: Hörer und Leser von Literatur im 4. Jahrhundert v. Chr.* Tübingen.

———. 2003. "Isokrates und sein Adressatenkreis: Strategien schriftlicher Kommunikation." In Orth 2003:18–33.

Usher, S., trans. 1974. *Dionysius of Halicarnassus: The Critical Essays* I. Cambridge, MA.

———, ed. 1990. *Greek Orators: Isocrates.* Warminster.

Vallozza, M. 2003. "Isocrate, il ποιητικὸν πρᾶγμα e la τέχνη impossibile." In Celentano 2003:17–29.

Velardi, R. 1991. "Le origini dell'inno in prosa." In Cassio 1991:205–231.

Viano, C. A. 1967. "Aristotele e la redenzione della retorica." *Rivista di filosofia* 58:371–425.

Vierhaus, R., ed. 1966. *Dauer und Wandel der Geschichte: Festgabe für Kurt von Raumer zum 15. Dezember 1965.* Münster.

Walker, M. 2010. "The Utility of Contemplation in Aristotle's *Protrepticus.*" *Ancient Philosophy* 30:135–153.

Walzer, R., ed. 1934. *Aristotelis dialogorum fragmenta.* Florence.

Warren, J., ed. 2009. *The Cambridge Companion to Epicureanism.* Cambridge.

Weber, G. 1998–1999. "The Hellenistic Rulers and Their Poets: Silencing Dangerous Critics?" *Ancient Society* 29:147–174.

Wehrli, F., ed. 1974. *Hermippos der Kallimacheer.* Die Schule des Aristoteles: Texte und Kommentar, Suppl. I. Basle.

Weil, R. 1980. "Aristote et Isocrate: Un conflit d'influences à Chypre." In Yon 1980:193–201.

Wendland, P. 1910. "Beiträge zu athenischer Politik und Publicistik des vierten Jahrhunderts" I ("König Philippos und Isokrates") and II ("Isokrates und Demosthenes"). Nachrichten von der königlichen Gesellschaft der Wissenschaften zu Göttingen: Philologisch-historische Klasse 1910:123–182 and 289–323. Göttingen.

White, S. A. 1994. "Callimachus on Plato and Cleombrotus." *Transactions of the American Philological Association* 124:135–161.

———. 2007. "Platonic Eros: Some Early Hellenistic Echoes." Paper presented at the "Hellenistic Plato" seminar, annual meeting of the American Philological Association, San Diego.

Wilamowitz-Möllendorff, U. von. 1900. "Lesefrüchte." *Hermes* 35:533–566.

Wittern, R., and P. Pellegrin, eds. 1993. *Hippokratische Medizin und antike Philosophie*. Hildesheim.

Wormell, D. E. W. 1935. "The Literary Tradition concerning Hermias of Atarneus." *Yale Classical Studies* 5:57–92.

Worthington, I., ed. 1994. *Ventures into Greek History*. Oxford.

Yon, M., ed. 1980. *Salamine de Chypre: Histoire et archéologie*. Colloques internationaux du CNRS 578. Paris.

Zajonz, S. 2002. *Isokrates' Enkomion auf Helena: Ein Kommentar*. Göttingen.

Zwierlein, O. 1996. *Die Rezitationsdramen Senecas*. Beiträge zur klassischen Philologie 20. Meisenheim am Glan.

Index of Primary Sources

Anaximenes of Lampsacus
  Trikaranos, 184n147.
  See also "Aristotle"
Anonymus Iamblichi (page and line
  numbers, ed. Pistelli): 95.20–23,
  66
Antiphanes: fr. 111 K–A, 97–98, 154;
  fr. 186 K–A (*Proverbs*), 107
Aristides Quintilianus
  De musica 1.4, 74n53
Aristocles of Messene (ed. Chiesara
  2001): F 2, 123n20; F 2, §5,
  153n45; F 2, §7, 106n93
Aristotle
  Eudemian Ethics II 1 1219a17, 40n75;
    II 3 1220b21–27, 16n11; II 5
    1222a6–14, 16n11
  Eudemus, 42n78; fr. 44 R³, 124n27
  Fragments (*see also under titles
    of lost works*) fr. 127 R³, 97n62; fr.
    464 R³, 107; fr. 465 R³, 97n58; fr.
    673 R³ (*Encomium of Plato*),
    148n23
  Gryllus, 78, 108n99; fr. 68 R³,
    103–104, 145
  Hymn to Virtue (fr. 675 R³, 842 PMG)
    142n6, 148, 150, 153
  Metaphysics I 1 981a12–15, 49; I 2
    982a10–19 b27, 47, 48n97; XI 4
    1061b28–33, 40n75

Nicomachean Ethics I 2 1094a25,
  16, 27; I 9 1099b9, 31n52; I 9
  1099b18–21, 28 II 1 1103a18ff.,
  28; II 1 1103a31–b2 and b6ff., 18;
  II 2 1103b27–1104a2, 16, 27; II 2
  1104a3–10, 16, 27; II 2 1104a31–
  32, 32n55; II 4 1105a21–26, 16; II
  4 1105b27–33, 24; II 5 1106a6–10,
  28; II 6, 15n5; II 6 1106b1–2,
  16; II 6 1106b13–14, 16; III 2
  1112a11–12, 26; III 3 1112a34–b2,
  25; III 5 1114a24–25, 32n55; III 9
  1117b20–22, 16, 27; IV 6 1126b11–
  19, 20n25; IV 7 1127b14–15, 28;
  IV 8 1127b33–1128a1, 20n25; V
  10 1137b1, 31; V 10 1137b27ff.,
  15n6; VI 1 1138b26–29, 16; VI 4–5,
  18; VI 5, 16–17; VI 5 1140a24–31,
  21; VI 5 1140b1–7, 59n8; VI 5
  1140b6–7, 18–19; VI 5 1140b21–
  25, 19n18, 26n39; VI 7 1141b8–23,
  18; VI 8 1142a11–20, 40–41; VI 8
  1142a20–27, 18; VI 11 1143b11–
  14, 26n40; VI 13 1144b1–17, 28;
  VII 5 1148b15–1149a24, 27; VII 7
  1150b9, 96n56; VII 8 1151a18–19,
  28n45; IX 9 1170a11–12, 32n55;
  X, 41–42; X 5 1175a12–15, 54; X
  5–6, 54; X 7 1177b16–18, 19; X 9
  1179a34–b8, 38–39; X 9 1179b23–
  25, 38; X 9 1179b24–30, 28; X 9

Subject Index

CPSIA information can be obtained
at www.ICGtesting.com
Printed in the USA
LVHW030721020223
738080LV00001B/6